Site Planning and Design for the Elderly
Issues, Guidelines, and Alternatives

Diane Y. Carstens

VNR VAN NOSTRAND REINHOLD COMPANY
New York

Copyright © 1985 by Van Nostrand Reinhold Company Inc.
Library of Congress Catalog Card Number 84-23708
ISBN 0-442-21768-4

Printed in the United States of America

Designed by Jules Perlmutter

Published by Van Nostrand Reinhold Company Inc.
115 Fifth Avenue
New York, New York 10003

Van Nostrand Reinhold Company Limited
Molly Millars Lane
Wokingham, Berkshire RG11 2PY, England

Van Nostrand Reinhold
480 La Trobe Street
Melbourne, Victoria 3000, Australia

Macmillan of Canada
Division of Canada Publishing Corporation
164 Commander Boulevard
Agincourt, Ontario M1S 3C7, Canada

16 15 14 13 12 11 10 9 8 7 6 5 4 3

Library of Congress Cataloging in Publication Data

Carstens, Diane Y.
  Site planning and design for the elderly.

  Bibliography: p.
  Includes index.
  1. Aged—Dwellings—Planning. 2. Building sites—
Planning. I. Title.
NA7195.A4C3 1985   728.3'1'043   84-23708
ISBN 0-442-21768-4

The power that holds the planets in their course
And places limits on the restless sea,
Holds my life too, within its mighty keeping—
Always holds me.

And so I rest as a swan rests on the river,
Quiet and calm, amid life's troubled flow.
I know I am held by a power of love,
That will not let me go.

—ANONYMOUS

Contents

Acknowledgments

I am deeply indebted to the many colleagues, friends, and professionals from allied fields who have offered their guidance, insights, and support throughout the development of this manuscript. Perhaps most important are the many seniors whom I have come to know throughout the research phases of this work. Their life stories and presence, in mind and heart, serving as a delicate reminder of the true reason for writing a book such as this, motivated me during even the most trying of moments.

Foremost among colleagues and friends, gratitude is due to the faculty and students at the Department of Landscape Architecture and the Housing Research and Development Program at the University of Illinois, Urbana–Champaign, for their unfailing commitment to designing "for use," and their willingness to allow me the time and resources necessary to explore ideas and concepts. Among this large group, special gratitude cannot sufficiently express my indebtedness to several people: Sue Weidemann, for her continuous flow of enthusiasm and subtle direction; Robert Riley, for his patience and his commitment to a rather intangible department specialization—"Design-Behavior"; and Robert D. Katz, who supported much of the original research. Ms. Doris Ravlin, director of the Housing Authority for LaSalle County, Illinois, very kindly provided the opportunity to apply, test, and refine many of the original concepts presented in this work.

It is only with an open sharing of ideas that the complex environmental needs of senior citizens can be addressed. As with any substantial undertaking, the works of others have provided the necessary foundation of knowledge on which to build the present book. The dedication of these individuals and their contributions to the field are greatly appreciated. A particular note of thanks is also due to the many individuals and design firms who have kindly contributed their ideas and work for this publication.

Finally, this publication would not have been possible without the support, patience, and love of those closest to me: my husband and colleague, Ed Lubieniecki, for his insightful observations and gentle understanding of the frustrations involved; my mother, Louise Voloshin, for her editing assistance and constant encouragement; and Kay B. Litchenberg, who so kindly provided the ideal writer's hideaway.

Introduction

The issues and guidelines presented in this work address a particular design problem: the design of outdoor spaces surrounding planned housing developments for relatively independent older people. They are applicable to many development types, including low-rise, high-rise, and mixed developments.

The focus is on those issues and recommendations that are particularly important for older people—for the perceptual, functional, and social changes associated with the aging process. This book is intended to sensitize the designer to these issues in addition to outlining specific recommendations for spatial organization, design, and detailing of outdoor spaces. The recommendations presented are intended as general guides, based upon measured research, empirical knowledge, and opinion; they are not steadfast rules. Furthermore, the recommendations were developed with relatively independent older people in mind, such as those living in individual apartment units or those who require some minor assistance with daily living, such as meal services; more intensive-care facilities may require additional environmental supports for special needs and/or handicaps.

Designing outdoor spaces surrounding planned housing developments for older people deserves special attention for several reasons. First, planned housing has become a common housing solution for many of today's more than 25.5 million older people (1980 census) [1]. In addition, the number of older people residing in the United States is expected to reach at least 32 million by the year 2000 with a disproportionate growth among the elderly over 75 years of age [2, 3]. The demand for purpose-built housing is likely to show similar increases if present trends toward independent and age-segregated housing continue. Many housing alternatives for more integrated living within the community, such as echo housing, will also expand to accommodate the diverse needs of this growing population.

Second, although "older people, on the whole, are pretty much like the rest of us, . . . where the capabilities of older people do differ from those of younger people, unique needs requiring unique satisfiers may result" [4]. Designing for older people thus involves searching out design solutions that respond to these needs, enabling older people, regardless of their limitations, to live as fulfilling and independent lives as possible.

Finally, much progress has already been made in many of the design fields toward providing high-quality planned housing for the elderly. Guidelines for indoor spaces are readily available, and the differences that these are making in the quality of life for elderly residents are evident in projects across the country. The design of outdoor spaces, however, has lagged far behind; some gerontologists note that outdoor spaces are so consistently unresponsive to the needs of older people that it appears they must have been intentionally planned that way!

This book is intended to close that gap by providing an overview of issues and recommendations for the design of outdoor spaces that surround planned housing for relatively independent older people.

Designing outdoor spaces, however, is but a small part of the ongoing process of providing high-quality housing for older people; it requires a flexible concept of aging that maximizes choices for older people and pays attention to all aspects of the housing environment. This includes choices in housing and service arrangements, responsive management and activity programming, as well as ongoing service and design evaluation.

Those whom we call "elderly" encompass a great diversity of physical and mental abilities, preferences, and life-styles. To meet these varied needs adequately and maximize opportunities for independence, environmental choices must be integrated into all aspects of housing.

1

On a macrolevel, environmental choices include choices in housing arrangements, such as single-family homes, low-rise, or high-rise living, as well as purchase or rental housing. The options for age-segregated or age-integrated housing are expanding along with options for service delivery. The older person can choose from wholly independent living, to supplementary support services in the home, to life-care contracts offering a range of support services and intensive-care facilities.

An extremely important concern for those involved in designing outdoor spaces for older people—but one that is often overlooked—is the dynamic interaction between design, management, and activity programming. Management and activity programming are vital components of a successful design, particularly for older people who may be less willing or less able to instigate a new activity, to change their physical surroundings, or to change management and programming policy. The designer is implored to consider the impact of these services and programs upon older residents and their use of the designed environment. Also vital is ongoing review of management, service, and activity programming, as well as evaluation of the design itself throughout the life span of the project.

The provision of high-quality housing for older people presents many special design challenges, such as the dual need of providing support for the frail when it is needed while offering challenges for more able residents. Small design issues become very important, particularly as the health of residents declines and more reliance is placed upon the immediate environment for the fulfillment of needs. Factors such as declining mobility and perceptual and cognitive losses not only affect very straightforward "hardware" decisions, such as doorknobs, ramps, and rails, but also the basic design concept. Loss of orientation in a large undifferentiated space, or difficulty in maintaining a conversation because of surrounding distractions, or benches that are not close enough for their occupants to hear each other speak, are issues that designers can and must address. The challenge is to provide a total housing package that responds to the varied needs of those involved in the aging process, offering support, variety, challenge, and opportunities

for control and independence in daily living, but not fixed solutions. It is hoped that the information presented in this book will serve as a basis for creative and informed decision making on the part of designers, not as a source of fixed stereotypical solutions.

Economic restraints and construction trade-offs are a part of every design decision, but by the year 2000, 32 million older people will require housing that allows them to fulfill their potential as mature adults. The challenge is to design with an understanding of the aging process and a commitment to the quality of life throughout the life span.

To be useful for designers, this work is organized similarly to the design process: from general issues and design concepts through to site detailing.

Part One examines some important issues for design, presenting background information on housing alternatives and the aging process. Within this context, specific objectives for design are discussed, including the spatial requirements of older people and considerations for safety and security, comfort and access. Part Two examines the impact of neighborhood conditions on site development and site-development patterns. The location, spatial characteristics, amenities, and detailing of major site-planning components (such as the site entry, parking, and pedestrian circulation) are discussed. Part Three examines some special types of outdoor use, as well as site components for recreational and pleasure use of the outdoors. Design detailing for special areas and amenities, such as pedestrian crossing areas, seating, and lighting are reviewed. Part Four summarizes the major points covered throughout this book and discusses future trends in the areas of aging, housing, and design.

Evaluations of actual projects from across the United States demonstrate how many of these issues fit together. Conceptual illustrations and examples from actual site designs are used to demonstrate the application of the basic concepts presented.

A wide range of topics is covered. Those less central to design but still important to keep in mind, such as the role of staff and management, are briefly discussed. With some complex design topics, such as site planning for larger mixed developments, those concerns that are most relevant to designing for older people are presented. The intent is to familiarize the designer with the range of issues and design considerations that may affect the daily lives of older people.

References

1. "AIA Round Table Explores Designing for the Elderly," *American Institute of Architects Journal.* 7, no. 8 (August 1982): 68.
2. "AIA Round Table," p. 68.
3. "Elderly Migration Patterns Changing," *Provider News.* 2, no. 2 (January 27, 1984): 2.
4. Lawton, M. Powell. *Environment and Aging.* Monterey, CA: Brooks/Cole, 1980, p. x.

Defining the Issues

A variety of housing and service alternatives is evolving to meet the diverse needs and changing character of the rapidly growing older population. Present population trends, for example, indicate that those over the age of 75, who generally require more care, will represent a larger percentage of the population than ever before. A new generation of active seniors is also evolving as a result of healthier life-styles, advances in medicine, and changing birthrates. These elderly represent a more discerning and selective housing consumer group, one that is more highly educated and financially secure than past generations.

Designing housing for senior citizens has therefore increased in complexity, requiring a broad-based understanding of the needs and circumstances of the aging and the role of design in limiting or promoting satisfaction in daily living and outdoor enjoyment. Recent research, for example, suggests that general life satisfaction and even the health of older people may be related to the design and management of their housing.

In this section, information intended to serve as the foundation of understanding and designing for the elderly is presented. Present housing options, aspects of the aging process that may affect design, and the relationships between housing type, design, and residents' ability level are discussed. Key issues are identified, and a range of design approaches outlined, including such important areas as designing for social interaction, wayfinding, and independence.

Low- to High-Rise Housing for Relatively Independent Older People

The variety of purpose-built housing types has been expanding in recent years, along with a growing trend toward independent living arrangements among older people. Fewer older people are living with their children, while less than 10 percent of the elderly are under long-term care [1, 2]. Low- to high-rise developments for senior citizens offer a range of housing alternatives for many of these independent older people.

Whether low- or high-rise, planned housing for relatively independent older people represents one point along a continuum of care and independence offered through a variety of housing alternatives. The range includes independent apartment units for the elderly (providing the greatest level of independence); congregate housing that provides some level of services and programs, such as meals; and geriatric hospitals, providing an acute-care setting. Some planned developments, such as life-care communities, may offer a full range of housing options, from single-family residences to congregate facilities and nursing homes, allowing the older person to remain in the same housing development in spite of advancing infirmities.

Many new types of housing alternatives are being tested, including the conversion of single-family homes to apartments for seniors, with the rent supplementing the income of the in-resident owner (also a senior citizen) and echo housing (or "granny" flats). Community support services in the home (such as meal deliveries and visiting nurse services) enable many older people to remain in their own homes.

Housing and service type may have important implications for the design of outdoor spaces, especially the provision of recreational facilities. A complex relationship often exists among the type of housing, service level, and the ability level of residents. This relationship may affect the use of outdoor space. Housing that includes independent units with kitch-

ens in every unit generally attracts the more able person. At this kind of residence, more active types of outdoor recreation may be highly used. Outdoor recreational facilities may be especially successful if the projected sales image is one of an active resort/retirement community. In contrast, life-care communities and projects that offer central dining facilities rather than kitchen units may attract the more frail older person. In such communities, areas for socializing and more protected indoor-outdoor areas may be much more popular among residents than recreational facilities. There is always, however, a great range in ability level among residents, and use does not always indicate the value of a particular amenity. In addition, the relationship between facility provision and ability level of residents may be a two-way street: Projects that promote and provide for a more active life-style may attract more able-bodied residents, regardless of the type of services offered. It is important to recognize this interplay between facilities and residents' ability level and to provide appropriate levels of challenge and support. Some common types of planned housing and their attributes are listed in table 2–1.

Typical Project Characteristics

Although each housing project is unique in terms of facilities, services, and tenant characteristics, some general observations are useful.

Mid- to high-rise apartment buildings, typically averaging 170 units, are the most common planned housing solution today [3]. Efficiency of service delivery as well as land use and cost per unit for development are often cited as benefits. Thus, mid- to high-rise developments are frequently located in urban areas, where land is at a premium and services are nearby. Mid- to high-rise housing, however, may not be the first choice of many residents, most of whom

Table 2–1 HOUSING TYPES AND SERVICES

Housing Type	Ability Level	Description
Managed public housing; apartments for the elderly; retirement housing*	Independent	Self-contained units, may include meals; often government rent support; may include public spaces
Congregate care apartments	Semi-independent	Resident capable of own personal care; meals available; may include emergency staff and social services
Homes for the aged	Semidependent	Meals; personal and housekeeping assistance; may be a nursing staff
Intermediate care; nursing homes	Dependent	Licensed practical nurse; meals; personal assistance
24-hour skilled nursing facility	Dependent	Health-care facilities, 24-hour registered nurse; all meals; housekeeping, social services, physiotherapy
Geriatric hospital	Dependent	Acute care, diagnosis, medical supervision, therapy

*Retirement Community—typically these offer two or more types of facilities. Often expensive, these age-segregated housing facilities frequently emphasize leisure activities and a protected environment.

are accustomed to living at ground level, with easy access to their own living quarters, private gardens, and the street. In addition, the height of the building may promote concern over elevator use and fire safety, and further remove residents from outdoor spaces. Centralized indoor common spaces, however, may facilitate social interaction and a sense of community in these situations.

Low-rise housing can offer many amenities associated with the single-family home, such as a front and back yard and parking immediately adjacent to or attached to the unit. Potential problems with this type of housing include isolation of facilities and individual units, as well as unsheltered access, which is especially difficult in harsh climates.

Amenities, facilities, and services may vary widely from project to project. Mid- to high-rise developments, in particular, often include some indoor common space, such as a lounge, entry lobby, and laundry rooms. Others may also include recreational facilities such as craft or card rooms or on-site recreation and community centers.

Outdoor facilities may range from simply a parking lot and a small patio to golf courses and riding stables. Retirement communities generally have the broadest range of outdoor recreational facilities, while single-building mid- to high-rise developments often offer the smallest range, owing to limited space.

In-house services may include activity programming, medical clinics, counseling, and transportation services. Congregate housing is generally defined by some form of communal or dorm-style living; at a minimum, meal services are offered.

Tenant Characteristics

Apartment units for older people generally serve elderly females, although inner-city low-income projects, in particular, may house mostly men. Some residents may be handicapped, use a walker or wheelchair, or be partially blind. Although many public housing projects designed explicitly for senior citizens require residents to be 62 years of age or older, or the spouse of a person 62 or older, no age restric-

8

tions apply to the handicapped. Thus, many housing projects may house both senior citizens and younger handicapped adults. Private developments may have lower age restrictions.

The range of abilities and needs among residents varies widely within and among projects. Some residents who require additional care and services may not desire or be financially able to move into more intensive care and service facilities. In some cases, particularly in rural areas, other housing options may not be available nearby. Consequently, some frail elderly may extend their residency in independent housing units. Many other residents may be active, physically able, and mentally alert.

Thus, although designing for independent elderly usually means designing for relatively able older people, it still requires a sensitivity to a range of abilities and handicaps, regardless of the housing type.

References

1. Lawton, M. Powell. *Environment and Aging.* Monterey, CA: Brooks/Cole, 1980.
2. Lipscom, Bentley E. (minority staff director of the Senate Special Committee on Aging). Quoted in "AIA Roundtable Explores Designing for the Elderly." *American Institute of Architects Journal.* 7, no. 8 (August 1982): 68.
3. U.S. Department of Housing and Urban Development, Office of Policy Development and Research. *Housing for the Elderly and Handicapped: The Experience of the Section 202 Program from 1959 to 1977.* HUDPDR301. Washington, DC: U.S. Government Printing Office, 1979.

CHAPTER

The Aging Process

Those we call "elderly" represent a great diversity of physical and mental abilities, preferences, and lifestyles. To design for older people requires an understanding of how the aging process can affect the way in which an older person perceives, interprets, and negotiates the environment; it also demands an understanding of what it means to grow older in our society. Some important aspects of the aging process that affect design are discussed in this chapter.

"Aging is universal and normal, a process that begins at birth" [1]. Throughout the aging process, positive changes occur that provide growth and maturity. To all persons, the aging process also means adaptation to a series of subtle and/or critical changes in social and functional roles, physical health, sensory acuity, and physical ability. Unfortunately, with the onset of retirement, an older person is often considered obsolete. These changes may be viewed generally on an "Age Loss Continuum," on which a series of changes slowly takes place over the span of later years (see table 3–1).

The challenge of providing high-quality housing for the elderly of today and tomorrow demands a flexibility of design response rooted in understanding the aging process. Such an understanding is critical for design, for the following reasons:

Although the most important generalization in gerontology may be that older people are, on the whole, pretty much like the rest of us, there is an important message: where the capabilities of older people do differ from those of younger people, unique needs requiring unique satisfiers may result. Hence the suggestion that what is good for people in general will be good for the elderly is only partly true [2].

Consequently, the elderly cannot be placed in a stereotypical group, nor can stereotypical solutions for housing the elderly fully satisfy or respond to the great diversity of the older population.

In this chapter we examine some physiological, social, and functional aspects of the aging process that may directly influence design and affect the lives of elderly residents. It is hoped that this approach will serve as a basis for informed and creative decision making in the planning and design of outdoor spaces surrounding housing for older persons.

Physiological Aging

The process of aging brings many physiological and psychological changes that affect the functioning of the individual and his or her interaction with the environment.

Real aging is determined by the body's loss of reserve or ability to maintain its equilibrium [3]. Environmental variables and cultural norms, however, may hasten the aging process. These are discussed later in this chapter.

To maximize the options for daily living for older people, design can and must respond to changes in sensory processes and perception, the central nervous system and cognitive functions, and health associated with the aging process.

Sensory Processes and Perception

Changes in sensory processes throughout the aging process affect the individual's ability to receive information about the physical and social environment and about the body itself, thereby profoundly affecting the way the individual responds to the environment [4].

Sensory losses typically begin around the age of 65. Changes in hearing and vision are particularly important, as they are the primary senses through which

10

Table 3–1 THE AGE-LOSS CONTINUUM

Losses:*	Age	30	40	50	60	70	80	90
Separation of children				•				
Death of peers					•			
Loss of spouse					•			
Motor output deterioration						•		
Sensory acuity losses					•			
Age-related health problems						•		
Reduced physical mobility						•		

*These losses do not happen as precisely indicated for each age category, nor are they necessarily experienced by any one individual.

SOURCE: Leon A. Pastalan. "Privacy as an Expression of Human Territoriality." In *Spatial Behavior of Older People*, edited by L. Pastalan and D. Carson. Ann Arbor: University of Michigan Press. 1970, 98. Reprinted with permission.

most information about the environment is gathered. Sensory information acts as a conveyor of the meaning of the environment. Some important changes will be examined.

Vision. This is the primary mechanism for receiving and interpreting information about the environment. As one ages, however, the lens of the eye thickens, yellows, and may become increasingly opaque. These changes can impair color vision. The yellowing of the lens filters out violet, blue, and green, particularly along the dark end of the spectrum. Yellow, orange, and red are thus easier to see than darker colors or those in the blue-green range.

Depth perception may also be impaired. The juxtaposition of advancing and receding colors or deep shadows contrasting with light, for example, may give the false impression of a change in elevation.

Aging and disease may make it difficult to discriminate fine detail or even faces, particularly after the age of 70 [5].

The quality and quantity of light required for focusing on an image increase with age. Adaptation to light and dark may take longer, and periods of temporary blindness may be experienced while the eye slowly adjusts to changes in illumination. Wearing heavy eyeglasses may also increase sensitivity to glare. [6].

Tunnel vision may occur with age, reducing ability to negotiate space and perceive motion because peripheral vision acts as a warning and guiding system [7].

Hearing. Sounds relate a person to the environment, provide important warning signals, and allow conversation. Sounds also aid in monitoring the environment.

Two main types of hearing losses with age are "flat loss" and "selective loss" [8]. Flat loss is loss of hearing at all frequencies. Selective loss generally affects the reception of higher pitches. Thus many older people prefer music with lower-pitched sounds, usually of uniform intensities. This may have implications for the design of sound sculptures and other acoustic design elements.

The intensity or loudness required to hear may increase with age, although in many cases sheer volume will not increase reception. Men over 55 years of age generally have greater hearing difficulty than women over 55 [9].

Touch, Taste, and Smell. Older people are often slower in evaluating objects through taste, touch, and smell. They are more cautious and less capable of reaching a decision about identifying an object. One implication is that older people generally prefer spicy foods and more tactually loaded environments. Some authorities have speculated that an older person's preference for "clutter" and his or her tendency to move closer to a conversation partner may be an attempt to compensate for sensory losses.

Central Nervous System and Cognitive Functions

The main change in the central nervous system is the loss of cells. This may account for a slowing of reaction time.

Overall, intellectual processes remain basically unchanged; however, several diseases and general senescence may affect cognitive functioning. Stored information and verbal information are generally sustained, although concept formation and other functions may decline [10]. Reaction time may also be rigid; therefore, elderly persons may need a more constant environment. New environments may cause confusion. Some older people may find it difficult, for example, to form a "cognitive map" of a new area, and they easily become disoriented.

Related to loss of orientation is the confusion experienced because of the inability to discriminate between background noises and foreground sounds and a tendency to confuse and misinterpret the two. Background noises may make it more difficult for elderly persons to follow a conversation. However, "the most important factor in maintaining mental skills into old age seems to be an environment which allows the mental faculties to be exercised" [11].

Muscular and Skeletal Systems

Elderly persons may experience a reduction in agility, strength, and muscular control. Muscle strength peaks between 20 and 30 years of age and then declines. A person in his or her mid 70s, for example, has approximately half the strength of a 30-year-old [12]. Walking and exercises involving the leg muscles improve circulation and strength.

Walking gait. Older persons may also experience changes in their walking gait and posture. Their gait becomes more reserved, with broader and shorter strides to improve stability. Some may shuffle their feet while walking and focus their vision on the ground plane directly in front of them in order to "see" it.

Tremor. This occurs when a person is tired, and it reduces the ability to discriminate small motor movements and make controlled adjustments.

The Skeletal system. This becomes less resilient with age and more vulnerable to accident or injury. Fractures of the pelvis, femur, and spine are common. Bones do not heal as readily as they do in younger people.

Adaptation to Temperature

Many elderly persons experience a reduced ability to adapt to temperature, either high or low. This may be caused by changes in metabolism, hormones, and muscular responses.

Disease

"Health affects participation in most social roles, life satisfaction and the way we are treated by others" [13]. Older persons are most often afflicted with chronic conditions (long-term or permanent conditions, such as heart trouble). Common chronic conditions among the elderly population include arthritis and rheumatism, heart disease and high blood pressure [14]. The most obvious implications of these conditions are the limitations that they place upon activity participation.

Arthritis. This is a very prominent and disabling condition. Control and motion are severely affected. Activities requiring gross movements of the body or fine dexterity, for example, are difficult for those with arthritis. "Although movement should be restrained and limited so as not to aggravate the condition, overresting or too much caution may advance the disease" [15].

Cardiopulmonary organs. The heart of an older person has a slower rate and lower output. The capacity of the lungs to oxygenate the blood is reduced with age. Under stress there is less reserve; therefore, the older person may tire more easily.

Kidney cells. These are reduced in number with age. Incontinence may be a distressing discomfort associated with progressive age and kidney disease (see table 3–2).

Table 3–2 CHECKLIST OF PHYSIOLOGICAL CHANGES WITH AGE AND SOME DESIGN IMPLICATIONS

Sensory Process and Perception

Age-related sensory losses occur with vision, hearing, taste, touch, and smell. One possible and practical design response to these losses is to load the environment with redundant sensory clues. This includes special attention to:

1. the quality and quantity of light
2. the use of color (brighter colors and those in the orange-yellow-red spectrum are easier to distinguish)
3. contrasts of light and dark shadows and advancing and receding colors as they distort depth perception
4. the intensity and pitch of sounds (lower-pitched sounds are more easily heard)
5. tactual cues that may be more easily "read"

Central Nervous System and Cognitive Functions

Although many cognitive functions do not change with age, concept formation ability and reaction time may be reduced. To facilitate orientation and promote safety, special attention must be given to:

1. decreased concept formation ability affecting orientation or wayfinding
2. slower reaction time
3. difficulty in distinguishing and interpreting background noises from foreground sounds

Muscular and Skeletal Systems

Muscular strength, agility, and fine motor control may diminish with age. The reduced resiliency of the skeletal system requires attention to safety, security, and environmental negotiability, as injury may be more devastating for older people. These have special implications for the design of:

1. ground surfaces and changes in elevation
2. facilities requiring fine and/or gross muscle movement

Temperature Adaptation

The reduced ability to adapt to changes in temperature requires amenities and detailing for temperature moderation/control.

Disease

Susceptibility to chronic diseases restrains activity. Special considerations for health-related problems include:

1. providing easy access to nearby restrooms
2. providing options for those with various levels of reserve/energy
3. limitations on fine motor control and gross movements due to arthritis

Social and Functional Roles

The aging process also brings many changes in social and functional roles. These changes tend to reduce older people's sense of security and control over their lives, diminish self-confidence, and reduce social networks. Other age-related changes affect economic security and reduce the older person's sphere of activity.

Social and environmental variables such as retirement, lack of exercise, and poor nutritional habits may hasten the aging process. Even death itself is not necessarily a result of the aging process.

Recent research . . . shows that one of the most reliable predictors of death among elderly who have been transferred from one setting to another may be the loss of desire to penetrate the social and physical environment [16].

Three major social and functional role changes that may occur with age include changes in the family structure and work roles, reduced income, and an increasingly smaller range of activity.

Family Structure and Work Roles

By the time the parent is 55 years of age, children typically move and start their own lives away from home. By 65, friends, relatives, and spouse may be lost through death or a move.

Retirement often brings a loss of the work role with its accompanying status. Retirement may be a particularly difficult adjustment for those generations imbued in the work ethic who have generally not developed leisure-time pursuits nor feel that leisure is worthwhile; therefore, existing or new social contacts and meaningful roles may become very important for the older person [17].

Income

An ever-present problem with retirement is loss of income. Social security, retirement plans, and personal savings are often insufficient. Many older persons find that they cannot afford to maintain their house, pay taxes, or afford many leisure activities or equipment.

Mobility and Sphere of Activity

Loss of health, mobility, income, and social roles may reduce the aging person's sphere of activity. Older persons may find it increasingly difficult to get out into the community, to take trips to the city core,

shopping centers, and vacation spots. Daily and weekly activities take place within a progressively smaller range, closer to the home. This restriction in range of activities is compounded by the lack of opportunities for establishing meaningful roles in the community. The situation is, however, much brighter for aging adults than ever before. A recent U.S. Department of Housing and Urban Development study indicated that in 1980 more elderly persons enjoyed better health and depended less upon friends and family than ever before [18].

References

1. Green, Isaac, et al. *Housing for the Elderly: The Development and Design Process.* New York: Van Nostrand Reinhold, 1975, 10.
2. Lawton, M. Powell. *Environment and Aging.* Monterey, CA: Brooks/Cole, 1980.
3. Koncelik, Joseph, A. *Designing the Open Nursing Home.* Community Development Series no. 27. Stroudsburg, PA: Dowden, Hutchinson & Ross, 1976.
4. Atchely, Robert C. *The Social Forces in Later Life: An Introduction to Social Gerontology.* Belmont, CA: Wadsworth Press, 1972.
5. ————. *The Social Forces.*
6. ————. *The Social Forces.*
7. ————. *The Social Forces.*
8. Koncelik. *Designing the Open Nursing Home.*
9. Atchely. *The Social Forces.*
10. Koncelik. *Designing the Open Nursing Home.*
11. Atchely. *The Social Forces,* 71.
12. Koncelik. *Designing the Open Nursing Home.*
13. Atchely. *The Social Forces,* 113.
14. ————. *The Social Forces.*
15. Koncelik. *Designing the Open Nursing Home,* 19.
16. ————. *Designing the Open Nursing Home,* 14.
17. Lawton. *Environment and Aging.*
18. Rabushka, Alvin, and Bruce Jacobs. *Old Folks at Home.* New York: Free Press, 1980.

Designing for the Elderly—General Issues

4

We have seen that the aging process involves a series of subtle and/or critical changes that can affect the older person's perception and interpretation of the environment. Some general concepts for design that respond to many of these important age-related changes are outlined in this chapter. These include:

- adopting a "prosthetic approach" to design [1]
- providing variety and choice
- promoting a sense of autonomy, independence, and usefulness
- allowing personalization and control over the environment
- providing for adaptability of design—the constant and accommodating models
- providing access to community services, facilities, and information
- establishing management policies on use of facilities and activity programming

The issues and concepts outlined in this chapter are not intended to present a thorough discussion of each topic, nor to exhaust all general topics related to designing for the aged. Rather, they represent a few major concerns important to keep in mind when designing for older people.

Issue: A Prosthetic Approach to Design: Challenge and Support

Objective

The overriding design concept must be to provide a "prosthetic environment" that offers appropriate levels of challenge and support when needed.

Rationale

A prosthetic environment is one that permits the optimal functioning of the individual by offering support when needed, but allows for independence, challenge, and learning. It allows the individual to function in spite of any handicaps. This involves recognizing the disabilities of the elderly and searching for environmental supports that facilitate a higher level of functioning [2]. Many of these supports are examined in the design chapters of this book.

Appropriate levels of challenge and support are important for outdoor use and for the well-being of residents. Incremental "doses" of challenge and support should be available for the practice of skills and independence for all levels of ability. When environmental challenges exceed the individual's ability to cope, frustration, anxiety, or withdrawal may result. If the environment does not provide enough challenge, boredom and lethargy may result. The long-term effect of reduced demands and opportunities for skill practice may be the loss of those skills and abilities [3].

Appropriate site location, spatial arrangements, detailing, and site hardware may aid in the optimal functioning of the elderly with perceptual disabilities and limited cognitive and self-maintenance skills.

Examples

Challenge and support for a prosthetic environment may be offered by providing variety in:

- the topography of walking routes (e.g., routes with an incline as well as flat routes)
- length of walking routes
- exposure to weather (e.g., covered outdoor areas, shady and sunny areas)
- prosthetic devices or elements to encourage participation by less able residents
- recreational options, from watching activity to walking, shuffleboard, and so on
- access to facilities and services both on- and off-site
- walking surfaces that are easy to negotiate (e.g.,

nonslip, nonglare, without ridges or abrupt edges), and those that present more challenge, such as rough garden paths

Issue: Variety and Choice

Objective

A variety of outdoor areas and activities should be available to residents.

Rationale

To respond to the variety of preferences and abilities among elderly residents, variety and choice must be offered in the outdoor environment. This is particularly important in planned housing, where a number of individuals must share the same housing environment, and where less able residents will spend more time at home and depend more upon their immediate environment for the fulfillment of needs.

Where environmental choices are available, older people generally tend to choose those that match their ability level [4]. The number of spaces and options, however, should not be so great that the actual number of people in a space is diffused, as the presence of other people is a strong determinant for use of a space [5]. In addition, each space should provide a unified image or message to reduce the possibility of confusion [6].

Examples

Environmental choices and variety may be offered by providing:

- formal and informal spaces
- places for social interaction as well as intimacy and privacy
- choices in scale of spaces
- clarity and ambiguity

Issue: Autonomy, Independence, and a Sense of Usefulness

Objective

Design and management must allow residents to perform tasks for themselves to reinforce a sense of autonomy, independence, and usefulness.

Rationale

Some autonomy is sacrificed in housing environments offering group services and facilities [7]. In addition, retirement often brings the loss of important roles and a sense of uselessness. A design and management policy that responds to a variety of ability levels and allows residents to perform tasks themselves reinforces a sense of autonomy and usefulness. Privacy is also tied to autonomy.

Examples

The exercise of independence and autonomy may be facilitated by a design that provides for:

- easy access to facilities
- comfort and ease of use
- options for control of privacy
- opportunities for participation in activity programming, service delivery, and activity organizing
- opportunities to participate in outdoor maintenance, share responsibility for recreational equipment, and so on
- environmental negotiability (see chapter 4)
- orientation and wayfinding (see chapter 4)

Issue: Personalize, Change, and Control the Environment

Objective

Residents must be able to personalize, change, and control the environment to suit their own needs, abilities, and personalities.

Rationale

Personalization and control over the environment is important for self-esteem and satisfaction, particularly for aging persons who experience a closing off of life's options, and those in planned housing, where options for control and personalization may be limited. Being able to change and personalize the environment allows individual needs and preferences to be satisfied. A sense of control also increases the feeling of home and the use of a space while decreasing the institutional character of planned housing. Management policies as well as design are important for a sense of control.

Examples

Personalization and control of the environment may be facilitated by a design and management policy that provides:

- movable (versus fixed) site furniture, for residents' control over placement
- space for residents' own garden amenities, such as bird feeders
- display and garden areas for residents' own use
- individual/unit patios or balconies
- unit entry vestibules with space for personalization (flowers, etc.)

Issue: Adaptability of Design— Constant versus Accommodating Model

Objective

Design must be able to accommodate, to a degree, the changing interests, preferences, and abilities of residents and the gradual aging of the population within the project. A decision must be made, however, as to the extent of design and service adaptability.

Rationale

In general, tenant turnover in planned housing tends to be very low [8,9]. Over time, the average age of tenants increases; thus, their abilities may decline. In addition, residents' preferences for outdoor use may change over short periods of time, requiring some flexibility in design and management.

To a certain point, variety, choice, and design flexibility may accommodate changes in residents' abilities and preferences. A decision must be made whether the environment is to provide a fairly constant level of environmental support or accommodate long-term changes in the resident population by providing additional support to maintain a tenant as long as possible [10].

In continuing to try to serve the most independent as well as those whose capabilities have grossly decreased, [planners] risk the evolution of a service and social environment with potentially negative impact [11].

Issue: Access to Community Services, Facilities, and Information

Objective

Easy access to neighborhood resources, transportation, and information about services and events should be available.

Rationale

Poorer health and loss of income and social roles associated with later years are often accompanied by a reduction in "sphere of activity," where connections to the community become increasingly limited. This may be a result of the circumstances surrounding the aging process, rather than a conscious choice [12].

Access to neighborhood resources and information is important for general life satisfaction, morale, and the optimal functioning of the individual, as well as for avoiding isolation from the rest of the community. On-site services and facilities may discourage trips to the surrounding community; this negative effect should be carefully weighed.

Examples

- close and convenient public transportation, stops, and routes
- bulletin boards with community events and service information
- safe and convenient walking routes to community facilities
- on-site facilities for events involving the community at large, such as a craft display or cookouts
- scheduled trips to the community, for plays, tours, and so on

Issue: Management Policies on Use of Facilities and Activity Programming

Objective

Management policies on use of facilities and activity programming should encourage independence and use of facilities.

Rationale

Management policies on use of facilities and activity programming are critical for encouraging independence, use of facilities, and the optimal functioning of the individual. Management and programming may have a strong impact upon the success or failure of a design and use of facilities.

Elderly persons, in particular, are more likely than younger people to accept existing conditions, "rules," or policies on use of facilities, and are less likely to instigate a change in their physical or social environment. Management policies on the use of facilities may be quietly accepted by residents, although they may not accommodate residents' needs and may actually discourage use and satisfaction with the surrounding environment.

Programming activities, particularly for "new" activities or facilities, may encourage use. Coaxing, however, should not be used to encourage participation.

Examples

- A system by which residents can voice their concerns and opinions about the design and provision of on-site facilities may increase the responsiveness of facilities to residents' needs. A resident design board at Leisure World—Laguna Hills, California, is one successful example. The board has the power to evaluate, review, and propose changes or additions to on-site facilities. Some of the board's achievements have included the addition of several clubhouses, and the development of a standard design for those residents who choose to have their balconies enclosed.
- Programmed events, of special interest to residents, may increase use of facilities and interest in developing other activities that utilize the facility. An "ethnic day," held once a month on the terrace of one project, for example, spurred residents' interest in holding other events on the terrace.

- Ongoing reviews of management and programming, both by those outside of the project and by residents, can provide many insights into the appropriateness of policies on use.

References

1. Lindsley, O. R. "Geriatric Behavioral Prosthetics." In *New Thoughts on Old Age*, edited by R. Kastenbaum, New York: Springer, 1964. The term *prosthetic environment* was coined by Ogden Lindsley.

2. Lawton, M. Powell. "Planner's Notebook: Planning Environments for Older People." *American Institute of Planners Journal.* 36 (1970): 124–29.

3. Nahemow, Lucille, and M. Powell Lawton. "Toward an Ecological Theory of Adaptation and Aging." In *Proceedings of the 4th Annual Environmental Design Research Conference*, edited by W.F.E. Preiser. Stroudsburg, PA: Dowden, Hutchinson & Ross, 1973.

4. Lawton, M. Powell. "Ecology and Aging." In *Spatial Behavior of Older People*, edited by L. Pastalan and D. Carson. Ann Arbor: University of Michigan, 1970.

5. Lawton, *Planner's Notebook.*

6. DeLong, A. J. "The Micro-Spatial Structure of the Older Person: Some Implications of Planning the Social and Physical Environment." In *Spatial Behavior of Older People*, edited by L. Pastalan and D. Carson. Ann Arbor: University of Michigan, Institute of Gerontology, 1970.

7. Lawton, M. Powell. *Environment and Aging.* Monterey, CA: Brooks/Cole, 1980.

8. U.S. Department of Housing and Urban Development, Office of Policy Development and Research. *Housing for the Elderly and Handicapped: The Experience of the Section 202 Program from 1959 to 1977.* HUDPDR301. Washington, DC: U.S. Government Printing Office, 1979.

9. Lawton, *Environment and Aging.*

10. ———. *Environment and Aging.*

11. ———. *Environment and Aging*, 97.

12. ———. *Environment and Aging.*

Formulating Design Objectives

Designing for outdoor use demands a sensitivity to the spatial requirements, preferences, needs, and concerns of older people. This chapter focuses on those issues that affect the concept stages of design; Part A reviews the spatial requirements and preferences of older people, and Part B outlines important concerns such as safety and security, comfort, ease of access, and environmental negotiability.

Part A
Spatial Requirements and Preferences

One aspect of designing for outdoor use involves the way that the environment is perceived or understood. This subsection addresses how age-related changes in the sensory system and cognitive functions affect the way older people perceive and negotiate the environment. These changes suggest particular spatial organization schemes and general design responses to facilitate:

1. Orientation and wayfinding in the environment
2. Predictability of a space to reduce confusion and conflicts over appropriate uses
3. Socializing, mastering, and claiming of a space
4. Sensory stimulation and environmental comprehension

The issues and recommendations are based upon the observation that age-related changes in sensory processes may act as a "perceptual screen," filtering out certain kinds of information about the physical and social environment [1].

Cognitive changes may also affect the way older people perceive and negotiate the environment. Thus, many older people may depend more upon different sensory information when interacting with others, finding their way around an outdoor space, or interpreting clues for the appropriate use for a space [2, 3]. They may have unique spatial requirements that should be met through design to allow the individual to function optimally and to encourage outdoor use.

Issue: Orientation and Wayfinding

Objective

The arrangement and design of outdoor spaces should facilitate orientation and wayfinding.

Rationale

Failing memory and difficulty in forming a new mental concept make it more difficult for older people to orient themselves or find their way in a less familiar environment [4]. This is especially true in large planned developments or in monotonous undefined areas, where fewer clues are available for orienting. Orientation may also be difficult in areas where a number of directional options or distractions are present. Age-related losses may compound problems with orientation by reducing the number and strength of sensory clues perceived [5]. Therefore, the basic site-planning scheme or pattern should be easy to recognize and identify. Landscape detailing must also support orientation.

Recommendations

1. A spatial organization pattern that is easy to recognize and identify is basic for orientation and wayfinding. It is most applicable to larger low-rise and mixed developments, where finding one's way around the site may be more difficult.

Several common organization schemes or patterns that are easy to recognize include the radial plan, the linear plan, and the familiar street and address plan [6]. They may be applied to outdoor spaces surrounding a single high-rise building, or to low-rise and cluster developments. Some variations on these two plans are illustrated in figures 5–1 and 5–2, along with other spatial organization requirements for orientation and wayfinding.

2. Spaces should be point-integrated, with each space developed as a point along a referenced route [7, 8]. This also provides the older person with an easily identifiable reference system for orienting and wayfinding.

3. Spaces should be identified with a unique feature or focal point and supported by other design elements, such as architectural detailing unique to each housing cluster, and changes in the color, texture, and sound of the surrounding landscape. This provides sensory clues supporting the basic organization scheme.

4. Spaces should be arranged in hierarchies, with a dominant space [9, 10]. A hierarchy of space may be achieved, for example, with a community center serving as the focal point from which other spaces radiate. Creating a hierarchy of spaces ensures spatial clues for orientation.

5. Views from one area to another and views of landmarks promote orientation and wayfinding by enabling the individual to locate his or her position in relation to the rest of the site.

6. When spaces are located some distance away from each other, directional clues, such as signs, may be necessary (see "Signs" in chapter 10).

7. Directional and locational aids, such as color coding and special site layouts are generally most effective when residents are familiarized (by management, for example) with the directional-aid system employed. Maps and tours of the site also facilitate wayfinding.

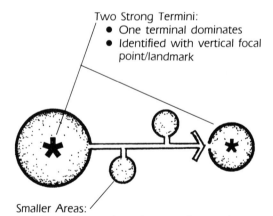

Central Area:
- One dominant focal area
- Vertical landmark
- Visible from other areas

Smaller Areas:
- Access identified by directional clues
- Visible from central area

5-1.
The radial plan is easily identified, promoting orientation and wayfinding.

Two Strong Termini:
- One terminal dominates
- Identified with vertical focal point/landmark

Smaller Areas:
- Located as points along a referenced route
- Visible from other areas and route

5-2.
The axial or linear plan promotes orientation and wayfinding by providing an easily identifiable pattern. Access routes, however, may become excessively long.

Issue: Predictability of a Space and Control

Objective

The design of outdoor spaces should suggest definite types of use as well as indicate if use is intended for a certain group, such as residents of a particular housing cluster.

Rationale

Large undefined spaces for general use are frequently found in planned housing. Yet these spaces may be a false economy and underused. Confusion and social conflicts over appropriate uses, and lack of a sense of ownership and control over the space may discourage use. Spaces that have been clearly designed for particular uses and groups and that have been differentiated from other spaces may solve many of these problems. However, these spaces should not be totally isolated, as connection to ongoing activities is popular among the elderly. Views also promote safety and security.

Recommendations

1. Spaces for use by various groups should be clearly defined and differentiated from each other. For mid- to high-rise developments, this may include defining public outdoor areas, areas for residents' use only, and areas for more intimate or private use. For low-rise and cluster housing, this may also include defining areas that "belong" to the cluster, as well as those that "belong" to individual units.

2. Landmarks and detailing suggesting particular types of use may further help identify areas and their uses. A formal landscape treatment may help define the "public" main entry of a mid-rise building, while an informal treatment may define areas for residents' casual use.

3. The size of areas may also indicate appropriate uses. Smaller defined areas, for example, suggest a private and intimate use.

4. However, outdoor spaces should not be isolated. They should present some degree of visual and physical connection to other spaces and activity.

5. Multipurpose spaces should be avoided, as confusion over use may result, especially among mentally frail older people.

Issue: Spatial Preferences—Space for Socializing, Mastering, and Claiming

Objective

Spaces should support social interaction. Some should be easily "claimed" by residents.

Rationale

In addition to the need for clear and unambiguous uses for spaces, smaller spaces are generally more appropriate for socializing and are preferred by older people. Smaller spaces are more easily negotiated and more easily claimed and mastered, particularly by the less able, who may have difficulty defending a larger space for themselves [11].

Smaller spaces facilitate social interaction and conversation. The frailer person is often intimidated and confused by larger spaces and groupings of people. In addition, larger spaces with numbers of people and other distractions may contribute to the loss of a trend of thought or confusion over who was speaking or even what was being said. Older persons who have difficulty hearing, for example, often have to concentrate so much on what is being said that they lose track of the conversation [12]. Older people may also find it more difficult to switch from concentrating on one voice to another. Listening to a single person speak from a single location may make conversation easier.

Although smaller gathering areas tend to encourage social interaction and the claiming of favorite areas and chairs, these areas should not be isolated from the action: connection to "activity" is a primary reason for the use of a space.

Recommendations

1. The general site plan and landscape treatment should create a series of smaller, more intimate spaces. These spaces are generally more appropriate

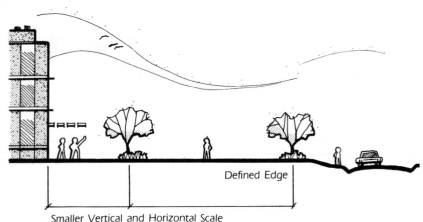

Defined Edge

Smaller Vertical and Horizontal Scale

for older persons than larger spaces are. Choices should be available (see figs. 5–3, 5–4).

2. Undefined larger multipurpose spaces should be avoided. Large group areas, such as community patios, can accommodate both small and large groups, if smaller subareas are subtly defined within the larger space. When larger spaces are necessary, smaller subareas within the space may be created through the use of overhead and vertical planes, such detailing as changes in ground-plane texture and color, as well as by manipulating the character of the area.

3. A smaller vertical scale is also important, particularly for areas near high-rise buildings and for larger open sites. Elements to reduce the apparent height and scale of mid- to high-rise buildings and to define large open spaces should be incorporated into the design of outdoor areas, particularly those for socializing and intimacy.

4. Areas with definite edges or boundaries suggesting the extent of an area reduce ambiguity.

Issue: Sensory Stimulation and Environmental Comprehension

Objective

The environment should be sensorially loaded to provide for sensory stimulation and to facilitate environmental comprehension.

Rationale

Sensorially loading the environment is one approach to compensating for age-related sensory losses.

A sensorially loaded environment is one that provides tactual, visual, and auditory stimulation to reach those with one or more sensory impairments. Tactual spaces and elements are especially important, as vi-

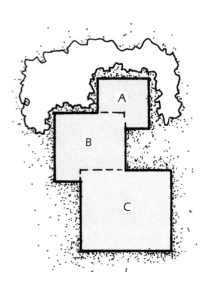

5-4.
Plan view of larger area with smaller subareas for socializing, intimacy, and claiming. Smaller subareas (A, B, and C) connect to form a larger contiguous area for group activities.

22

sion and audition are typically the first senses to decline with age.

A sensorially loaded environment may facilitate environmental comprehension, increase ease of use and confidence, reduce frustration, and encourage participation in a wider range of activities and outdoor environments. If older people cannot read the environment, they may compensate by enhancing environmental stimuli (e.g., touching a conversation partner or turning up the radio) or by reducing their dependence upon the environment [13]. The latter may result in a restriction of activity and environment to the more immediate and familiar, where fewer informational cues are necessary.

Recommendations

1. A greater level of detailing in outdoor spaces may be preferred by many older people to open spaces lacking detail. Caution must be exercised, however, to present a unified image to reduce the possibility of confusion. A balance between the level of detail and degree of uniformity is needed.

2. Visual, auditory, tactual, and kinesthetic stimulation should be available to convey the image or message of the space and to provide interest and stimulation.

3. Tactual cues are very important as they may be more easily "read" by many elderly people than auditory or visual cues. Changes in paving texture, for example, may signal upcoming stairs.

4. Where differentiation between colors is desired, yellows, oranges, and reds are more easily perceived. Blues, greens, and violets, particularly along the dark end of the spectrum and when juxtaposed, are not easily differentiated, due to the yellowing of the lens of the eye with age.

5. The intensity, quality, and quantity of light required to see may be greater than that for younger people. Night lighting outdoors is important for older people, whose eyes may not readily adjust to changes in illumination.

6. Sounds of a lower pitch and a greater intensity may be more easily heard by older people, although in some cases increased loudness will not improve reception. This has important implications for the design of audible warning and guiding systems (such as street-crossing buzzers), sound sculptures, and so on.

Part B
Safety and Security, Comfort, Ease of Access, and Environmental Negotiability

---

Designing for outdoor use not only requires a sensitivity to the spatial requirements of older people, but also a sensitivity to their feelings about outdoor use. Many older people are concerned about the safety and security of outdoor use, as well as comfort, ease of access, and environmental negotiability, or ease of use. These are very real problems for many older people, who experience declining health and susceptibility to physical injury among other changes associated with growing older. Once sensitized to these issues, however, a planner can make relatively straightforward design responses in spatial organization and simple detailing to support use of the outdoors by older persons.

The relationship between indoor and outdoor areas is central to many of these issues. Unfortunately, this relationship has generally received the least attention of any design aspect in housing for older people. Access to outdoor areas around high-rise housing, for example, is often limited to an indirect route through the front door that exits onto an exposed concrete slab. This presents abrupt and dramatic changes in environmental demands and provides no opportunity for preparation or adjustment. Important aspects of indoor–outdoor relationships examined here include visual and physical access and physical and psychological transitions between indoor and outdoor spaces.

23

Spatial organization schemes and general design responses that address safety and security, comfort, ease of access, and environmental negotiability are also examined.

Issue: A Safe and Secure Environment

Objective

The design of outdoor spaces should promote real and perceived security and safety.

Rationale

Fear of crime is the number one personal problem for many older people [14]. Stolen property is often irreplaceable, not only for its sentimental value, but also because the limited fixed income of many older people allows few purchases.

In addition, concern about falling or being attacked and not being seen or aided is high among older people. They are more vulnerable to long-term disabilities caused by a fall or an attack.

The rate of more serious crimes (e.g., assault) against the elderly is lower than among other age groups. However, less violent crimes do affect older people, including purse snatching, vandalism, and theft of social security checks from the mail. The statistics on crime rates, however, do not reduce fear among many older people. Thus measures for safety and security, as well as negotiability, are critical for promoting outdoor use.

Recommendations

1. Frequently used outdoor areas must be located to allow visual surveillance by residents and staff. Visual surveillance is particularly important for building entries, areas for socializing, and main connector walkways. These areas, for example, may be visible from the main office, lounge, or other areas frequented by staff and residents (see fig. 5–5).

2. Frequently used outdoor areas should be located for physical protection, such as that offered by two sides of an L-shaped building or by an area enclosed within a cluster. Such areas, which promote use by offering a sense of security and safety, are often prized by many older people. Building entries and social/seating areas, in particular, require protection (see fig. 5–6).

3. A clear transition from neighborhood public space to private space increases control over use and defines areas, or territories, for residents only. A series of spaces for public, communal, cluster, and individual or unit use is particularly important for large open sites—those which offer space for neighborhood use and those in areas with security problems (see fig. 5–7).

4. A clearly defined edge condition may encourage a sense of security, safety, and control over a space. In neighborhoods with security problems, this may involve enclosing part or all of the site, as in the popular courtyard arrangement. Larger sites may require fencing and guarded gates, though the problem of isolation from the community must be carefully weighed.

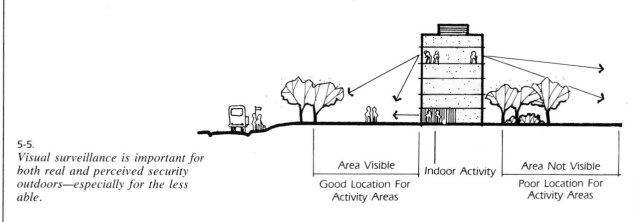

5-5.
Visual surveillance is important for both real and perceived security outdoors—especially for the less able.

Area Visible | Indoor Activity | Area Not Visible

Good Location For Activity Areas

Poor Location For Activity Areas

24

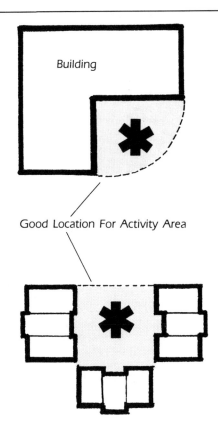

Good Location For Activity Area

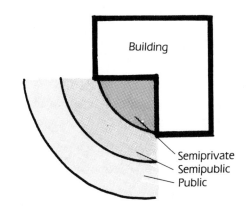

5-7.
Defined zones, from private to public spaces, help to define appropriate uses for a space while promoting safety and security.

5. Detailing, such as lighting, low-growing or high-branching plant materials that allow for surveillance, and elements for negotiability, such as handrails, promote a sense of security and safety (see chapter 10). Emergency call boxes and telephones are options, particularly for larger sites and where residents are more frail.

Issue: Ease of Access—Transitions for Physical and Psychological Comfort

Objective

Comfortable and easy access between indoor and outdoor areas and between different types of outdoor areas should be available.

Rationale

Areas of access and transition between two different types of environments are particularly important for

5-6. (left)
Physical protection provided by a building edge or cluster of units offers a needed sense of security for many outdoor spaces, especially those for socializing and for use by the more frail.

less able elderly, who may be unsure of their ability to participate in activities or their ability to negotiate environments demanding more physical and/or psychological effort.

Many older people require time to evaluate and prepare for changes in the environment. A halfway zone, where the environment presents only limited demand and allows for vicarious participation, can provide this opportunity.

The greater the change in demands for adapting to social or physical changes in the environment, the greater the necessity for a transition or a series of transitions. Where transitions and easy access routes to facilities are not available, use of the area may suffer.

Recommendations

1. Transition areas for access should be available between major indoor and outdoor areas. These

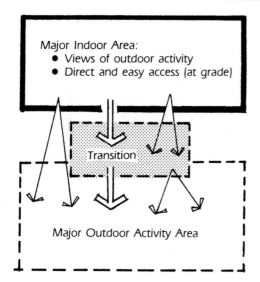

5-8.
Indoor-outdoor transition areas promote outdoor use by allowing for physical and psychological adjustment to the demands of the outdoor environment. These transition areas (e.g., porch) should offer: (1) views to and from indoors; (2) easy and direct access; (3) protection from weather/glare; (4) comfortable seating; and (5) a sense of enclosure and human scale.

should act as halfway zones, offering seating and viewing opportunities and easy, direct access to indoor and outdoor areas. Protection from weather and glare should also be available.

These areas allow for evaluation, preparation for participation, or just vicarious participation. A screened porch connecting a lounge and patio area, for example, offers protection from weather and a sense of security for less competent residents, who might otherwise find the outdoors too demanding (see fig. 5–8).

2. Transition areas between two different types of outdoor areas should provide opportunities for viewing the upcoming activity area and for vicarious participation. A transition area should be provided between an active recreation area and passive seating areas, for example, or between the site and the neighborhood (see fig. 5–9).

3. A single element or feature may provide subtle psychological and physical transition. A handrail for a moment's hesitation, an overhang for gradual adjustment to changes in illumination and protection from

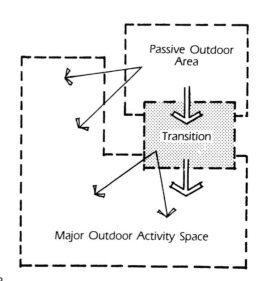

5-9.
Outdoor transition areas between two different types of use areas should provide a comfortable and protected place for viewing activity and for preparation before participation. These areas are essential for those who are less sure of their own abilities.

weather at minor building exits, or a window for a brief view are examples of design elements that serve as the first step in evaluation, preparation, adjustment, and participation.

Issue: Visual and Physical Access to Outdoor Areas

Objective

Clear visual and physical access should be available between indoor and outdoor activity areas.

Rationale

Views of the outdoors are the first invitation to outdoor use. Indoor areas for viewing outdoor activity, with close, direct, and easy access to the outdoors, may encourage outdoor use. This may be particularly important for mid- to high-rise housing and for developments that house more dependent older people, whose access to the outdoors may seem more diffi-

26

cult. Transitions should be incorporated into the access route, providing easy physical and psychological passage (see "Ease of Access," above).

Recommendations

1. A variety of views and access routes should be available to outdoor areas. Formal and informal views and access routes are some examples (see fig. 5–10).

2. Indoor viewing areas should be available with direct and easy access to and from major outdoor areas. A viewing area adjacent to the lobby of a mid-rise building, for example, may overlook the entry drive (see fig. 5–11).

Issue: Comfort and Environmental Negotiability

Objective

The design of outdoor areas should provide for comfort and environmental negotiability.

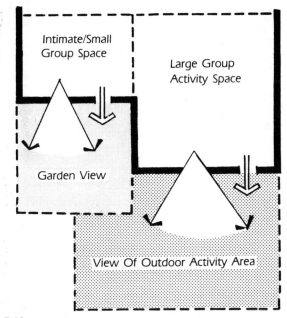

5-10.
Views and direct access between indoor and outdoor spaces maximize use of both; connections between similar types of spaces can reinforce appropriate use, especially for those who are easily confused. Too many access points, however, are also confusing.

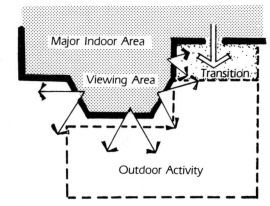

5-11.
Connections between key indoor and outdoor areas (e.g., lobby and arrival court) require special attention for maximizing views and providing direct access through a transition space. Door stoops should be visible from inside the building.

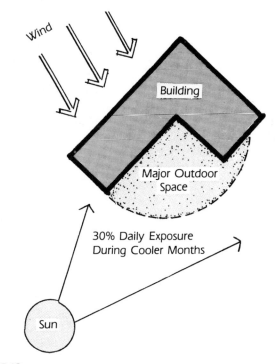

5-12.
Building orientation and the location of major outdoor spaces should maximize sun exposure during cooler months and moderate extremes in weather. Thirty percent daily sun exposure during fall, winter, and spring is ideal for major outdoor spaces.

27

Rationale

Comfort and negotiability, or ease of use of the outdoors, are major concerns for many senior citizens. Some aids to negotiability and comfort are relatively straightforward, such as wheelchair ramps, and rails. Others are more subtle, such as lighting levels, reflections of light on surfaces, glare from windows, hazardous ground-plane textures, chair design, package shelves at entries, and others. These require an understanding of the aging process. Many specific design responses for comfort and negotiability are covered in Part Three.

Recommendations

Comfort, access, and negotiability are especially important for high-use areas, such as building entries and activity areas. Orientation for maximum protection from wind, snow, excessive sun, and heat is an important concern. In colder climates, sun exposure during winter months can help melt snow and ice (see fig. 5–12).

References

1. Delong, A. J. "The Micro-Spatial Structure of the Older Person: Some Implications of Planning the Social and Physical Environment." In *Spatial Behavior of Older People*, edited by L. Pastalan and D. Carson. Ann Arbor: University of Michigan, 1970.

2. ———. "The Micro-Spatial Structure of the Older Person."

3. Pastalan, Leon A. "How the Elderly Negotiate their Environment." Paper presented at Environment for the Aged: A Working Conference on Behavioral Research, Utilization and Environmental Policy, at San Juan, Puerto Rico, December 1971.

4. Koncelik, Joseph A. *Designing the Open Nursing Home*. Community Development Series no. 27. Stroudsburg, PA: Dowden, Hutchinson & Ross, 1976.

5. Atchely, Robert C. *The Social Forces in Later Life: An Introduction to Social Gerontology*. Belmont, CA: Wadsworth Press, 1972.

6. Green, Isaac, et al. *Housing for the Elderly: The Development and Design Process*. New York: Van Nostrand Reinhold, 1975.

7. DeLong. "The Micro-Spatial Structure of the Older Person."

8. Pastalan. "How the Elderly Negotiate their Environment."

9. DeLong. "The Micro-Spatial Structure of the Older Person."

10. Pastalan. "How the Elderly Negotiate their Environment."

11. ———. "How the Elderly Negotiate their Environment."

12. Rabbit, Patrick. Quoted in "The Twilight of Memory." *Time*, July 1981, 81.

13. Lawton, M. Powell. "Planner's Notebook: Planning Environments for Older People." *American Institute of Planners Journal*. 36 (1970): 124–29.

14. Lawton, M. Powell. *Environment and Aging*. Monterey, CA: Brooks/Cole, 1980.

Housing provision, more than any other type of designed environment for the aged, must address a vast range of issues, needs, and abilities. The importance of the housing environment, as a supplier of daily needs, friendship, and self-fulfillment, grows with advancing years. Thus, providing a "home," not an institution, is a foremost goal. This involves balancing independence with care, and the functional with the social and aesthetic. The advancing frailties of age must be addressed, but assistance should only be offered when older persons cannot manage on their own. Some degree of flexibility is also needed to accommodate the changing needs of the tenants through the planning and design of housing. A custodial approach that robs people of their personal independence is not the answer.

In this section, important site-planning concepts and design recommendations for major site-planning elements illustrate how functional considerations, such as unit clustering or building entry, can meet the special needs and concerns of the older population. Case examples of actual projects illustrate the application of many concepts.

Site-Development Patterns: The Surrounding Neighborhood and On-Site Conditions

An important part of designing housing for senior citizens is the overall site-planning scheme or pattern and the various subpatterns that support it, such as patterns of open space, circulation, and low-rise clustering. Some important site-planning patterns that respond to the special needs of older people are outlined in this chapter. These patterns address behavioral issues, or goals, such as orientation, or wayfinding, and social interaction. Other factors that may influence the site-planning pattern are also discussed, including the characteristics of the site and surrounding neighborhood; the development (e.g., high-rise or low-rise), and service type (e.g., independent or dependent living). Examples of actual projects illustrating the various points are also provided.

Particularly strong or unique site and neighborhood characteristics may affect much of the site-development pattern and the way in which the needs of older people are met. A site with great variation in topography, for example, may suggest a particular circulation pattern for easy access; a neighborhood with safety and security problems may suggest an inwardly oriented development. Many important aspects of the surrounding condition, however, are more appropriately addressed through careful site selection.

The Surrounding Neighborhood

The condition of the surrounding neighborhood may have a strong influence upon the site-development scheme or pattern. This may be especially true in those neighborhoods with a discernible social character (e.g., problems with safety and security, or a close ethnic community), as well as those with a strong physical character, such as a highly developed neighborhood (e.g., urban). Due to physical proximity, smaller sites may be more affected by surrounding conditions.

The availability and ease of access to neighborhood services and facilities are important aspects of site planning, especially where few on-site services and facilities are available to residents. Some important responses to the surrounding condition are outlined below.

1. In general, the development zone should be located and oriented for easy and direct access to neighborhood services and facilities, including stores (e.g., grocery and drug stores); public transportation routes and stops; neighborhood activity centers; attractions (e.g., a park); and places of worship (see table 6–1).

Access to services and facilities may be important for ease and satisfaction with daily living; it is essential for less able older people and when few services and facilities are available on-site.

2. In some instances, the sharing of project and neighborhood facilities may be appropriate and mutually beneficial to both the community and project residents. This is especially true in communities with strong social ties. Site planning and design considerations for security, however, are essential for shared on-site facilities; separate resident and nonresident building entrances, a location that is easy for nonresidents to identify, and controlled access to residential areas within the project contribute to security (see Fig. 6–1).

3. The overall layout should maximize exceptional off-site views, especially of activity if such views are not available on-site. Views of off-site activity often draw people, thus generating use of on-site facilities.

4. The development should not be oriented toward those off-site areas that present safety and security problems, visual blights, or excessive noise. A buffer should be established between these areas and the development.

Table 6–1 CRITERIA FOR PROXIMITY TO SERVICES FOR THE ELDERLY

	Independent Apartments (feet)	Congregate (feet)
Mandatory services		
Food store (with competitive prices)	1,500	2,000
Drugstore	1,500	1,500
Transit stop (where transportation exists)	1,500	1,500
Desirable services*		
Department or clothing store	2,000	2,000
Bank	2,000	2,000
Medical services	2,500	2,500
Beauty parlor	2,500	2,000
Barbershop	2,500	2,000
Restaurant	3,000	3,000
Post Office	3,000	3,000

*Selection priority should be given to sites offering as many of these services within the prescribed (or shorter) distances as possible.

SOURCE: After: Isaac Green et al. *Housing for the Elderly: The Development and Design Process.* New York: Van Nostrand Reinhold, 1975, 40. Reprinted with permission.

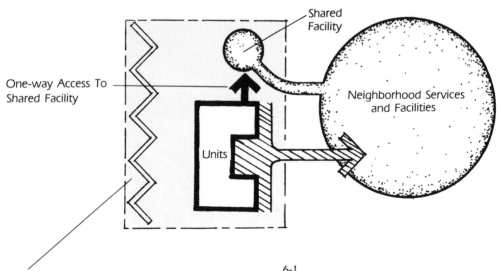

One-way Access To Shared Facility

Shared Facility

Neighborhood Services and Facilities

Units

Buffer Excessive Noise/Security Problems

6-1.
The development orientation should maximize access to key neighborhood services and facilities. On-site facilities for use by the community (e.g., day care) enhance opportunities for age-integrated activity; however, community access should not require passing through residential areas.

Neighborhood Services and Facilities

5. Totally enclosed sites and inwardly oriented developments marketed as secure, and/or private communities are becoming increasingly common in both safe and unsafe neighborhoods.

The problems of creating an institutionalized image and of isolating residents from community activity, however, must be carefully considered. A site plan that maximizes visual surveillance of the site and defines areas that "belong" to the project and residents also enhances security (see fig. 6–2).

6. Pedestrian access to neighborhood facilites should not involve a cumulative slope greater than 5 percent off-site, or access grades greater than 10 percent running longer than 75 feet (see fig. 6–3). [1]

6-2.
An inwardly oriented development can promote a sense of community and security within the project. Isolation from the community and an institutional image, however, may result—especially if primary services are provided on-site and residents' mobility is limited. Some connection to the neighborhood is desirable.

6-3.
The development should be located on that portion of the site where access to neighborhood services does not involve a cumulative slope greater than 5 percent overall. Building entry areas should have a maximum slope of 2 percent (no steps or ramps).

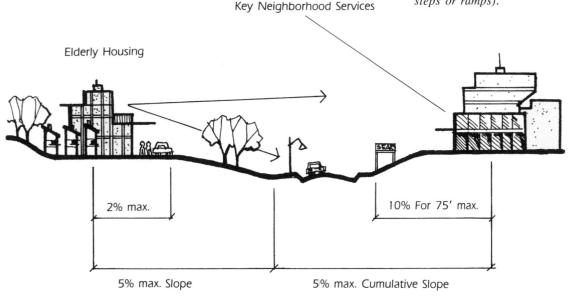

Key Neighborhood Services

Elderly Housing

2% max.

10% For 75' max.

5% max. Slope

5% max. Cumulative Slope

On-Site Conditions
and Development Patterns

The overall site-development pattern may affect many facets of outdoor use, from relatively straightforward aspects such as access to facilities to the more subtle, but equally important issues, such as feeling safe and secure outside or having opportunities to meet others—or not to meet them!

Some general goals for site planning are outlined in the remainder of this chapter, along with special considerations for developing patterns of circulation, social spaces, low-rise unit clusters, and housing for a range of ability levels. Where applicable, special note is made for common on-site conditions, such as variations in topography and unique natural features.

The size of the site and type of development affects the site-planning pattern. This may be illustrated through a comparison of two common design situations: (1) a single high-rise building on a small site and (2) a low-rise development on a larger site.

The very nature of mid- to high-rise housing often includes a strong indoor center of activity, partly because indoor communal spaces and residential units are housed within the same building, thereby reducing the likelihood of outdoor use. This indoor orientation suggests that outdoor spaces should be developed with a strong relationship to indoor activity spaces. An architectural transition to outdoors helps to provide a human scale that contrasts with the mass of the building. Although activity may be indoor oriented, the value of well-designed outdoor spaces for recreation and pleasure is not diminished. Outdoor spaces may provide a very needed opportunity for enjoying nature and relief from the high-density living of high-rise buildings.

A small site with low- to mid-rise development often suggests a dual concept of protected courtyard-type spaces, and street or neighborhood-oriented spaces. This arrangement affords the choice between security and activity, while enhancing a sense of place (see fig. 6–4).

A large site with low-rise development presents a different set of site-planning challenges, although the basic goals may be quite similar to those of high-rise developments on smaller sites. Residential units and indoor activity spaces are often located in separate buildings throughout the site, and there is a lower density of development. Thus outdoor spaces, while serving as the connecting fabric between on-site facilities, may become activity spaces in themselves. The larger scale and greater variety of potential outdoor spaces also present special challenges, such as facilitating wayfinding, defining outdoor activity spaces (especially on open sites), and creating a center (or centers) of activity that serves as a focal point for the development as well as establishes a sense of place (see fig. 6–5). Housing developed as a continuation of the neighborhood fabric (such as the standard street and address plan) reduces the potential for isolation from the neighborhood and an institutionalized image, although the provision of shared services and facilities may be more difficult, making this type of arrangement more suited to housing for independent seniors (see fig. 6–6).

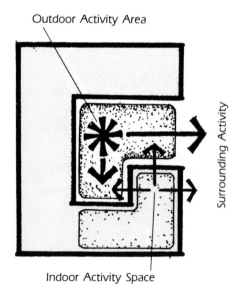

6-4.
Indoor and outdoor activity spaces are generally most successful when offering a dual orientation toward secure/protected areas and surrounding activity.

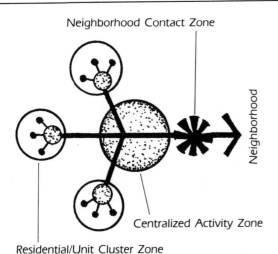

Neighborhood Contact Zone

Neighborhood

Centralized Activity Zone

Residential/Unit Cluster Zone

6-5.
Defined zones of activity and a focal point for the development promote a sense of community and ownership while enhancing wayfinding. Activity zones may include a neighborhood contact zone, central activity area, residential cluster zones, and individual unit space.

General Recommendations

1. To facilitate wayfinding, the site plan should present an overall pattern that residents and visitors may easily identify and recognize. This is important for larger developments where less able residents may find it difficult to find their way about the site without a reference system. A strong center (often the main arrival court or community building) generally promotes wayfinding as well as a sense of place (see "Orientation and Wayfinding" in chapter 5).

The radial plan, the axial plan, and the more traditional street and address plan are some examples of site patterns that are easy to recognize and identify.

2. A site-development pattern that provides a hierarchy of spaces, from public to private, promotes a sense of place and ownership for communal areas as well as for cluster and unit areas. These hierarchies must be integral with the larger overall pattern.

3. Creating defined zones of activity can help make the general layout of the site easier to understand as well as focus activity (see fig. 6–5). These zones can include:

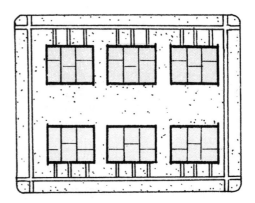

6-6.
Housing developed as a part of the neighborhood fabric, as in the standard street-and-address plan, is particularly viable for independent living. Services, shared facilities, and security are more difficult to provide and monitor, however, with a decentralized pattern.

- the zone of contact between the site and the neighborhood
- common space, building, and private-unit entry zones
- recreation zones (both active and passive, as well as areas for the development as a whole and those for unit clusters)

A Centralized Pattern

In general, a tight, or centralized, site-planning pattern is preferable to a sprawling one. Well conceived, a tight site-planning pattern should provide easy and direct access between all residential units and on-site facilities. This is a significant consideration for larger sites with low-density development, where a sprawling pattern may isolate facilities and make access difficult.

A tight site plan should strive to accomplish the following goals (see fig. 6–7):

1. Minimize the distance required for access to major on-site services and facilities, providing direct access from all residential units to parking, community centers, and other major facilities.

This is of real value in harsh climates, where long walking distances in rain, snow, or excessive heat may discourage use of facilities. Covering main access routes or even enclosing them are options for extreme climates.

2. Provide visual connections between on-site activity areas. This results in greater opportunities for vicarious participation in activities and increases the likelihood of impromptu social interaction as well as the sense of outdoor safety and security.

3. Reserve areas on-site for recreational and pleasure uses that require larger parcels of land or a location removed from activity (such as retreats or even a golf course).

4. Maintain or enhance natural features on-site through appropriate siting of the development zone. The development may be oriented for views and access to areas of natural beauty. Wooded areas, for example, may be maintained for enjoyment and exploration, while open areas on-site may be developed for residential units.

5. Develop activity centers and residential areas on that portion of the site where on-site pedestrian access will not involve a slope greater than 5 percent [2].

This is most important in colder climates, where snow and ice pose an increased threat for safety and negotiability on a slope, and for those areas that house less agile older people (see "Circulation," below).

6. Indoor and outdoor recreational and social spaces should be grouped to create a focal point for activity, maximizing options for activity participation. Some options include the following:

- Outdoor activity centers may be linked to a separate recreational building. This arrangement provides relative design freedom for a recreational center; with high-rise buildings it enables the development of a more intimate scale for the recreation center.
- Linking outdoor activity centers to indoor facilities establishes a strong center for activity. Some type of architectural transition, however, may be required for larger buildings to ensure a human scale for outdoor activity centers.

Housing for a Range of Competency Levels

Many developments offer a range of housing types and services for older people of different competencies. The location of housing and facilities for the more dependent resident, and the relationship of this housing and facilities to those for the more competent, however, is a complex social and design issue that is not easily resolved. Some of the concerns are outlined below; the appropriate design response must be evaluated for each individual project and group of residents.

1. Separation of on-site facilities for residents of different ability levels is a common design approach. Several points can be noted in favor of this arrangement:

- People tend naturally to group themselves. In many projects, more able residents prefer not to mingle on a daily basis with the less competent.

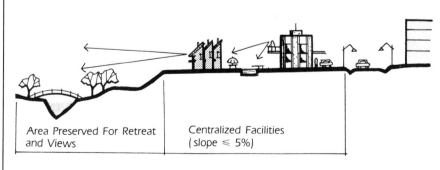

Area Preserved For Retreat and Views

Centralized Facilities (slope ≤ 5%)

6-7.
A centralized pattern of development that establishes visual and physical connections between key areas on- and off-site maximizes opportunities for participation and use. Centralized development also enables the preservation/enhancement of natural features.

- More able residents, if housed adjacent to facilities for the frail, may associate this physical proximity as a personal closeness to death and dying.
- Integration of intensive-care facilities (especially in large complexes) with more independent living may promote a "hospital" image for the development as a whole, rather than an image of "living."
- The social costs of separation may be reduced by a management that encourages volunteer interaction, such as visiting, reading for the visually impaired, and so on.

2. Integration of facilities for those of all competency levels, especially for those requiring acute care, is not a common housing arrangement in the United States. Grouping intermediate- and acute-care facilities with separate facilities for independent living is somewhat more common, as is grouping of independent and intermediate facilities with separate facilities for acute care. The rationale for shared facilities includes the following:

- Financial incentives encourage shared services and facilities. This rationale, however, also allows for separate housing linked by common support facilities and services.
- Integration promotes sharing, mutual assistance, and self-help, as well as providing a powerful source for social learning.
- Segregated facilities often require the eventual movement of residents and the separation of spouses and friends. Such a move can have very negative effects upon the residents' health.
- Shared facilities may be more appropriate for some ethnic groups with strong family and social ties.

3. The decision to create separate zones or to integrate care facilities must be carefully weighed. Options for spatial arrangements include the following (see also figs. 6–8, 6–9, 6–10):

- Separating housing zones for independent living, congregate, and more intensive-care facilities.
- Clustering intermediate- and acute-care facilities and support services together or separating them subtly (e.g., separate building wings), while providing a separate zone for independent housing.
- Establishing physical distance between various care

levels. A gradient of care across the site, based upon the level of services required, and shared facilities is one example. This arrangement, however, places limitations upon access to facilities and isolates residents.
- A shared meeting ground of common spaces, but separate residential areas and facilities suitable for each ability level.
- A radial arrangement, with common facilities and social areas as the central element, is another possibility. Services and facilities common to various levels of care can establish housing adjacencies on the radial arrangement.
- A clear change in landscape treatment or topography can provide separation without physical distance and isolation. This arrangement allows for physical closeness, promoting a sense of security among the less able.

4. Special provisions for the safety of the mentally frail are necessary if outdoor use is to be encouraged, or even allowed. Some residents may wander into potentially hazardous areas; therefore, staff may restrict outdoor access to times when an escort is available (which may not be very often). The importance of safety considerations is underscored by the experience at one project, where several residents were found walking along a major freeway in Los Angeles.

- A good location for outdoor areas serving the frail older person is one that is protected from potentially hazardous areas or places in which one can easily get lost.
- A location near housing for more able residents can promote a sense of safety and security for the more frail; a subtle distance between the two facilities, however, may be appropriate so that housing for the more frail does not serve as a constant reminder of care for the more able [3].
- An enclosed outdoor space, such as a courtyard, in addition to more open areas, may accommodate a range of ability levels.

5. Many of the considerations mentioned throughout this chapter, such as access and wayfinding, are of special importance for the more mentally and physically frail resident.

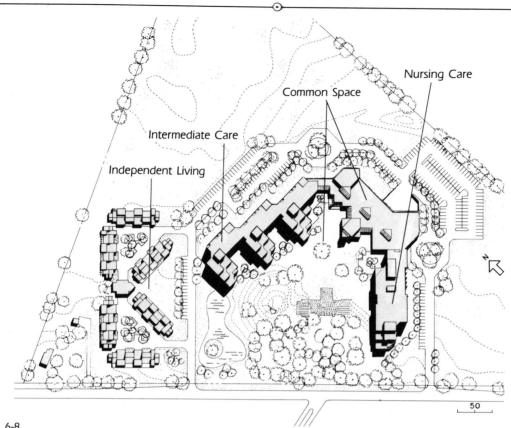

Independent Living

Intermediate Care

Common Space

Nursing Care

N

50

6-8.

Maple Knoll Village, Ohio: Town houses developed as a separate complex promote an image of independent living. The nursing and intermediate-care facilities are housed in separate wings; shared common space (lounge, chapel, therapy, and outdoor spaces) provides opportunities for interaction. The Gruzen Partnership, Architects and Planners, New York. Landscape Architect: M. Paul Friedberg and Associates, New York. Reprinted with permission.

Circulation

The layout of pedestrian, vehicular, and bicycle circulation systems should establish a pattern that, like the overall site plan, is easy to recognize and identify. Circulation systems should also accomplish the following goals (see fig. 6–11):

1. Provide easy and direct access to on- and off-site facilities, allowing for the natural flow of movement.

2. Support social interaction. The general layout of pedestrian circulation systems may be developed as a feeder or collector system to achieve this. Walkways leading from units, for example, may converge on a cluster walkway, and cluster walkways converge on a major access route. This arrangement provides greater opportunities for meeting others by collecting people en route, as well as supporting the hierarchy of public to private spaces established through the overall site plan.

3. Access to residential units should not require passing directly through activity areas, nor should access to activity areas require passing through semi-private residential areas.

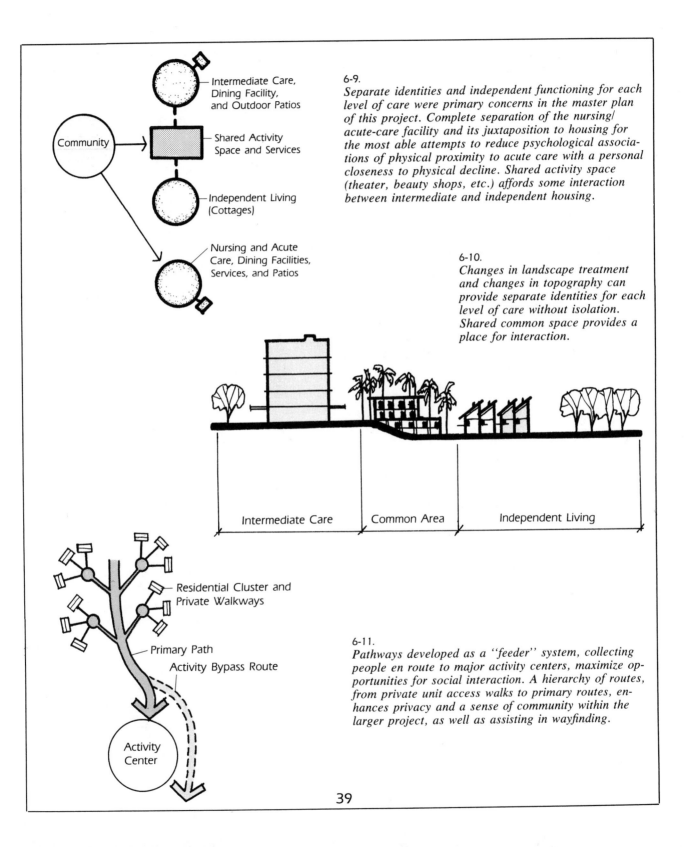

Intermediate Care,
Dining Facility,
and Outdoor Patios

Community

Shared Activity
Space and Services

Independent Living
(Cottages)

Nursing and Acute
Care, Dining Facilities,
Services, and Patios

6-9.
Separate identities and independent functioning for each level of care were primary concerns in the master plan of this project. Complete separation of the nursing/ acute-care facility and its juxtaposition to housing for the most able attempts to reduce psychological associations of physical proximity to acute care with a personal closeness to physical decline. Shared activity space (theater, beauty shops, etc.) affords some interaction between intermediate and independent housing.

6-10.
Changes in landscape treatment and changes in topography can provide separate identities for each level of care without isolation. Shared common space provides a place for interaction.

Intermediate Care | Common Area | Independent Living

Residential Cluster and
Private Walkways

Primary Path

Activity Bypass Route

6-11.
Pathways developed as a ''feeder'' system, collecting people en route to major activity centers, maximize opportunities for social interaction. A hierarchy of routes, from private unit access walks to primary routes, enhances privacy and a sense of community within the larger project, as well as assisting in wayfinding.

Activity
Center

4. Crossing pedestrian, vehicular, and bicycle systems poses a safety problem, particularly for older people who may have poor vision and slower reaction times.

5. Major access routes located for maximum protection from strong winds, or excessive glare promote comfort. In cold climates, consideration for maximum sun exposure in fall, winter, and spring, to allow the snow and ice to melt, increases safety.

6. Major access routes that are within view of activity areas allow for surveillance, safety, and security.

7. Major on-site pedestrian access routes should not involve a slope greater than 5 percent [4].

8. The layout of pleasure routes should consider providing "goals" in the landscape to encourage walking.

9. Pathway and pedestrian control is important for security. Pathways should not provide a convenient shortcut for nonresidents, especially diagonal access from two right-angled streets.

Parking Requirements

Parking is essential for elderly persons to maintain their independence. Many factors, however, will affect the number of parking spaces required at a particular development, including the level of care offered and the site location. More intensive care facilities, for example, generally require fewer resident parking spaces and increased staff parking. Unfortunately, little research has been undertaken to determine the appropriate parking/unit ratio for various situations. What information does exist tends to be disparate. Important factors to consider in determining parking requirements are noted below. Parking lot design and detailing are covered in chapter 7.

1. Market analysis of prospective residents' use of the automobile is ideal for determining parking requirements. Local zoning requirements for parking ratios should be used only as a general guide, as they are based upon averages, while housing developments for the elderly and the elderly themselves do not represent homogenous groups. Dependence on so-called standards or other assumptions may result

in too many parking spaces or, more commonly, too few.

One example that illustrates the pivotal role of parking is that of a recently constructed continuum-of-care project, where town house sales were virtually negligible. Expecting that "retiring" seniors would be attracted by the level of services and care offered, developers provided very little resident parking (services and facilities included meals, project-owned limousine and van services, and key neighborhood services within two blocks). The development was, however, drawing more able-bodied prospective buyers. Only with additional parking (bringing the ratio to slightly over 1:1) did the units actually sell. Although parking is still inadequate, the management expects that, as the average age of residents increases over the years, car ownership will decline, and with it the demand for parking.

2. The site location (urban, suburban, rural, etc.) and its proximity to basic services and transportation also influence parking requirements. As noted, however, present guidelines are often contradictory, although all indicate a general increase in parking requirements as neighborhood services and public transportation become less proximate (see table 6–1 for proximity to services requirements).

For example, the Michigan State Housing Development Authority (MSHDA) recommends almost four times the amount of parking than does the Central Mortgage and Housing Corporation of Canada (CMHC) (see table 6–2).

3. Adequate long-term parking for residents and staff and short-term parking for visitors must be available. Resident and visitor parking should be located for close and easy access to units and major facilities.

4. Smaller parking lots associated with particular units and facilities are preferable to larger lots.

Social Spaces

Views for safety and security, a sense of protection, and connection to activity are especially important for social spaces. (see "Issue: Spatial Preferences" in chapter 5, fig. 6–12, "Shared Patios and Terraces" and "Unit Patios and Balconies" in chapter 9).

Table 6–2 COMPARISON OF PARKING RATIO REQUIREMENTS

Site Characteristics	Comparison of Parking Ratios* (CMHC)	(MSHDA)
Urban site, good access to full range of services and public transportation	.167	.5
Suburban site, with fair access to services and public transportation	.2	.75
Rural/small town site with poor access to facilities and public transportation and/or high rate of local car use	.25	1.0

*Number of parking spaces per unit.

SOURCE: For MSHDA—Isaac Green et al. *Housing for the Elderly: The Development and Design Process.* New York: Van Nostrand Reinhold, 1975, 15. Reprinted with permission. For CMHC—Central Mortgage and Housing Corporation. Minister of State of Affairs. *Housing the Elderly.* Ottawa, Canada: CMHC, 1975, 5.

1. Social spaces that are easily accessible from indoor activity spaces are generally the most successful, especially at projects housing the more frail.

2. Social spaces should provide a hierarchy of options, from private unit spaces and intimate or small-group spaces, to community-wide spaces for meeting others (see fig. 6–12).

3. Spaces with a dual orientation toward both protected or secure areas and active areas, such as the neighborhood, provide greater options for meeting others as well as control and security. One example is a partially enclosed courtyard with views and controlled access to the street.

4. A smaller scale and sense of protection and enclosure may be more appropriate for most social spaces. Structures and landscaping on-site should be arranged to create intimate protected social spaces outdoors, such as a warm pocket created by a U-shaped building or a cluster of units while maintaining views of activity.

5. It is possible to have too many social spaces, and as a result the people using a social space can become too dispersed so that spaces may seem empty.

6. A location protected from too much sun, heat, and wind promotes use of social spaces by all. A primarily northern exposure is not appropriate; a westerly exposure requires design features to reduce glare and excessive heat.

7. Social spaces that provide a natural reason for being there are ideal. Examples include those near major pedestrian routes or groupings of functional facilities, such as laundry areas.

Low-rise Unit Clustering

Many basic site-planning issues for developing unit cluster patterns have been covered throughout this chapter, including easy access, ease of wayfinding, and so on. In addition to these concerns, some special site-planning considerations for unit clustering are outlined below (see figs. 6–13 and 6–14).

1. Clusters that are easy to recognize and identify, with a unique character, promote orientation as well as a sense of place and belonging.

2. A socially oriented arrangement of units is ideal.

- Clusters of up to approximately 20 units promote a sense of neighborhood [5].
- Unit layouts that define common space for the units and control access (e.g., U-shaped, circular, or elliptical arrangements) enhance social interaction and security.

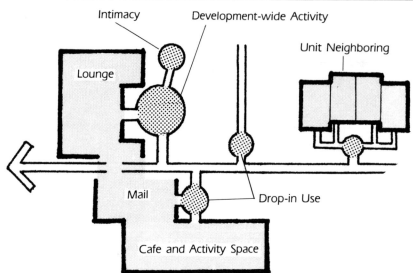

Intimacy   Development-wide Activity

Lounge

Unit Neighboring

Mail

Drop-in Use

Cafe and Activity Space

6-12.
Key locations for outdoor social spaces are those connected to activity generators (e.g., mailboxes, cafe) or along pedestrian routes. Options for intimacy, visiting neighbors, and development-wide socializing are ideal.

- Grouping functional facilities for the cluster, such as mailboxes and laundry facilities, promotes a sense of community within the cluster.

3. Unit clusters should be arranged to provide opportunities for meeting others in the cluster while maintaining unit privacy and identity. Walkway layouts are an important element in this. One possible design response is to orient units so that individual patios or balconies line both sides of a common walkway or social space.

- Easy and equal visual and physical access from all units to the common space provides opportunities for drop-in socializing by all residents, enhancing the feeling of "equal" ownership.
- A viewing distance of approximately 20 to 100 feet between units and shared activity spaces, for example, will allow most residents to recognize others or identify activity, while maintaining unit privacy [6].

4. Access walks leading to a cluster of units should be separate from access walks for the development as a whole. This arrangement enhances cluster identity and increases residents' control over access. Private unit walkways are also desirable.

5. The front and back of units should be clearly defined. This arrangement enables unit entries to function as they would in a private residence—the front entry serving as a formal display and symbolic greeting area, the back functioning for everyday purposes.

6. Small parking clusters relating to the units enhance the sense of community and are most convenient, especially for the less mobile older person (see "Parking Requirements," in this chapter, and "Parking and Building Access," in chapter 7).

Case Examples

Many aspects of the surrounding neighborhood and the overall site plan are important when designing housing for senior citizens. It is nearly impossible to integrate all of these considerations into one particular project. The following examples, however, illustrate how some of these principles have been applied to the site planning of actual projects.

Case Example: Redevelopment of a Multilevel Care Facility

Motion Picture and Television Country House and Hospital
Woodland Hills, California
Architects: Bobrow/Thomas and Associates

This project demonstrates many issues for the site

planning of larger developments. The unique nature of the group of residents is of special interest, as is a series of planning solutions to accommodate many levels of care on-site. The final proposal more closely matches residents' preferences for maintaining the country character of the project and for separation of housing based upon level of care.

Background and Setting. The Motion Picture and Television Fund operates the project on 41 acres in Woodland Hills, California. The layout and design of the existing facilities provide for three somewhat distinct communities: a lodge with a hotel atmosphere for the semidependent, semiattached country-type cottages (for semi- to fully independent living) and a modern acute-care facility (see fig. 6–15). The slightly rolling hills and native California plant materials lend a relaxed, country/campus atmosphere to much of the project. Recreational facilities are minimal.

Residents of this project, although they come from varied backgrounds, share one common bond: they have all worked in the motion picture and television industry and have contributed to a fund over a period of years to guarantee their life care. Stagehands, sound technicians, and others (often with little means of support) outnumber the stars, who have included Mary Astor, Larry Fine (of the Three Stooges), and Regis Toomey.

Many vestiges of Hollywood enliven and warm the hearts of residents and visitors. Residents are quick to offer photographic advice, or point out a "real star." The on-site theater shows a bevy of films. Even the signage is reminiscent of a sound stage.

Because of the variety of housing and care offered, residents exhibit a wide range of abilities and dependency. Although a move to the project is usually prompted by health problems, more able residents may be found strolling along the meandering pathway system, while the less able often find a comfortable spot near building entries to watch the day's activities.

Shared Activity Building

To Activity Areas

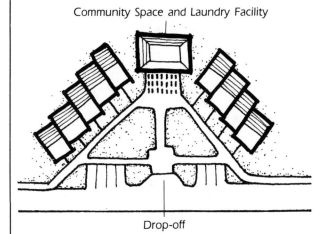

Community Space and Laundry Facility

Drop-off

6-14.
A centralized social space within view of unit entries and the drop-off area maximizes opportunities for visiting neighbors and drop-in use.

6-13. (left)
This cluster of units defines a common "backyard" space for activity; access through the space to development-wide activity areas enhances use. Equal access from units and visibility from private patios promote a sense of ownership and control. Nearby parking is a plus.

43

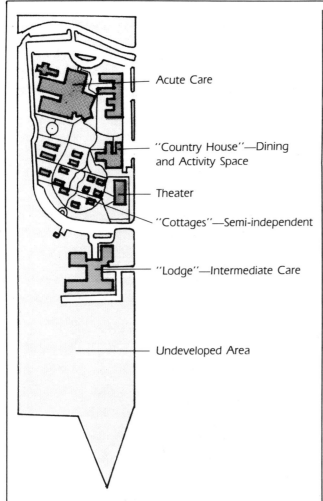

Acute Care

"Country House"—Dining and Activity Space

Theater

"Cottages"—Semi-independent

"Lodge"—Intermediate Care

Undeveloped Area

6-15.
Existing site at the Motion Picture and Television Industry Fund Country House and Hospital.

Preliminary Master Plans for Expansion. In response to the need for additional facilities, the architectural firm of Bobrow/Thomas and Associates developed a series of master plans. Some features of the preliminary plans included:

- a strong central pedestrian spine, with centralized community/recreation facilities to promote wayfinding while providing a focus for community-wide activity
- automobile access generally confined to a perimeter loop road, reducing conflicts with pedestrians

- site zoning organized on a gradient, based upon the level of care, from acute care through to semi-independent living, enabling a sharing of support facilities (see fig. 6–16)

A survey of the residents, however, suggested several points for reconsideration. Residents liked the existing country atmosphere, rather than a "harder" architectural solution. In addition, a strong sense of community existed within each of the housing types, and proximity to more intensive-care facilities was associated with a personal nearness to death and dying. It was felt that the original proposal for a gradient of care across the site might heighten this concern.

Revised Master Plan. The revised master plan, completed in 1983, addresses many of the concerns and issues the original proposals elicited. These are summarized below (see fig. 6–17):

1. Site zoning—housing/service type

Level of care is not indicated by a gradient across the site: instead, each is developed as a separate entity in separate buildings.

Separate facilities and use of landscape materials address the problem of associating physical proximity to more intensive-care facilities with a personal closeness to death. The design also considers the residents' desire to maintain a sense of community within their housing type.

- Landscape treatment and plant materials are employed to help define each area, or zone, rather than relying heavily upon "distance," which can isolate residents and increase concern over security.
- Special attention was given to the question of identifying the hospital area as a separate zone in order to reduce the feeling of continuity with death and dying. The hospital is most distant from the common facilities, minimizing the "hospital" image for the site as a whole (separate services and facilities are provided in the building).
- Intermediate care (the lodge) is closest to the common facilities and dining area, enhancing access and security for the less able but still ambulatory resident.

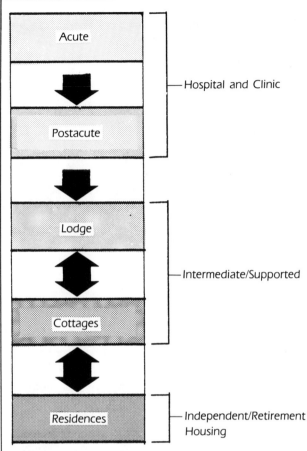

Acute	⎫
↓	⎬ Hospital and Clinic
Postacute	⎭
↓	
Lodge	⎫
↕	⎬ Intermediate/Supported
Cottages	⎭
↕	
Residences	⎫ Independent/Retirement ⎬ Housing ⎭

6-16.
Preliminary proposal for the Motion Picture and Television Fund Country House and Hospital: site zoning on a gradient by level of care; adjacencies by similarity of required services and sharing potential.

- Semi-independent housing (cottages) for the more able is slightly more distant from the dining area and common facilities, accommodating independent living and a greater ability to traverse the distance.

2. Pedestrian access, orientation, and wayfinding

Common facilities are located in the center of the site, maximizing access from all locations. The linear site, however, results in rather long walks from some locations.

- A covered walkway between common facilities enhances comfort and convenience.
- A more informal pedestrian spine connects units to central facilities while providing a transition to a more residential scale.
- Plant materials, rather than a strong architectural spine, guide residents around the site, helping to identify the site edge and providing identity for each use area. Use of vegetation to direct and orient residents includes clusters of native vegetation (same species) to identify areas, crescents of hedgerows to enclose space and guide the walker, and a row of very tall palm trees visible from many parts of the site to serve as a landmark.
- The layout of cottages, using a variation of the standard street and address plan, is easy for residents to identify and provides a sense of community and independence. Few common spaces relating to these units, however, are available for socializing.

3. Parking and building access

Vehicular traffic is restricted primarily to the perimeter of the site, reducing vehicular and pedestrian conflicts.

- Perimeter parking with drop-off areas at key access points around the site may be more acceptable in this instance than in others, as regular use of a private car is not especially common. Project-owned transportation is available, and the need for frequent trips to the grocery store is limited since meals are provided on-site.
- Small trams transport residents around the site and to neighboring shopping centers.

4. Natural features

- A natural knoll and ravine (to the far south end of the site) are preserved. The adjacent area is developed for lower-density cottage housing and a recreation center.

5. Safety, security, and privacy from the curtain call

The existing facility is relatively open to the surrounding community. Security guards make regular rounds on foot and in electric carts. There are several unique security problems, however, with the existing

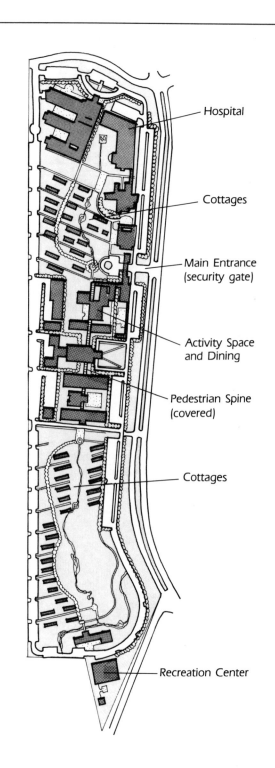

Hospital

Cottages

Main Entrance
(security gate)

Activity Space
and Dining

Pedestrian Spine
(covered)

Cottages

Recreation Center

site. Control over privacy is a special concern for management and those residents who want to retire from the limelight. Unannounced "visits" by journalists may result in a splashy story in a gossip magazine, depicting the demise of a star. The range of abilities among residents also requires special attention to safety. Some less alert residents have been found wandering off the site.

- The proposed master plan addresses these concerns by enclosing the site and providing security-guarded gates at all entrances. The hospital location, however, remains closest to major traffic streets and a freeway.

Case Example: Retirement Community and Multilevel Care Facility

Regents Point
Irvine, California
Architects: Neptune and Thomas Associates

Regents Point, a retirement community owned and operated by the Southern California Presbyterian Homes, provides eighty-six semiattached low-rise units (independent living), eighty-six personal care units in a four-story apartment building, and skilled nursing-care facilities in a two-story building. The main focus is on services to retain independent living rather than on recreation. Thus residents demonstrate a range of ability levels. Most are of the upper-income bracket.

The layout makes the most of views of the neighboring park; however, automobile circulation and parking dominate much of the site, to the detriment of the pedestrian. Parking was expanded for marketing purposes. Highly centralized recreational and service facilities are shared by the independent and semi-independent residents—nursing care is developed as a separate complex. Some elements of special interest are outlined below (see fig. 6–18).

6-17.
Final proposal for the Motion Picture and Television Fund Country House and Hospital focuses upon establishing separate identities for each level of care. Pedestrian spines and plantings help to guide the pedestrian. Bobrow/Thomas and Associates, Architects, Los Angeles.

1. Maximizing outstanding views

- Views of the neighboring park are maximized by siting low-rise units downslope, along the edge of the park, while the midrise buildings are upslope.

2. Pedestrian and vehicular circulation

- The loop drive provides direct access to almost all units and is easy to follow, but parking dominates much of the site.
- Although traffic is light, pedestrians must cross the road to reach the community building. Walkways give way to automobile routes and are not well developed as a system and have little value as an amenity.
- Covered drop-off areas at main buildings and parking (mostly carports) in front of low-rise units ensure convenience.

    It must be noted that much of the parking was added after the initial construction, due to marketing needs. When the project was new, prospective residents were generally "young," mobile, and active. Although they desired a more service-oriented life-style, the automobile was seen as key for maintaining independence in Southern California.
- The loop layout maximizes access to the communal facilities from most units and is easy to follow. Variations in unit placement and arrangement assist in identification.

3. Site zoning—housing–service type

- Centralized services and recreational facilities are provided for independent and semi-independent residents.
- Walk-up condominium apartments located around the site perimeter reflect independence.
- Apartments (generally for the less able) are adjacent to the community center/dining room, assuring easy access (through a glassed corridor) and greater security for those who require it most.
- The skilled-nursing facility, which functions independently, is developed as a separate zone, thereby confining the hospital image to one end of the site.

4. Focal point for activity

- A clustering of indoor and outdoor community facilities in a central location supports use of both, and provides many options for participation. Facilities include a dining room, lounges/meeting rooms, craft/exercise rooms, a library, a small sidewalk ice cream parlor, swimming pool, Jacuzzi, and lawn bowling.
- Outdoor recreational facilities are nestled between the community and apartment buildings, enhancing security and visual connections. Outstanding views are maximized.
- Although centrally located, access walks to this facility suffer somewhat by the change in grade and the lack of easy and direct routes from many units.

Case Example:
Independent Low-rise Living

Heaton Court
Stockbridge, Massachusetts
Architects: Goody, Clancy and Associates

This 50-unit project illustrates a sensitive site planning of low-rise apartment units for relatively independent living, although the landscape design is somewhat barren. Some key elements in the success of this informal courtyard scheme are outlined below (see figs. 6–19 and 6–20).

1. General

- Containing the development to a small portion of the site maximizes access from units to shared facilities while reserving areas on-site for retreats and views.
- The informal courtyard arrangement, with parking behind units, provides safe and convenient access from most units to common spaces and parking while enhancing a sense of community.

2. Unit orientation and placement

- Three-story units located upslope and one- to two-story units downslope maximize views of the Berkshire Mountains.
- The unit layout blocks northerly winds into the courtyard space and maximizes exposure of walkways and common spaces to the sun.

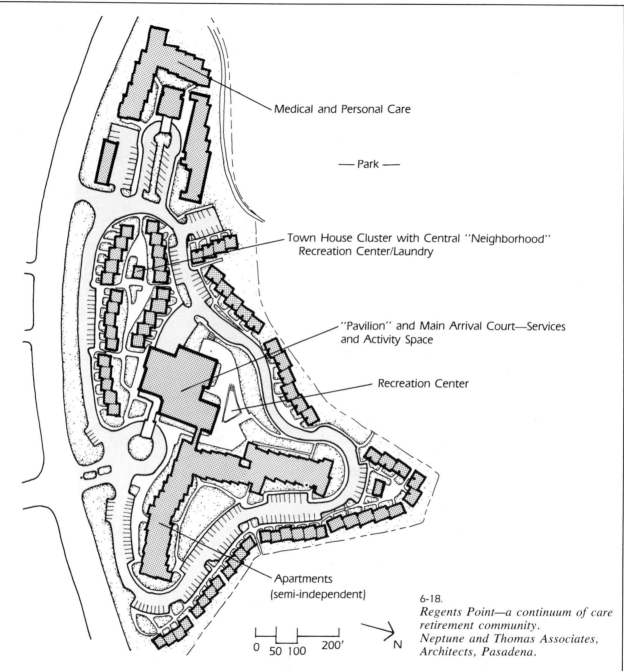

Medical and Personal Care

— Park —

Town House Cluster with Central "Neighborhood" Recreation Center/Laundry

"Pavilion" and Main Arrival Court—Services and Activity Space

Recreation Center

Apartments (semi-independent)

0 50 100   200'

N

6-18.
Regents Point—a continuum of care retirement community.
Neptune and Thomas Associates, Architects, Pasadena.

- The front and back of most units are clearly defined, with parking and porches at the rear of units and a more formal front entrance through the courtyard and along the open-air galleries.

- Site grading enables development of common space on fairly level terrain.
- A widening of the central courtyard adjacent to indoor activity areas—social hall, crafts, and shop—is

48

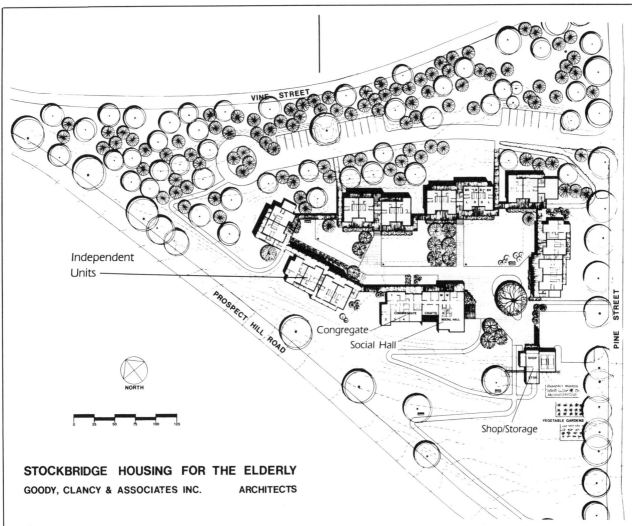

Independent
Units

Congregate

Social Hall

Shop/Storage

NORTH

0   25   50   75   100   125

STOCKBRIDGE HOUSING FOR THE ELDERLY

GOODY, CLANCY & ASSOCIATES INC.   ARCHITECTS

6-19.
Heaton Court—low-rise housing for independent living.
Goody, Clancy and Associates, Inc., Architects, Boston.
Reprinted with permission.

ideal for outdoor activity. A greater level of spatial
definition, with a transition from indoor common
spaces, and a greater level of landscape detailing
would support the basic layout.

3. Pedestrian and vehicular access

- A central drop-off area within view of the community building is ideal, although the walking distance
is too great.

- Parking upslope, connected to the intermediate
level of units by pedestrian bridges, reduces the
number of stairs necessary for access to most
apartments.
- Continuous covered porches and galleries around
the courtyard space provide comfortable covered
access between units as well as a place for sitting,
socializing, and admiring the view.
- Downslope, the traversing paths, with an easy
grade (approximately 1:18) and dotted with resting
spots, provide a place for comfortable retreat and
exercise.

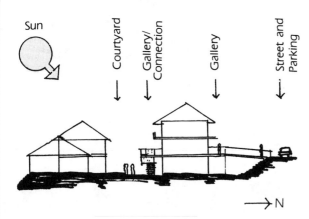

Sun
Courtyard
Gallery/
Connection
Gallery
Street and
Parking

→N

6-20.
Heaton Court: Placing cars on the uphill side of the slope, behind the units, allowed development of a central courtyard space on level terrain. Second-floor galleries and bridges connect to parking while the stepping down from three to one stories on the south side maximizes sun penetration into the courtyard and views of the mountains.
After: Goody, Clancy and Associates, Inc., Architects, Boston.
Used with permission.

Case Examples: Two Inwardly Oriented Courtyard Developments

Kings Road, East
West Hollywood, California
Architects: Bobrow/Thomas and Associates
and Charles Moore/Urban Innovations Group
Landscape Architect: Pam Burton and Company

Central City East
Los Angeles, California
Architects: David E. Crompton and Jenkins-Fleming
Landscape Architects: Peterson and Befu

These two low-rise apartment projects illustrate variations on the same basic site-planning pattern—an inwardly oriented courtyard scheme.

Both projects are similar in size and are three-story public housing projects. Central City East, however, as one of the first redevelopment projects in the Skid Row area, faces many problems with safety and security. Both designs respond to concern over security by defining the site boundaries, controlling access through locked gates, and providing a secure outdoor space for residents. Use of the two sites, however, is vastly different. The courtyard area at Kings Road is the focal point for activity; at Central City East, the building entry/porch area is the most popular spot.

Some important similarities and differences between the two sites include the following (see figs. 6–21, 6–22):

1. Both sites use a common courtyard scheme that ensures security and provides a protected social space.

- At Kings Road, courtyard use is supported by site entry directly into a vestibule space within the courtyard itself, and by strong connections to activity generators (e.g., units, mailboxes, views of the entry walk and street).
- At Central City East, factors that limit courtyard use include few views of or connections to the street, indoor activities, and units. The courtyard becomes more of a throughway to units and the front porch/lounge area, with walkways bypassing the main seating area. Easy access from the courtyard to warming kitchens, however, enables use of the space for special events.

2. Both sites provide for unit access through the central courtyards. which supports use of the space.

- At Kings Road a subtle separation between unit access routes and the seating area encourages drop-in use without invasion of privacy.
- The primary seating area at Central City East, however, is removed from unit access routes; a greater degree of effort and commitment is required for casual drop-in use.

3. Site access through one main controlled access point enhances a sense of security at both Kings Road and Central City East while providing a potential focal area for meeting.

- At Kings Road the interior courtyard space serves as the site "entry" area, as well as an outdoor "lounge," although a drop-off/waiting area nearer the street is needed.

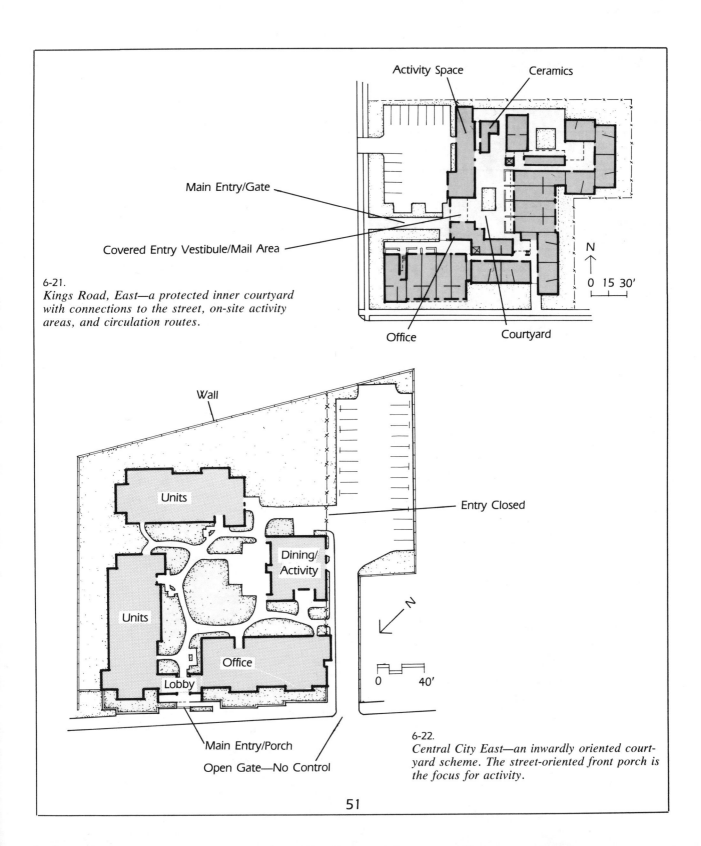

Activity Space   Ceramics

Main Entry/Gate

Covered Entry Vestibule/Mail Area

N

0 15 30'

6-21.
Kings Road, East—a protected inner courtyard with connections to the street, on-site activity areas, and circulation routes.

Office   Courtyard

Wall

Units

Entry Closed

Dining/
Activity

N

Units

Office

0   40'

Lobby

Main Entry/Porch

Open Gate—No Control

6-22.
Central City East—an inwardly oriented court-yard scheme. The street-oriented front porch is the focus for activity.

- At Central City East the activity potential of the site entry area is enhanced by the development of a "front porch" and strong ties to the indoor lounge/reception desk and street life.

4. Both sites have small parking lots outside of the "secure" area, which could be problematic.

- Parking at Kings Road is highly visible from the street and entry walk, enhancing security. Access to parking from the back units, however, is indirect.
- Central City East has some security problems, as parking is isolated from activity and view. Fairly direct access to units is available, but one route is closed due to lack of surveillance from the main office and reception desk.

Case Example: Shared Facilities and Neighborhood Orientation

Little Tokyo Towers
Los Angeles, California
Architects: Ogren, Juarez and Gibes
Landscape Architects: Peterson and Befu

Located adjacent to Little Tokyo in downtown Los Angeles, this 300-unit high-rise development demonstrates both a successful neighborhood connection that supports a mutual sharing of facilities and friendship and a problematic connection. The tightly knit social fabric of the neighborhood, surrounding land use, and comfortable walkways with seating at prime locations (offering views of major connecting walkways) are key elements at this site. Pedestrian connections and other design elements that contribute to the successful sharing of facilities are noted below (see fig. 6–23).

1. Neighborhood orientation

- The site entry is problematic, as it is oriented away from on-site and neighborhood activity and toward the less secure side of the site, frequented by vagrants rather than residents.
- Other pedestrian walks, however, heavily landscaped in a Japanese theme, provide the needed connection between key facilities: an on-site dining room for use by residents and community seniors, an adjacent senior citizen center, the Little Tokyo

shopping district, and a neighboring Buddhist temple.

2. Pedestrian walks connect key facilities

- Building security is ensured by a separate side entrance for dining, reducing concern over nonresident access to the building. Social activity focuses on this route.
- Key connecting walkways are completely separate from automobile traffic and are within view of seating areas and the building, enhancing safety and security.

3. Social activity is centered at walkway intersections

- Ample seating and resting spots at walkway intersections support the hub of community and resident activity along the walks, especially around mealtime.
- Views of those coming and going as well as visual surveillance from inside the building promote use.
- A large Japanese-style sculpture provides a focal point for the area.
- The sense of scale, in contrast to the high-rise building, is fairly well defined by heavy use of plant materials and the large sculpture.
- The two patios are less central to social activity. More removed from the pedestrian flow, they are occasionally used for intimate groupings. The smaller patio is rarely used; an orientation toward the less active side of the site and lack of access from other outdoor spaces are particular problems.

Case Example: A Recreationally Focused Retirement Community

Leisure World—Laguna Hills
Laguna Hills, California
Developer: Rossmoor Corporation

The second largest retirement community in the United States, Leisure World—Laguna Hills offers recreationally focused retirement living for active seniors within the walls of a secure environment. The scale of the project is underscored by the recent move toward

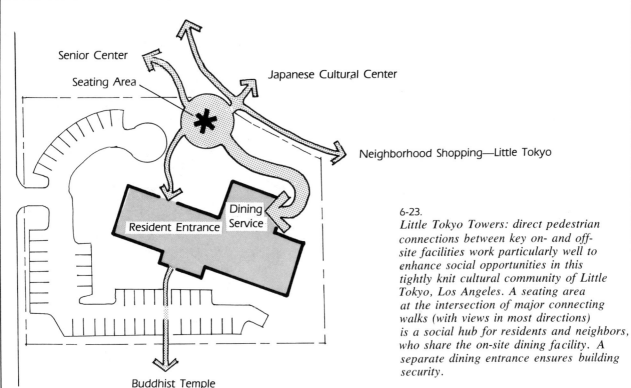

Senior Center

Seating Area

Japanese Cultural Center

Neighborhood Shopping—Little Tokyo

Resident Entrance

Dining Service

Buddhist Temple

6-23.
Little Tokyo Towers: direct pedestrian connections between key on- and off-site facilities work particularly well to enhance social opportunities in this tightly knit cultural community of Little Tokyo, Los Angeles. A seating area at the intersection of major connecting walks (with views in most directions) is a social hub for residents and neighbors, who share the on-site dining facility. A separate dining entrance ensures building security.

incorporation as a separate city. The facilities are staggering:

1,660.9	total acres
2,584	buildings
13,100+	units (12,400+ low-rise; 622 newer high-rise congregate units)
6	clubhouses
5	swimming pools
18	shuffleboard courts
6	tennis courts
1	auditorium/theater (seats 850)
1	stable facility (40 stalls, 3.5 miles of equestrian trails)
2	golf courses (36 holes)
2	garden centers
14	security gates
2	recreational vehicle storage areas (413 spaces)
22,000+	residents

Developed over several decades, the site-planning process as a whole has been, understandably, spotty. Some noteworthy elements, however, are summarized below (see fig. 6.24).

1. Orientation and access to neighborhood facilities

- The site is inwardly oriented and entirely enclosed by a 6-foot wall (barbed wire has recently been added), with 14 guarded entry gates. A pass is required for nonresident access. Security is a big selling point.
- Availability of neighborhood services was originally provided through the sale of adjacent lands to key service and facility providers, for restaurants, supermarkets, and shopping malls. These perimeter developments have now expanded to include, among other things, housing offering greater levels of care than what is available at Leisure World.

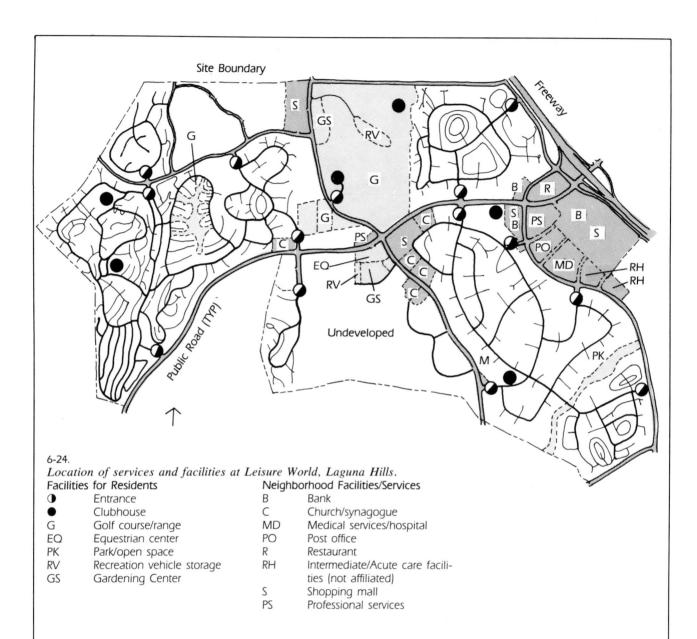

6-24.
Location of services and facilities at Leisure World, Laguna Hills.

Facilities for Residents		Neighborhood Facilities/Services	
◐	Entrance	B	Bank
●	Clubhouse	C	Church/synagogue
G	Golf course/range	MD	Medical services/hospital
EQ	Equestrian center	PO	Post office
PK	Park/open space	R	Restaurant
RV	Recreation vehicle storage	RH	Intermediate/Acute care facili-
GS	Gardening Center		ties (not affiliated)
		S	Shopping mall
		PS	Professional services

- Private cars, golf carts (often used in conjunction with the extensive in-house bus system), and the bus system itself, provide adequate access to and from this large community and the sprawling neighborhood. The site is far too large for almost anyone to traverse on foot. Covered bus-stop areas, located at major points around and within the site, add convenience.

2. Project layout

- The layout of residential units is similar to that of many suburban housing developments that emphasize self-sufficient living. Social contacts are supported through recreation centers and clubs.
- The use of cul-de-sac street systems creates more intimate neighborhoods within the development,

although the layout is somewhat confusing. The lengthy Spanish street names add to the confusion, as few residents are Hispanic.

3. Social and recreational facilities

- Six clubhouses, scattered throughout the site, provide focal points for recreational and social activities. Each clubhouse, in addition to providing base facilities (generally a swimming pool and activity rooms), addresses the needs of special-interest groups, such as dancers and workshop enthusiasts. At the clubhouses, residents can meet others with similar interests.
- The sense of safety and security on-site is an important element in allowing residents the freedom to use all outdoor recreation areas, including nature walks along the remote Aliso Creek.

4. Facility ownership and management

- Residents play a critical role in facility ownership, management, and development, thereby reinforcing independence. Property owners (all residents) belong to one of seven housing corporations responsible for housing and the operation of their lands.

All "community" facilities (bus system, security, clubhouses, and so on) are managed by these corporations in conjuction with a larger management body, the Gold Rain Tree Foundation. Development of new facilities and reviews of construction proposals are among the board's responsibilities, and assure design and community compatibility.

References

1. Green, Isaac, et al. *Housing for the Elderly: The Development and Design Process.* New York: Van Nostrand Reinhold, 1975.

2. ———. *Housing for the Elderly.*

3. Lawton, M. Powell. *Planning and Managing Housing for the Elderly.* New York: John Wiley & Sons, 1975.

4. Green et al. *Housing for the Elderly.*

5. Zeisel, J., G. Epp, and S. Demos. *Low Rise Housing for Older People.* U.S. Department of Housing and Urban Development, Office of Policy Development and Research, HUD-483 (TQ)-76. Washington, DC: U.S. Government Printing Office, 1977.

6. ———. *Low Rise Housing for Older People.*

Major Site-Planning Elements

Specific recommendations for major site-planning components, such as site and building entry areas and circulation systems, are outlined in this chapter. A range of design stages is covered for each component, from the location to amenities and detailing, tying together many of the issues examined in the previous chapters and demonstrating their application. Actual examples of projects illustrate the application of many design concepts.

Although often considered only as functional elements of site design, many of the areas addressed in this chapter are the most popular spots for socializing and recreation. Building entry areas, in particular, can be the most active, entertaining, and highly used outdoor places on the site. When designing, it is important to keep all possible uses in mind.

The type, number, location, and size of each major site element will depend in part on the development type (e.g., low-rise or high-rise) and the number of units, not to mention financial limitations. The site-planning elements discussed in this chapter are not exhaustive of all possibilities, nor should the guidelines limit the creativity of the designer in addressing the needs of older people.

The Site Entry/Exit

The site entry area is important for resident and visitor access, as well as for the community image. Safety and ease of recognition and access are primary considerations.

The type and number of entries included in the site-development plan will depend to a large extent upon the development type and the size of the site. Off-site factors may also influence the site-entry scheme, such as the safety, spatial scale, and characteristics of the surrounding streets and neighborhood, and the location of amenities and services. Regardless of the site entry type, safe and convenient access to

on- and off-site facilities is a must for any development.

Two main types of entrances are the drive-by entrance and the entrance drive. While a drive-by entrance or small circular drive is a viable option for smaller sites, larger ones generally require entrance drives. Many options are available for larger low-rise and mixed developments:

- If the development is planned as a continuation of the neighborhood fabric, a site entry area may be replaced by some other form of entry, such as individual unit entries that relate to the neighborhood scale.
- For larger sites and those developed as a complex separate from the neighborhood, a site entry should provide a sense of entrance to the site and help residents and visitors to identify and gain access to facilities.
- More than one site entry may be necessary to provide an easy and direct route to larger sites.
- In some cases, the site entry may also be the building drop-off area, particularly at small urban sites with a single building, where space is at a premium.

Some important considerations that apply to most types of site entries are examined below.

Location

1. The orientation of the site entrance to surrounding streets and the neighborhood often involves a choice between major and minor traffic streets [1].

- Major traffic streets offer high entrance visibility and easy access.
- Minor streets offer increased safety but reduce ease of recognition.

The trade-off between easy recognition and safety is best decided by an examination of site-specific qualities, including the visual quality and safety of the surrounding area (fig. 7–1).

2. For easy recognition and safety, site entries should be located for adequate sight distance from both directions on the street [2] (fig. 7–2).

3. Site entries should be located for direct and easy access to on- and off-site facilities, particularly supermarkets, drugstores, and transit stops. Site entries should be planned as part of the overall site access scheme, enabling an easy progression from site identification and entry to building identification, front-door drop-off, and parking.

4. Where some facilities on-site are for community/neighborhood use, the site entry location should allow for easy access to these facilities, without requiring general access through on-site residential areas.

5. Multiple site entries may be necessary for easy access to and from larger sites. Where multiple entries are provided, each entry should be easy to identify and recognize as different from the others.

6. A separate site entry for delivery and service vehicles may be desirable, particularly for those developments, such as congregate facilities, that require frequent deliveries.

Spatial Characteristics

1. The type and size of the entry should be in proportion to the surrounding neighborhood and compatible in image with it. It should be easy to recognize, but not overpowering (see figs. 7–3, 7–5). Some special considerations for the drive-by entrance and the entrance drive are outlined below:

- Entrance drives may take many forms. Island entries and one-way drives must be carefully planned, designed, and detailed to reduce confusion over which side or direction is for entering and which one is for exiting.

- Drive-by entrances are most common for smaller sites with a single building. Ample space must be provided for passing cars and dropping off passengers (see "The Main Entry/Arrival Court," below). Again, special attention needs to be given to one-way drives.

2. Drop-off and seating areas at the site entry are convenient. In some neighborhoods, however, these areas may become favorite hangouts for vagrants or others who may intimidate residents. A seating area that seems to "belong" to the site rather than to the

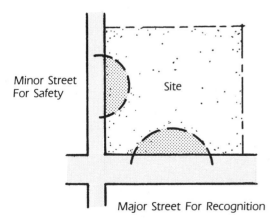

7-1.
Orientation of the site entry toward minor streets offers safety, while major streets offer ease of recognition.
After: Isaac Green et al. Housing for the Elderly: The Development and Design Process. *New York: Van Nostrand Reinhold, 1975, 52.*

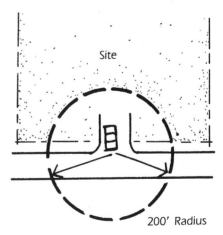

7-2.
Site entry location for adequate sight distance to ensure safety.
After: Isaac Green et al. Housing for the Elderly: The Development and Design Process. *New York: Van Nostrand Reinhold, 1975, 52.*

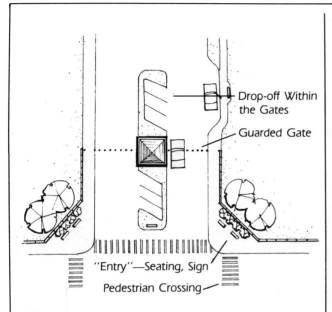

"Entry"—Seating, Sign

Drop-off Within the Gates

Guarded Gate

Pedestrian Crossing

7-3.
Site entries at Leisure World are easy to identify. The design guides the driver into the site. Choice between seating and drop-off inside or outside of the gates (with easy turnaround) is ideal.

street and does not provide for concealment can help to alleviate this situation.

Amenities and Detailing

1. A covered transit stop, taxi stand, or waiting area is desirable at the site entry (see fig. 7–4). Amenities such as newspaper stands and public mailboxes add interest and support use.

2. High-branching plant materials or low ground covers that do not obscure vision for drivers and pedestrians or provide areas for concealment are appropriate for site entries. Visibility is a major consideration for safety and security in high traffic areas, as older people may have difficulty perceiving motion and have slower reaction times (see fig. 7–4).

3. Pedestrian and bicycle access may be incorporated into the site entry route. Adequate separation among pedestrian, bicycle, and automobile traffic ensures safety.

4. Pedestrian and bicycle crossings should be clearly marked by changes in paving. Crossing lights

should be timed to provide ample time for slower-walking pedestrians (see "Pedestrian Street Crossings" in chapter 10).

5. Signs and lighting to identify the site entry and for directional information on larger sites should be incorporated into the site entry (see figs. 7–4, 7–5, and 7–6, "Outdoor Lighting" and "Outdoor Signs" in chapter 10).

6. Entry-gate control may be desirable for some developments, especially in neighborhoods with safety and security problems, and for those developments that offer a "secure community." Entry-gate control, however, may set the project apart from the community, promoting an image of isolation and institutionalization.

Case Example: Security Entry Gate For Pedestrians and Golf Carts

Leisure World—Laguna Hills, California
Developer: Rossmoor Corporation

This pedestrian and golf-cart gate solves a unique neighborhood access problem for a very large but secure site. The gate provides several convenient access alternatives to those who do not wish to drive their cars off-site, but cannot walk or carry packages any distance. The area also serves as a hub for informal meeting and socializing. The system works exceptionally well in this warm, sunny climate. Major attributes of this entry are noted below (see figs. 7–7, 7–8).

1. Location

• A central location, near on- and off-site transit services and adjacent to an on-site clubhouse and large off-site shopping center, is ideal for convenience and social interaction.

• Offset from the main traffic street and with a minor access road to the adjacent shopping center, this gate provides a safe access route for pedestrians and golf carts in this very car-dominated area.

2. Features

• A parking lot and bus stop within the gates increase safety and convenience for intermodal transportation.

• A shopping cart stand located directly outside the

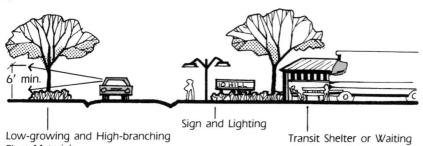

6' min.

Low-growing and High-branching Plant Materials

Sign and Lighting

Transit Shelter or Waiting and Drop-off Area

7-4.
Site-entry amenities and detailing should enhance safety, visibility, comfort, and access to the site and surrounding neighborhood.

Kings Road (East)

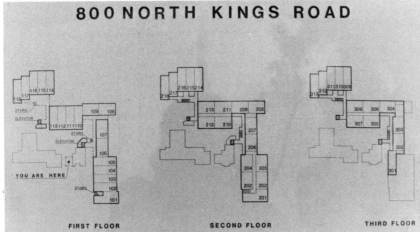

800 NORTH KINGS ROAD

Locational Map

7-5 and 7.6.
The scale of the pedestrian site entry at Kings Road, East, is consistent with that of the surrounding residential neighborhood. The gate allows for previewing before exiting and for views of street activity from the inner courtyard, thus increasing safety and adding interest. A large, easy-to-read map at the gate (similar to one at Kings Road, North, illustrated here) assists in wayfinding. The addition of a shaded seating area near the street and a package shelf by the gate would enhance convenience.

gate enables use of private cars or the on-site bus system to traverse the large site, and grocery carts to transport packages the short, one-quarter- to one-half-block route to and from the shopping area. Others choose to use their golf carts for the entire trip, which does not require traveling along the major street.

- Immediately outside of the gate, covered bus stops with ample seating increase the versatility of the area.

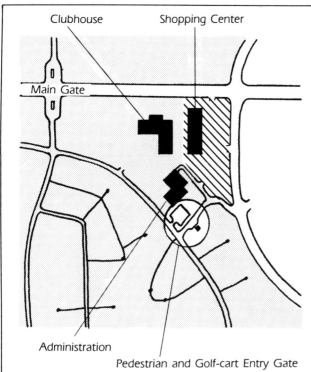

Clubhouse   Shopping Center

Main Gate

Administration

Pedestrian and Golf-cart Entry Gate

7-7.
Leisure World: A separate site entry for pedestrians and golf-carts, with an access route to the adjacent shopping center bypassing a major boulevard, ensures safety and convenience. The clustering of facilities on- and off-site creates a hub of pedestrian and social activity.

- Monitoring of the entrance gate by a guard who is also a resident adds to the sense of community and improves service at the entry gate by providing information, directions, and assistance with carts.

Case Example: Site Entry and Entry Drive

Regents Point, California
Architects and Engineers: Neptune and Thomas Associates

Safe and convenient automobile access is afforded by this site-entry arrangement; but provisions for the pedestrian are not as well conceived. Some of the major attributes and problem areas are noted below (see fig. 7–9).

1. Location

- The main building entry and drop-off area (set off from the main on-site loop road) are easy to identify on entering the site, making wayfinding easier; conversely, the site entry is visible from the main drop-off area and building entry.

2. Spatial characteristics

- The separation of inward- and outward-bound traffic at the site entry is easy to identify and follow.

7-8.
Leisure World: Those who prefer not to drive off-site, park just inside the site entrance and walk to the adjacent shopping center; shopping carts are left at the gate upon return. Vehicular use of the gate is limited to golf carts (used for short trips) and the on-site bus system.

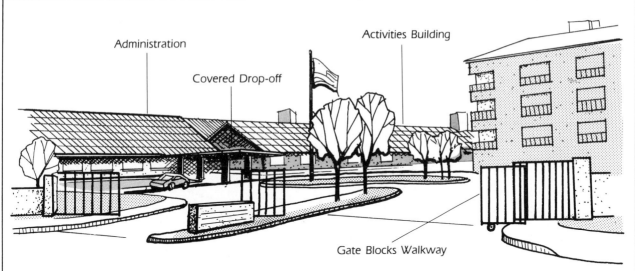

Administration

Covered Drop-off

Activities Building

Gate Blocks Walkway

7-9.
Regents Point: The site entry and entry drive provide for convenient and direct vehicular access to a central drop-off point. Circulation, amenities, and detailing for the pedestrian, however, are not well addressed.

- A circular drop-off drive and covered building entry area, separate from the main access road, provide a safe separation from the main traffic flow and add to convenience.

3. Amenities and detailing

- No seating/waiting area is available at the site entry.
- Once inside the gate of this larger development, little signage is visible to direct visitors and residents to the office, units, and so on.
- The fencing and gates (added by the management) block off the pedestrian walk, requiring pedestrians to use the entry drive itself. The running track of gate is also hazardous, with a lip protruding a half inch above grade.
- The entry sign, with lettering chiseled on a neutral gray stone block, lacks contrast and is not easy to read; no address is given.

The Entry Drive

Entry drives should provide for safe and direct access to site facilities as well as for passenger drop-off at all building entries. Some form of loop drive is often desirable for convenience. Small sites with a single building may need only one entry drive or just a drop-off area, while larger developments may require several entry drive systems for direct and easy access to on-site facilities. Many variations on the standard loop drive are possible for larger low-rise and mixed developments.

Several functional considerations for entry drives are outlined below (see also chapter 6).

Location

1. The layout of entry drives should create a pattern that is easy to recognize and identify, providing safe access for both pedestrians and vehicles. Interior drives should be aligned with off-site drives in favor of inwardly in-bound traffic; this traffic generally moves more quickly than out-bound traffic (see fig. 7-10).

2. Entry drives should be located for close and convenient drop-off at building entries, but should allow space for arrival court or unit entry development (see fig. 7-11 and "The Main Entry/Arrival Court" and "Low-rise Unit Entries," below).

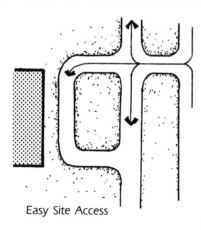

Easy Site Access

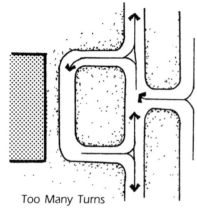

Too Many Turns

7-10.
An entry drive alignment that favors faster-moving inbound traffic and requires fewer turns is safest and least confusing.

Spatial Characteristics

1. The radii and width of entry drives at major building entries should permit maneuverability of cars, vans, buses, and ambulances, allowing enough space for wheelchairs and open car doors (see fig. 7.11). The Michigan State Housing Development Authority recommends the following standards [3]:

- Single two-way road: curb-to-curb minimum width of 25 feet.
- Boulevard: each way minimum width of 20 feet and median minimum width of 15 feet. The design and layout of these drives, however, must be

clearly defined and direct vehicles to the "correct" side of the boulevard. Some people may be confused by single-direction roads.
- Arrival court drop-off area: minimum interior curb radius of 33 feet and minimum exterior radius of 57 feet.

2. Drop-off areas require adequate access aisle space for safe passenger loading (see fig. 7–12).

- An access aisle 48 inches wide adjacent to the pull-up space is necessary for safe loading of the handicapped.
- If curbs are used, a curb ramp leading directly to the access walk is necessary.

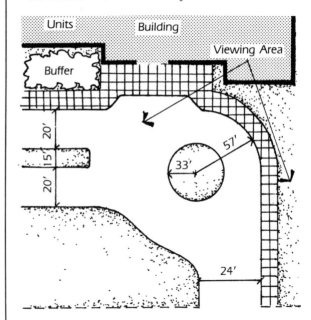

Heavily Traveled Drive—Separate From Drop-off Loop

7-11.
Entry drives located for close building drop-off and visibility from key indoor spaces maximize convenience. Where entry drives are heavily traveled, a separate drop-off loop with adequate space for arrival court development and vehicle turnaround is necessary for safety.
After: Isaac Green et al. Housing for the Elderly: The Development and Design Process. *New York: Van Nostrand Reinhold, 1975, 131.*

3. The use of both one-way and two-way drives is often confusing for the older driver. The design and layout should be consistent. Intersections with boulevard-type drives should clearly direct the driver to the correct side of travel.

4. Where apartment units on the first floor face the entry drive, a buffer should be established between the entry drive curb and the building face.

5. Temporary parking (short term) may be provided for visitors near unit or building entries (for long-term resident parking, see "Parking and Building Access," below). Local ordinances should be consulted for minimum parking ratios, but additional parking is often necessary (see also table 7–1).

Amenities and Detailing

1. Traffic intersections and stop signs (particularly one- or two-way stops) must be clearly marked and easy to identify; cross-traffic should be highly visible (see fig. 7–13).

The Main Entry/Arrival Court

The arrival court of apartment buildings and other major structures, such as community centers, are important for building access and community image. They are also use areas in themselves. They should consist of two main functional areas: (1) an access way to and from the building and (2) an outdoor

Table 7–1 SUGGESTED SHORT-TERM PARKING RATIOS FOR MID- TO HIGH-RISE BUILDINGS

up to 100 units	6 short-term spaces
101–200 units	10 short-term spaces
201–300 units	12 short-term spaces

SOURCE: Isaac Green et al. *Housing for the Elderly: The Development and Design Process.* New York: Van Nostrand Reinhold, 1975, 53. Reprinted with permission.

seating and waiting area. Oftentimes, particularly with small urban sites, these functions may be combined with the site entry area.

The high level of activity usually found at the main entrance of apartment and community buildings makes this a favorite spot for sitting and watching activity or for waiting for assistance on a short walk or to run errands. Ample space must also be provided for loading and unloading passengers and packages, some light delivery, and waiting for rides and other residents or visitors.

Ease of access and comfort, image, security, and indoor–outdoor relationships are very important elements.

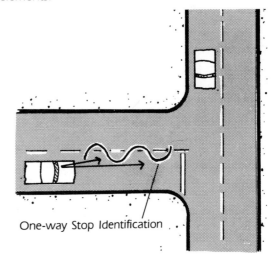

One-way Stop Identification

7-13.
Traffic intersections, particularly one-way stops, must be easy to identify. A broad yellow wavy line painted along the center line at one project clearly identifies one-way stops. Textural warning strips are also a good option.

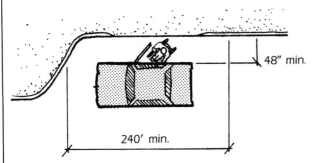

48" min.

240' min.

7-12.
Minimum access aisle space for safe passenger drop-off.
After: American National Standards Institute. Specifications for Making Buildings and Facilities Accessible to and Usable by Physically Handicapped People. New York: ANSI, 1980, 22.

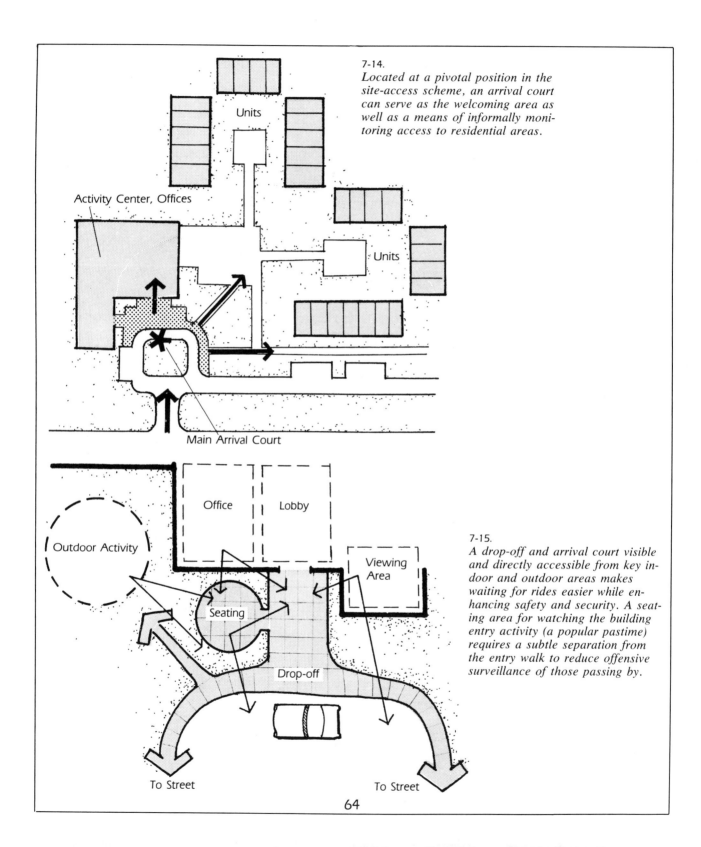

7-14.
Located at a pivotal position in the site-access scheme, an arrival court can serve as the welcoming area as well as a means of informally monitoring access to residential areas.

Units

Activity Center, Offices

Units

Main Arrival Court

Office

Lobby

Outdoor Activity

Viewing Area

7-15.
A drop-off and arrival court visible and directly accessible from key indoor and outdoor areas makes waiting for rides easier while enhancing safety and security. A seating area for watching the building entry activity (a popular pastime) requires a subtle separation from the entry walk to reduce offensive surveillance of those passing by.

Seating

Drop-off

To Street

To Street

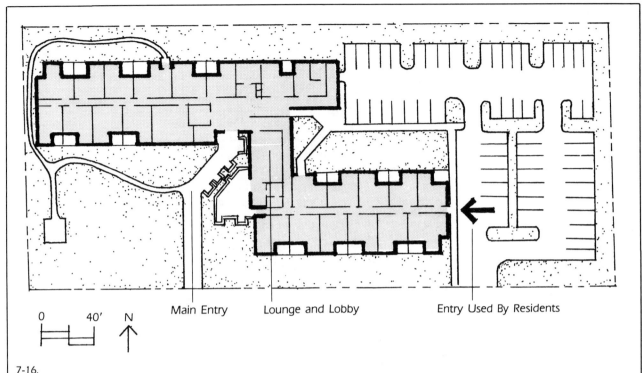

0   40'   N

Main Entry   Lounge and Lobby   Entry Used By Residents

7-16.
*At this site in the Los Angeles area, the purpose of the main entry and lobby
was sabotaged by a layout that isolates the arrival court from the street.
The main entry is seldom used; residents waiting for rides use the more convenient side entrance. The recent addition of a bench by the side entrance is
greatly appreciated.*
Original evaluation by: Sociotech, Santa Monica, California.

Location

1. The arrival court should be located for maximum protection from extremes in weather, such as
cold winds and excessive heat and glare. In cold climates, exposure to the sun in fall, winter, and spring
will accelerate melting of ice and snow and is critical
for safety.

2. Easy and direct access from the arrival court to
on- and off-site facilities is ideal (see fig. 7–14).

- The arrival court may serve as the pivotal point in
  the site-entry scheme for visitor welcome, direction,
  and security monitoring.
- Entry walks to the building doorsill should not involve a slope greater than 2.5 percent (1 percent
  minimum). Steps and ramps must be avoided [4].

3. Views and access among the arrival court, street
and/or drop-off area, and the lobby are essential for
easy recognition of approaching cars or persons, as
well as for adding interest to sitting/waiting areas.
Lack of such connections may decrease use of the arrival court area (see figs. 7–15, 7–16, 7–17).

4. Views of the arrival court and drop-off area
from indoor spaces frequented by residents and staff,
such as the office and lobby, enhance safety and security as well as use of both (see fig. 7–15).

Spatial Characteristics

1. A seating/waiting area located slightly to the
side of the entry walk allows ample room for safe
and easy movement to and from the building. A sub-

7-17.
Many projects have a resident volunteer doorsitter who monitors the activity of the site or building entry. This resident-created seating area at the arrival court of one site is a popular spot. Raised but subtly separated from the walkway, the seating area affords an excellent view of others coming and going, the street activity, and the adjacent shopping center. Although ample seating is available in shade, additional seating in sun is obviously needed.

tle separation between the entry walk and the seating area reduces the likelihood of offensive surveillance of those entering and leaving the building while providing a comfortable area for conversation. Views of the entry walk, however, should be available (see fig. 7–15, 7–17).

2. Building access should be direct and simple to identify.

Amenities and Detailing

1. A canopy or cover offering protection from weather is a must for safe and comfortable entry to the building, especially in harsh climates (see fig. 7–18). Some special considerations for cover include the following:

- Cover should extend over the drop-off area to provide protection for less agile residents, who may take considerable time getting in and out of a car.
- Cover should be wide enough for several people to walk side by side, as well as for walkers and wheelchairs (6-foot minimum walkway width is best; 5-foot minimum allows two wheelchairs to pass very cautiously) and should offer protection from rain and snow when windy (siding is an option if it does not create a dark entry area).
- The cover should not create a dark entry area. Skylights or a translucent cover are possible solutions.

- Abrasive surfaces should not be used on canopy supports, which residents may grasp for stability or brush against when walking or falling.

2. Comfortable seating should be available in shade, sun, and under cover (see fig. 7–18).

3. A "front porch" is a good option for a seating and waiting area. It has a smaller enclosed space, protection from weather, and viewing opportunities, all of which promote social interaction, conversation, comfort, and a sense of safety and security. These areas, however, must be connected to indoor activity (e.g., lounge/lobby) and have views of interest.

4. The arrival court should be at grade with the entry drive. Bollards (5-foot minimum clearance between them) may be used to control automobile traffic at the drop-off area (see fig. 7–18).

- Steps, curbs, and curb ramps should be avoided in this area.
- Ramps, however, are not a substitute for stairs, as they require a change in gait that is not easy for marginally ambulatory people. A reduced sense of balance and the shuffling walk associated with growing older also make ramps and stairs difficult to negotiate.

5. Where curbs and curb cuts are necessary, support rails extending out to the point of the curb accommodate the less agile. A curb-cut width of 36 inches, excluding flairs, is generally recommended (see "Pedestrian Street Crossings" in chapter 10).

6. Areas of high pedestrian and vehicular movement, which demand fast reaction time, should be clearly marked and defined. Changes in paving color and texture should define the drop-off area and should separate vehicle and pedestrian areas (see fig. 7–18).

7. Support railings along the entry walk or other vertical elements that may serve as grab posts or "touchstones" make access easier for the unsure of foot. A secure and highly visible lamppost, for example, may provide opportunity for a brief rest. A distance of 15 feet from the car to building entry may seem a long way for some older people.

8. Lighting for safety and negotiability is a must. It should illuminate the pavement edge and not create glare or deep shadows in movement areas (see "Lighting" in chapter 10).

9. In regions with heavy snowfall, adequate space for snow removal and piling should be provided.

10. Grading for positive drainage is basic.

11. Low-level planters or other protrusions on the ground plane should be avoided in the entry area. Planters should be either at grade or a minimum of 30 inches in height (36 inches for the blind) to reduce the possibility of tripping [5] (see "Planters and Planting Beds" in chapter 10).

12. Walkways in this area should be a minimum of 6 feet wide. A nonslip, nonglare walking surface is a priority for building entries. Pavement type and texture may also help guide the visually impaired (see "Pedestrian Street Crossings" in chapter 10).

Case Example: Arrival Court and Drop-off Area

Motion Picture and Television Fund Country House and Hospital
Woodland Hills, California
Architects: Bobrow/Thomas and Associates

The entry and drop-off area of this congregate facility works well for the extremely light traffic at the site and for loading and unloading passengers using the small in-house tram system. Major attributes and key areas for improvement are noted below (see figs. 7–19, 7–20).

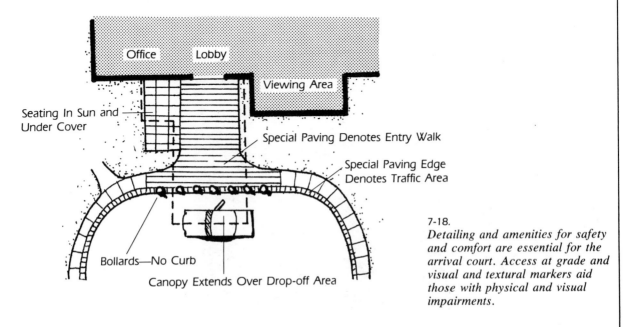

7-18.
Detailing and amenities for safety and comfort are essential for the arrival court. Access at grade and visual and textural markers aid those with physical and visual impairments.

1. Location

- The fact that the drop-off area is separate from the main drive and parking lot reduces congestion at the main entry and increases safety, although automobile turnaround is almost impossible.
- Adjacent to the indoor lobbies and reception area, the arrival court is a popular spot for sitting in the shade and watching the activity. The "back" patio is seldom used.

2. Spatial characteristics and amenities

- Additional space for vehicle turnaround and defined pedestrian walkways is needed for convenience and safety.

- Covered drop-off at grade and directly adjacent to the door enables easy pick-up of less agile passengers, many of whom use walkers. However, a slightly wider buffer area between the drop-off and door is desirable.
- Bollards to control traffic, textural markers to define pedestrian areas, and a seating area are needed. For seating, more able residents presently bring chairs from indoors.

7-19.
Motion Picture and Television Fund Country House and Hospital: The arrival court provides convenient access at grade and strong connections to the lobby, which are ideal for the less able. Automobile drop-off, pedestrians, and doorsitters require additional space and separation.

7-20.
Motion Picture and Television Fund Country House and Hospital: These gentlemen frequent the main entry of the "Lodge"—a prime seating spot directly connected to the lobby and office and right in the middle of the action.

Case Example: Arrival Court and Front Porch

Central City East
Los Angeles, California
Architects: David E. Crompton and Jenkins-Fleming
Landscape Architects: Peterson and Befu

The predominant activity in the Skid Row area is street-oriented interaction and travel. The residents, mostly men, are from the local area. The arrival court and front porch (which are the site entry) respond to this street-oriented life-style while providing design features for safety, security, and for control of site access. The overall concept works well, although accessibility for the less agile and definition of the site edge are not as well addressed (see fig. 7–21).

1. Location and street orientation

- To establish a presence on the street and enhance safety and security, the arrival court area abuts the public sidewalk. This arrangement also allows for full views among the porch, building entry, lobby, reception desk, and street and sidewalk, enabling previewing by residents before exiting the building, as well as monitoring by patrolling police.

2. Spatial characteristics

- Raised planters distinguish the public sidewalk from the "project" and porch area. These planters, however, being at seating level and belonging more to the street than to the project, are problematic; they are a favorite hangout for local nonresident vagrants as well as for ladies of the evening (after the social security checks arrive). This is a frequent problem when street-oriented spaces are not within the perceptual boundaries of the site; they are easily taken over and controlled by stronger, nonresident groups.
- For the less agile, access to the building is slightly difficult; no drop-off area is available, as it was felt that most residents would travel on foot. Steps or a narrow ramp must be negotiated for access.

3. Covered front porch

- A slightly recessed sitting porch establishes an active street connection while ensuring a safe, comfortable, and popular seating area. Connection to activity is generally essential for a successful front porch.
- The porch is defined as belonging to the site through a slight recessing from the street, a minor change in grade, planters, and overhead cover. The area feels safe while offering visual and physical connections to the street.

Recessed Porch

Lobby

Office and Reception

Entrance Controlled By Nonresidents

7-21.
Central City East: This street-oriented arrival court and front porch responds to the life-style of the Skid Row area, while views between the office, porch, and street enhance security. However, planters that belong more to the street and that are at an ideal height for sitting have become a favorite hangout for vagrants.

- Strong links to the indoor lobby and office enhance safety and security.
- Overhead cover provides ample shade for the westerly exposure and warm climate, while open railings enhance viewing.
- A slight separation between the seating areas and the building access route reduces opportunities for offensive surveillance between those seated and those passing by.

Low-rise Unit Entries

The unit entry area must provide for easy and direct access to and from the unit as well as adequate space for residents to personalize a "welcome" area. Where unit entries face areas of activity or interest, a comfortable place to sit and watch the activity is desirable.

Safety, security, and easy access are special concerns for entries. Each unit entry must also be easy to recognize and identify from other units. Areas for personalization also aid in entry identification and in establishing a sense of place. If well designed, the unit entry area can perceptually extend the size of indoor spaces, which are often quite small in retirement housing (see also "Low-rise Unit Clustering" in chapter 6).

Some special concerns for the design of unit entries are outlined below.

Location

1. Unit entries should be located for protection from extremes in climate. Intense sun or dark shadows, glare, and heat may pose problems for safety and security as well as for comfort. In colder climates, exposure to sun in the fall, winter, and spring is important in order to melt snow and ice.

2. Visibility from walkways and other areas frequented by residents is important for safety and security as well as for unit identification. A distance of approximately 20 feet (the minimum to ensure privacy) to 100 feet (70 feet being the preferable maximum) between unit entries and shared walkways will allow for recognition of entries and those passing by.

3. Direct and easy access from resident parking

areas to individual units is a must, although parking should not dominate primary views. Where parking is not near unit entries, a drop-off area is desirable (see fig. 7–22).

4. Individual unit access walks, which feed into access walks for a particular cluster of units rather than development-wide walks, promote a sense of safety and ownership (see fig. 7–22).

5. Access to unit doorsills should not involve a slope greater than 2.5 percent (1 percent minimum) [6]. Steps and ramps should be avoided at the entry area. A resident who develops ambulatory problems while living in a unit with steps may be forced into a premature move (see "Ramps and Stairs" in chapter 10).

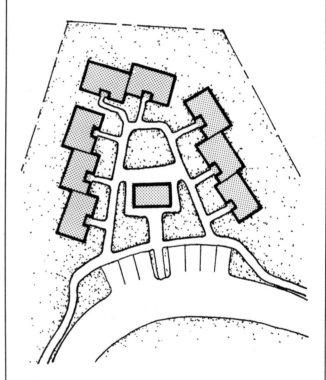

7-22.
Regents Point: Unit access through a series of walkways, from community-wide (along the street), to cluster and private walks, enhances a sense of neighborhood and privacy. The off-setting of units defines entries and provides privacy, while most entries are visible for security. Street parking along a secondary loop road is close for most units while not dominating entries and primary views.

6. The basic site-planning scheme may include a unit arrangement where unit entries face shared activity spaces or pedestrian routes. In this case, the location and orientation of unit entries should support viewing of activity and informal meeting and socializing (see fig. 7–23, 7–24). In other schemes the back of the unit or patio area may provide this connection (see "Unit Patios and Balconies" in chapter 9).

Spatial Characteristics

1. Unit access should be easy to identify and describe to visitors. The layout of units and circulation systems as well as the location, design, and detailing of unit entries should enhance unit identification and wayfinding.

2. A clear definition between private entryways and public spaces enhances security. Unit entries, however, should not be isolated from view, nor should they be isolated from areas frequented by residents.

3. The entry area should be wide enough for easy access, allowing several people to walk side by side, as well as for walkers and wheelchairs. Additional vestibule space is desirable for personalization by means of such items as planters or chairs (see figs. 7–25, 7–26, and "Unit Patios and Balconies" in chapter 9).

- A walkway width of 5 feet is recommended, allowing a minimum clearance for two wheelchairs.
- A minimum vestibule clear space of 78 by 60 inches is required for a smooth U-turn in a wheelchair.

Amenities and Detailing

1. Detailing should suggest the extent of space available for personalization. Unique paving, fencing, or planting are some options.

2. Adequate cover overhead, for protection from weather and glare, is very important for unit entries. The cover should not create a dark entry.

3. A place by the door to rest packages and purse while searching for keys makes unit access easier.

4. Ledges, railings, or other vertical elements for gripping are important, particularly where ice, snow, deep shadows, or glare may be a problem. Railings are a must for any change in elevation.

5. Lighting that illuminates the entryway, the door, and keyhole increases the ease and safety of access. Lighting should not create glare or deep shadows (see "Outdoor Lighting" and "Doors and Door Handles" in chapter 10).

6. Abrasive surfaces (such as coarse stucco or rough-hewn rock facing) should not be used on vertical surfaces near unit entries, as residents may grab them for support or brush against them.

7. Low-level planters or other protrusions on the ground plane should be avoided in the entry area. Planters should be either 30 inches in height (36 inches for the blind) or at grade to reduce the possibility of tripping [7]. Edging should not be used along unit access walks (see "Planters and Planting Beds" in chapter 10).

8. Paving must be nonslip and nonglare—it should be easy to negotiate (see "Pedestrian and Bicycle Circulation" in chapter 9).

9. For projects housing the more able, particularly in warmer climates, a place near the unit entry for locking bicycles is a good idea. Cover is desirable.

Secondary Building Exits/Entries

Access to outdoor areas is often so removed from indoor activity areas that residents have little exposure to the outdoors. This is a frequent problem with mid- to high-rise buildings, where the only access route available may be through the main entry or may be a route that exits to a parking lot. Circuitous routes discourage outdoor use by sheer distances involved and minimize opportunities for taking "sneak peaks" outside, to obtain extra chairs, equipment, and food, or to go to restrooms or coax friends outdoors.

Some major considerations for secondary building exits and entries are outlined below (see also "Ease of Access" in chapter 5).

Location

1. Secondary access routes between major indoor and outdoor activity spaces, such as patios, parking,

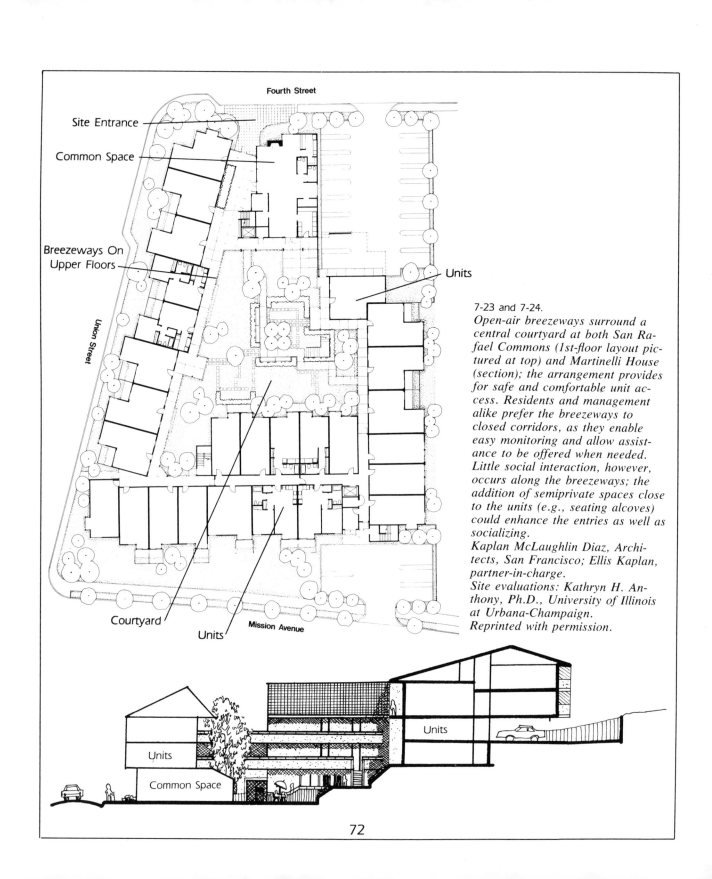

Fourth Street

Site Entrance

Common Space

Breezeways On
Upper Floors

Union Street

Units

7-23 and 7-24.
*Open-air breezeways surround a
central courtyard at both San Rafael Commons (1st-floor layout pictured at top) and Martinelli House
(section); the arrangement provides
for safe and comfortable unit access. Residents and management
alike prefer the breezeways to
closed corridors, as they enable
easy monitoring and allow assistance to be offered when needed.
Little social interaction, however,
occurs along the breezeways; the
addition of semiprivate spaces close
to the units (e.g., seating alcoves)
could enhance the entries as well as
socializing.*
*Kaplan McLaughlin Diaz, Archi-
tects, San Francisco; Ellis Kaplan,
partner-in-charge.*
*Site evaluations: Kathryn H. An-
thony, Ph.D., University of Illinois
at Urbana-Champaign.*
Reprinted with permission.

Courtyard

Units

Mission Avenue

Units

Units

Common Space

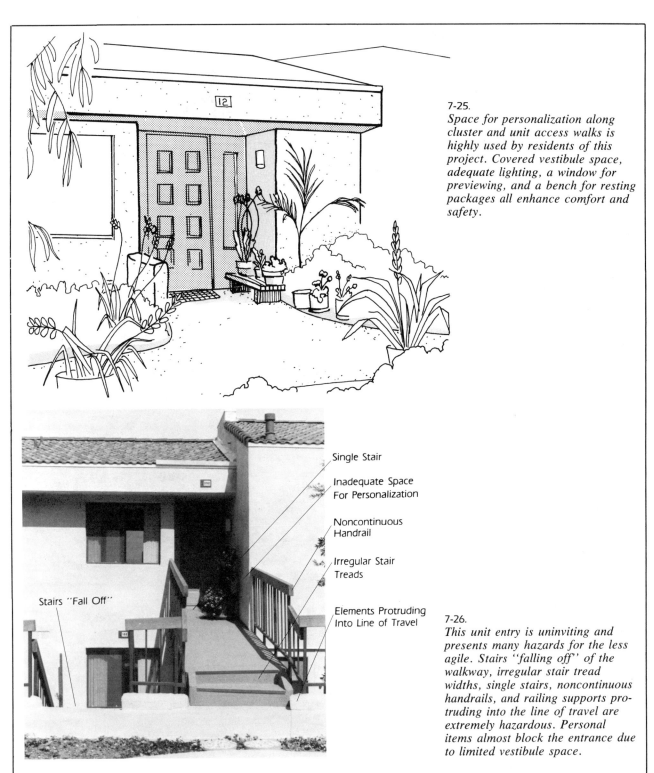

7-25.
Space for personalization along cluster and unit access walks is highly used by residents of this project. Covered vestibule space, adequate lighting, a window for previewing, and a bench for resting packages all enhance comfort and safety.

Single Stair

Inadequate Space For Personalization

Noncontinuous Handrail

Irregular Stair Treads

Elements Protruding Into Line of Travel

Stairs "Fall Off"

7-26.
This unit entry is uninviting and presents many hazards for the less agile. Stairs "falling off" of the walkway, irregular stair tread widths, single stairs, noncontinuous handrails, and railing supports protruding into the line of travel are extremely hazardous. Personal items almost block the entrance due to limited vestibule space.

lounge, and laundry rooms, promote outdoor use. One possible exception for not providing secondary exits and entries may be in cases of extreme concern over less alert residents who may absentmindedly wander off-site. A sensitive site design, one, for example, that includes an enclosed outdoor space, is generally a better alternative than limiting indoor-outdoor access points.

2. For staff monitoring, doorways for secondary access routes must be highly visible from indoor common space. In many cases, secondary access doors are permanently locked and their purpose thwarted by management concern over security (residents often forget that they propped such a door open).

Spatial Characteristics

1. Secondary exits and entries should provide a comfortable transition between indoor and outdoor areas, serving as a halfway zone that moderates exposure to weather and controls glare (see fig. 7–27). Exiting should not require direct exposure to rain, snow, or glare.

2. Exits and entries providing views to and from outdoor activity allow for previewing to generate interest in outdoor participation as well as enhance a sense of security and safety. Secondary exits and entries should not be isolated from view (see fig. 7–27).

Amenities and Detailing

1. A porch, bay window, or even an awning for comfortable viewing and sitting incorporated into major secondary exits and entries may accommodate less capable residents (see number 3, above, and fig. 7–27).

2. Access at grade is preferable to steps or ramps. If a change in elevation is necessary, both steps and ramps should be available to accommodate both ambulatory and nonambulatory residents (see "Ramps and Stairs" in chapter 10). A level threshold or a beveled one (8 percent maximum slope), ensures safe access.

3. An overhead cover providing protection from weather and glare is a good option.

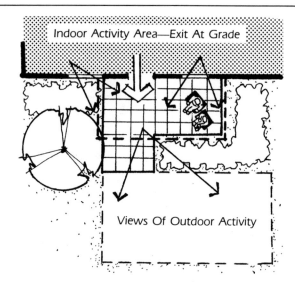

7-27.
Secondary building entries/exits can provide direct links to outdoor activity. If isolated, however, they may be permanently locked for security. An area of transition at the exit, with seating, views, and protection from weather and glare, promotes comfort and use.

4. A nonslip, nonglare walking surface is important (see "Pedestrian and Bicycle Circulation" in chapter 9).

5. Automatic locking doors operated by residents' keys or codes may help alleviate concern over security inside the building. In such cases, a ledge for resting packages or purse while searching for keys is especially desirable (see "Doors" in chapter 10).

6. Security lighting and lighting that illuminates the pavement edge promote safety. Lighting should not create glare or deep shadows (see "Outdoor Lighting" in chapter 10).

Parking and Building Access

Parking is an important site component for access to the community and for maintaining independence. Many older people may depend regularly upon their cars, particularly in rural areas or in areas without public transportation. Safety and ease of access and use are primary considerations.

Parking should be close and easily accessible from residential units and community buildings, yet should not dominate the site or building entries. Many options are available for providing safe and convenient parking and building access. Large parking lots for mid- to high-rise buildings may be divided into smaller clusters that are easier to negotiate, less visually dominating, and generally more secure due to easier visual surveillance. Secondary building entrances and drop-off areas may reduce congestion at the main building entry/drop-off area (see "Main Entry/Arrival Court" in this chapter). Small cluster lots with drop-off areas near units or some variation of the standard street or driveway parking arrangement near units are viable options for low-rise developments (see "The Entry Drive," above).

Subsurface or multilevel parking structures are options for larger developments, particularly in extreme climates and in urban areas where land is at a premium. But parking structures are not entirely desirable because they involve indirect building access, circuitous routes, changes in grade, and are difficult to monitor for security. Many of the requirements for exterior parking also apply to parking structures. Individual parking garages or carports are favored by many people. (For a discussion of parking ratios, refer to "Parking Requirements" in chapter 6.)

Location

1. A site layout that enables the natural progression from building approach and identification, to drop-off, to temporary or visitor parking, and to long-term parking aids in wayfinding and reduces confusion (see figs. 7–28, 7–29).

2. To ensure convenience, parking areas should be

Small Cluster Parking Associated With Units

Units

Apts.

Drop-off and Secondary Access Points For Larger Parking Lots

7-28.
Smaller cluster parking associated with units is preferable to larger lots. A drop-off and secondary building access route may be necessary for larger lots. Offsetting parking from the street is advisable for heavy traffic streets.

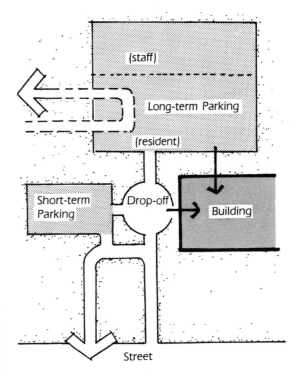

(staff)

Long-term Parking

(resident)

Short-term Parking

Drop-off

Building

Street

7-29.
A progression from site entry and building identification, to drop-off, short-term, and then long-term parking is easiest to follow. A separate entrance for long-term parking can reduce congestion at the main entrance and enhance convenience.

located close to residential and community buildings, but should not dominate primary views or building entries (see number 1 in "Spatial Characteristics," below).

3. Where parking must be located farther away from main building entries, a secondary entrance or a drop-off area is necessary for the less agile (see fig. 7–29).

4. To ensure safety, parking stalls should not be located directly along major traffic streets.

Spatial Characteristics

1. Although a setback or offset from buildings is desirable for aesthetic reasons, especially where units face parking, proximity to parking is often a greater priority for reasons of safety, security surveillance, and convenience.

2. The layout of parking areas should be straight-forward, consistent, and predictable (see fig. 7–30).

- Wide two-way aisles are generally preferable to one-way aisles and drives, which, unless carefully designed, may cause confusion. The tenacity of the older driver in pursuing his or her "own" direction suggests that mixing both one- and two-way aisles presents a severe safety hazard.
- Parking-lot layout should not require good driver vision to the extreme left or right of the line of travel. Poorer peripheral vision and lessened flexibility in turning the body or head make such situations difficult and hazardous for the older driver.

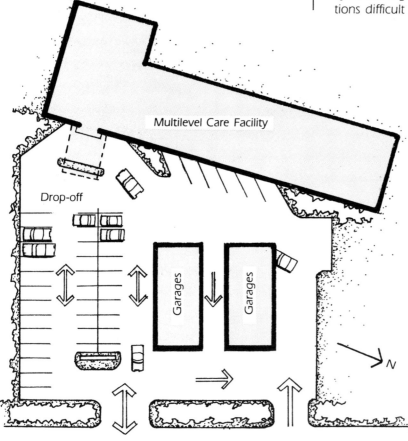

7-30.
Mixing one-way and two-way drives is most confusing. A reminder printed in the resident newsletter at this project highlights part of the problem: "Remember, the driveway north of the garages is marked for 'in' traffic only; the strip east of the garages, parallel to the street, is for northbound traffic only." Although building drop-off is convenient, access requires passing through the parking lot (pedestrians behind cars). The garage layout creates blind spots for those with poorer peripheral vision or those who cannot easily turn their head to see.

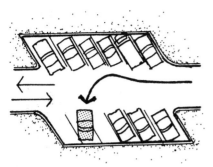

7-31.
Two-way angled parking can be confusing, resulting in misaligned parked cars.

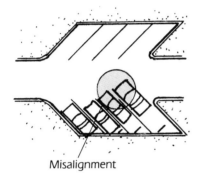

Misalignment

7-33.
Forty-five-degree parking is more likely to result in misaligned cars protruding into the access aisle, as older drivers, with poorer depth perception, may use the adjacent car to judge their own parking alignment.

3. Access aisles should be aligned with drives to favor inbound traffic, which is generally faster moving than outbound traffic [8]. The best layout is one that reduces the number of turns required in general.

4. Perpendicular and angled parking are both viable options. Turning into the stall is easier with angled parking than with 90-degree parking; it reduces the chance of nicking the adjacent parked car. Perpendicular parking, however, is familiar to many. Several points must be considered in choosing the appropriate parking type (see figs. 7–31, 7–32, 7–33):

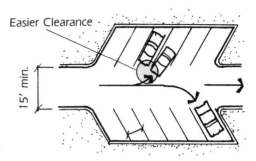

Easier Clearance

15' min.

7-32.
Sixty-degree angled parking makes turning into stalls easier; however, special attention to the overall layout of circulation and parking is needed to reduce confusion created by one-way drives.

- A parking lot type, layout, and required direction of travel that are consistent with the overall layout of on-site roads and drives are generally easier to negotiate.
- Angled parking with one-way aisles may be confusing unless the on-site vehicular circulation system is similarly designed and design elements such as reduced-turning-radii [5 feet] on "no-turn" corners are introduced that guide the driver along the correct line of travel.
- Angled parking with two-way aisles can result in parked cars angled in the wrong direction.
- Sixty-degree angled parking is more appropriate than 45-degree parking. The older driver, with poorer depth perception, may align the front of his or her car with that of the adjacent parked car; with 45-degree parking there is a greater likelihood that the rear of the car will protrude into the access aisle.

5. A layout that ensures pedestrian safety is essential (see fig. 7–34).

- Smaller cluster lots relating to the building or units are generally easier to negotiate for the pedestrian as well as for the driver.
- The layout of larger lots should allow for safe pedestrian movement in front of the cars, not behind them.
- Drop-off and seating/waiting areas near the build-

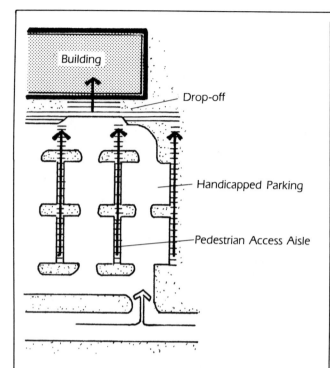

7-34.
A parking lot layout that minimizes pedestrian and vehicular crossing and does not require pedestrians (especially the handicapped) to pass behind parked cars increases safety. Pedestrian access aisles are one option for larger lots.

ing entry are important components for safe loading and unloading of passengers and packages, especially in larger parking lots or those more removed from building entries (see "The Main Entry/Arrival Court" and "Low-rise Unit Entries," above).

6. Visual surveillance of the parking area is a prime consideration, as parking lots often present security problems.

7. A reasonable number of parking stalls (5 percent is generally recommended) should be reserved for the handicapped; they must be close to the destination and not require people to pass behind parked cars to reach the walkway.

Amenities and Detailing

1. High-branching or low-growing plant material in parking areas ensures visibility and reduces opportunities for concealment (see fig. 7–35).

2. Parking lots should be well lighted for safety and security (see "Lighting" in chapter 10).

3. Parking islands at the ends of rows should allow no less than a 25-foot clear width for two-way traffic (24-foot minimum width between the stalls); if less than 25 feet, a one-way access aisle (minimum width 15 feet) is recommended [9].

4. Parking stall dimensions for the ambulatory should provide adequate space for easy maneuverability, and for those with walking aids, in getting in and out of the car (see fig. 7–36).

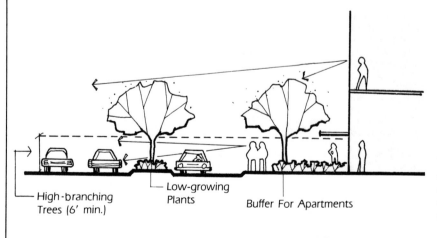

High-branching Trees (6' min.)

Low-growing Plants

Buffer For Apartments

7-35.
Parking lots should provide close and convenient building access. Elements for safety and security are essential; visual surveillance is key.

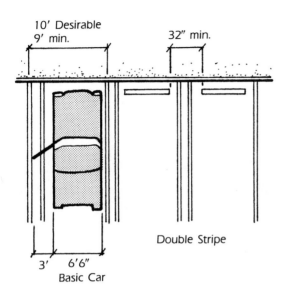

10' Desirable
9' min.

32" min.

Double Stripe

3' 6'6"
Basic Car

7-36.
Parking stall dimensions for the ambulatory should allow ample space for getting in and out of the car and for opening doors (basic vehicle requires 3 feet). Wheel stop placement should allow a 32-inch (min.) access aisle for pedestrian safety.

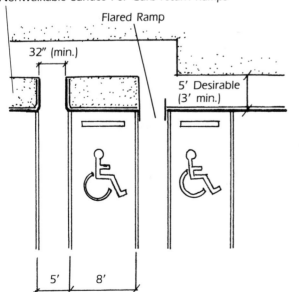

Nonwalkable Surface For Curb-return Ramps

Flared Ramp

32" (min.)

5' Desirable
(3' min.)

5'   8'

- A parking stall width of 10 feet is desirable (9 feet minimum), allowing a 3 foot, 6 inch space between two parked cars for opened doors (a standard car door requires a 3-foot clear space for opening).
- Stalls with double painted lines make it easier for the driver to align the car in the space correctly and to define pedestrian access aisles.

5. Parking for the handicapped must provide ample space for maneuverability of the wheelchair to and from the stall (see fig. 7–37) [10].

- A stall width of 8 feet with an additional 5-foot access aisle is recommended; the access aisle may be shared between two spaces.
- The location of curb cuts (32-inch minimum width) should provide a directly accessible route from the stall to the sidewalk that does not require the handicapped person to pass behind parked vehicles (see "Pedestrian Street Crossings" in chapter 10).

6. Walkways in front of parked cars should be a minimum of 3 feet wide (5 feet is more desirable), not including a vehicle overhang of 30 inches (see fig. 7–38) [11].

7. Wheel stops or bumpers deserve special attention, as they are not easily seen by pedestrians and can cause a fall (see figs. 7–36, 7–38).

- Wheel stops, if used, must be placed to allow a 32-inch (minimum) access aisle between parked cars.
- Special treatment, such as painting, to increase visibility is desirable.
- Where wheel stops are not used, an additional 30-inch overhang must be calculated for all walkways passing in front of parked cars.

7-37.
Parking stall dimensions for the handicapped should provide a 5-foot access aisle (may be shared between two stalls) directly accessible to the walkway.

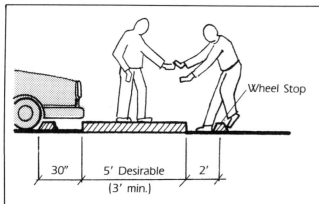

30"   5' Desirable   2'
              (3' min.)

7-38.
To ensure pedestrian safety and maneuverability, where wheel stops are not used, an additional 30-inch walkway width or buffer is needed for vehicle overhang. Wheel stops must be well marked and carefully placed to ensure a clear path of travel from car to walkway.

Service and Delivery Areas

Service and delivery areas are often considered visual blights that should be screened from view. Some residents, however, may enjoy watching the activity of a frequently used delivery area. Obviously, such areas should not dominate views or high-use spaces. A few special considerations for service and delivery areas are outlined below.

Location

1. Such areas should not interfere with resident access to and from on-site facilities or activity areas.

2. The location should consider the image presented to the community and residents at large.

3. Small delivery/service areas for residents' use may be especially useful for mid- to high-rise buildings. These areas may be used for transporting heavy objects and, if connected to the appropriate indoor spaces, for such activities as glass and paper recycling.

4. Opportunities for sitting and watching the activity of the delivery area are desirable, although the area should not dominate views.

5. Service areas, dumpsters, and so on, for residents' use should be easy to reach from units.

Spatial Characteristics

Adequate space for delivery and collection trucks and for extra refuse from "spring cleaning" is basic.

Amenities and Detailing

1. A sitting area/bench near frequently used delivery areas may provide a place for those who want to watch the activity.

2. Special paving to denote delivery and traffic areas maximizes safety.

References

1. Green, Isaac, *et al. Housing for the Elderly: The Development and Design Process.* New York: Van Nostrand Reinhold. 1975.

2. ———. *Housing for the Elderly.*

3. ———. *Housing for the Elderly,* 113.

4. ———. *Housing for the Elderly,* 130.

5. ———. *Housing for the Elderly.*

6. ———. *Housing for the Elderly,* 130.

7. ———. *Housing for the Elderly.*

8. Zolomij, Robert. "Vehicular Circulation." In *Handbook of Landscape Architectural Construction,* edited by J. Carpenter. Washington, DC: Landscape Architecture Foundation, 1976, 241–323.

9. ———. "Vehicular Circulation."

10. American National Standards Institute. *Specifications for Making Buildings and Facilities Accessible to and Usable by Physically Handicapped People.* A117.1–1980. New York: ANSI, 1980.

11. ———. *Specifications for Making Buildings and Facilities Accessible.*

Designing for Outdoor Use

Outdoor use for pleasure and recreation is perhaps the most difficult type for which to design and to provide facilities.

First, the abilities and preferences of older people vary greatly. Thus, outdoor areas should provide for a wide range of possible activities rather than a number of the same inflexible facilities. Variety and flexibility of outdoor space are the keys to recreational and pleasure use. Opportunities for social interaction are also essential.

Second, actual outdoor use is generally very low, especially when compared to indoor use. The design of outdoor areas, however, often does not respond to the special needs and requirements of older people, especially in terms of comfort, protection from weather, and safety and security. Although outdoor use may be quite seasonal in some regions, it is difficult to place a value either on enjoying the outdoors after a long winter or just knowing that the option to enjoy it is there.

Finally, for many older people, a move to planned housing often means a change in life routines. The provision of facilities that enable continuity with previous pastimes and environments is an important consideration. Greater emphasis upon health and leisure suggests that a broad range of sports and outdoor activities will become more popular among the aging.

In chapter 8, considerations for popular types of outdoor use are examined. Specific site elements for recreation and pleasure (e.g., patios) are examined in chapter 9; while special considerations for amenities and detailing are discussed in chapter 10.

Designing for Recreation and Pleasure Use of the Outdoors

This chapter is intended to give the designer an understanding of the types of outdoor use often preferred by older people. It also outlines design factors affecting use. Four popular types of outdoor use for pleasure and recreation are examined:

- outdoor areas for social interaction
- outdoor areas for enjoying nature
- areas for health and exercise
- enjoying the outdoors from inside

How one responds to these types of use in actual facilities is determined ideally by a survey of existing or potential residents.

In general, the best solution is to cluster outdoor activity areas together. This provides more opportunities for meeting others involved in different activities. Connection to indoor activity spaces also promotes outdoor use. For larger developments, smaller activity areas related to unit clusters as well as a focal point for development-wide activity is desirable.

Outdoor Areas for Social Interaction

"Social interaction" and "being near the activity of others" are primary reasons for the elderly's use of space. A frequent error is made in the assumption that older people prefer a "peaceful and quiet" environment. Sitting and watching, however, may be a very active form of participation for many seniors, enabling them to feel a part of the activity [1].

The structure and furnishings of a space, as well as the relationship between spaces and their orientation, are important considerations when designing areas for social interaction [2]. Safety, security, negotiability, ease of access, and comfort are basic considerations for all spaces, but are particularly important for outdoor areas for socializing, where less able elderly may congregate.

Location

1. A location near nodes of activity is ideal for social spaces and seating areas. Grouping community social spaces and recreation areas together as a focal point for activity on-site increases the potential for meeting others engaged in various activities as well as for meeting residents from other parts of a larger development (see fig. 8–1). Adequate space for accommodating the functional activities of an area (such as building access), as well as space for socializing or sitting and watching, is imperative but often overlooked, especially at building entries.

Some examples of popular activity nodes include the following:

- Building entry areas are generally the most popular spots to sit and watch activity and to meet and socialize casually.
- Community centers and recreational areas provide opportunities for meeting residents engaged in other activities.
- Areas adjacent to indoor activity spaces and frequently used services, such as lounges, lobbies, laundry facilities, and mail delivery areas, provide similar opportunities.
- Areas adjacent to unit balconies and patios provide opportunities for meeting others passing by.
- Walkway intersections, particularly those leading from units to activity areas, parking lots, community centers, or laundry rooms, are prime locations for seating areas and socializing.
- Areas near neighborhood activity, especially when at building entries, tend to attract interest and draw people.
- Areas adjacent to cafes or other food services and (group or individual) kitchens are good locations for social areas.

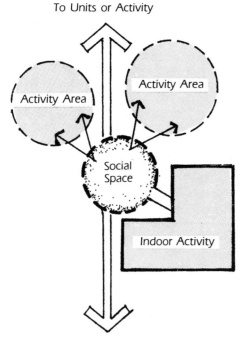

To Units or Activity

Activity Area

Activity Area

Social Space

Indoor Activity

To Neighborhood or Activity

8-1.
Clustering of social spaces near indoor and outdoor activity centers and along frequently traveled walkways maximizes opportunities for drop-in use and casual socializing. A viewing distance of up to 100 feet will enable most residents to recognize the activity (closer distance is required for recognizing individuals).

2. A visual distance of less than 100 feet between activity generators and social spaces (such as unit patios and a common walkway/seating area) will enable identification of the activity (fig. 8–1) [3].

3. Other noteworthy location factors for social areas include:

- location for safety and security, including visibility and physical protection offered from a building edge or partially enclosed corner, or an area protected by a cluster of units (see chapter 5, Part B)
- orientation for protection from climate (see "Comfort and Environmental Negotiability" in chapter 5, Part B)

4. A location for direct and easy access to and from indoor and outdoor activity spaces is especially

important for the less able who may frequent social areas. Steep grades, crossing of vehicular traffic, and other potential barriers should be avoided.

Spatial Characteristics

1. A smaller, more intimate scale is more appropriate for most social spaces, since such a scale offers a sense of closeness that supports social interaction. A variety of smaller spaces can also be more easily claimed by various social groups. Men, for example, may prefer to claim a small area for themselves where they can "get away from the women," but still see them from a distance (see "Issue: Spatial Preferences–Space for Socializing, Mastering, and Claiming" in chapter 5).

2. Spaces with defined edges or boundaries often provide a more comfortable space for social interaction.

3. A variety of spaces for meeting others, as well as intimacy and privacy should be available, from a private nook, to side-line seating, and seating in the middle of the action.

Amenities and Detailing

1. Comfortable seating offering a choice between right-angle conversation seating and street- or activity-oriented seating should be available for socializing. Movable furniture is preferable to fixed furniture (see "Shared Patios and Terraces" in chapter 9 and "Seating" in chapter 10).

2. Access to indoor facilities, such as restrooms and kitchens, increases comfort and use.

3. Pick-up games and game tables may encourage impromptu participation and socializing, providing a "reason" for use of a space.

4. Architectural devices offering protection from weather, such as extended overhangs or porches, are important.

Management and Activity Programming

1. Programmed activities involving residents and even the surrounding community can help activate areas and increase social connections if adequate space and facilities are available. Clubhouses with large patios and adjacent open space, for example, can accommodate a range of activities, from craft sales, neighborhood ice-sculpture contests, and holiday barbeques, to family reunions.

Planned activities, although often essential for sparking interest and use of facilities among the less energetic, can be successful only if the necessary facilities are available. A close working relationship with the activity programmer is helpful to anticipate group needs and necessary facilities, such as barbeque grills and dancing surfaces.

Outdoor Areas for Enjoying Nature

Enjoying nature is an important reason for many older people's use of the outdoors and is closely related to health and exercise [4]. Opportunities for enjoying nature encourage seasonal awareness and may aid in maintaining cognitive orientation to the passing of time. Some residents may be dedicated to growing their own garden, others may prefer to view a formal garden, while some may enjoy the solitude and variety of a natural area. Several important design factors are examined below.

Location

1. Nature areas should provide a variety of experiences, from formal gardens to nature trails and wildlife areas.

2. Pleasure gardens and nature areas visible from indoors can provide a window of entertainment for the housebound, especially during inclement weather. More distant areas may encourage exercise and exploration (see fig. 8–2).

3. Pleasure garden areas located near outdoor social spaces provide greater opportunities for meeting others by serving as an "attractor," and as a topic of conversation. Gardens can enliven and add interest to what might otherwise be a rather dull sitting area.

4. Places for residents' participation in nature are an important consideration. Small plots associated with units, balconies, and patios, and larger, more distant gardening centers are some options. The level of maintenance and the type of garden maintained by the residents (a presentation versus a working gar-

den) affect the location (see "Resident Gardening Areas" in chapter 9).

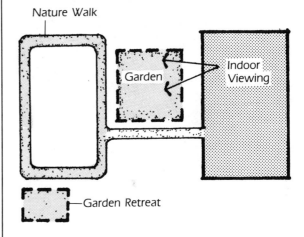

8-2.
A variety in type and location of gardens and nature areas is ideal. Nearby gardens for viewing from indoors are important for the housebound. Nature walks may encourage exercise and exploration. More distant nature areas may serve as needed retreats.

Amenities and Detailing

1. A variety of plant materials for seasonal color and attraction of wildlife as well as amenities like bird feeders add interest and activity.

2. Special facilities, such as locking tool sheds, raised working areas, and planting beds accessible to the handicapped, promote garden use (see "Resident Gardening Areas" in chapter 9 and "Planters and Planting Beds" in chapter 10).

Management and Programming

1. Management policy should encourage residents' personal use of the outdoors through gardening, for example, or adding their own bird feeders. Such use can be accommodated in a private patio or balcony area.

2. The addition of personal items like garden furniture and plants to common spaces may be appreciated by some residents, but not by others (see fig. 8–3). One option, especially for major site additions,

8-3.
Allowing the addition of personal items, whether small or large (such as garden furniture), promotes a sense of home. This bird, placed on the lawn by a resident, is one of the few homey details on this site.

is the formation of a resident-management design review board to evaluate residents' proposals.

Areas for Health and Exercise

Health and exercise are concerns of many older people and are prime reasons for outdoor use [5, 6]. Areas and facilities for health and exercise should provide a range of challenges while offering support for those whose health limits their range of activities. Interest in specific activities and recreational facilities may vary according to region, economic class, ability levels, and climate. For example, the level of care offered at a particular development will determine in part the relative success of active versus more passive recreational facilities (see fig. 8–4). Walking, however, is extremely popular among many seniors and is an activity in which most can participate. A survey of the potential residents is an ideal way to determine the specific facilities best suited to residents' preferences and ability levels.

Many residents may have health and mobility limitations on their use of the outdoors. Some feel that they are "just too old" or "tire too easily" to be outdoors. For such people, feeling the sun on their faces for a few minutes or looking at the flowers may constitute an activity that is good for their health while representing the most activity they feel up to. Others may be very active. Detailing for residents' diverse needs is important, as well as planning for general design issues of spatial quality and relationships, challenge and support, and the provision of specific recreational facilities. Recreational facilities for use by visitors and grandchildren are also a consideration.

Location

1. Areas for health and exercise, particularly those for mild exercise, if located close to residential units or indoor community spaces, promote use among

8-4.
Physically challenging recreation (such as this formation riding class) is highly popular among the "young" residents of this recreationally based retirement community.

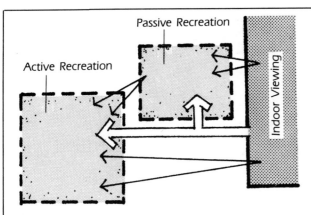

8-5.
Grouping active and passive recreation areas enhances participation. Passive areas, if located nearer the building, encourage use by the more frail.

persons of all ability levels. Proximity to indoor social spaces also maximizes opportunities for "showing off."

More "active" outdoor areas may be located farther away, but still within view of major indoor activity areas. As noted, views of activity are an important catalyst to participation (see fig. 8–5).

2. Activity areas may be related to unit clusters or to one or more central focal points on-site.

3. A location along frequently traveled pathways is ideal, increasing opportunities for drop-in use.

Spatial Characteristics

1. Providing exercise opportunities for the less mobile requires a richness and variety of outdoor spaces—just getting outdoors may be exercise for some.

2. Walkway loops, providing a series of longer and shorter routes, and variety of challenges by means of topographical design should be available. Walking is a very popular outdoor activity among many seniors at all levels of ability (see "Pedestrian and Bicycle Circulation" in chapter 9).

3. Bicycling, a popular activity in many regions, requires special considerations for separation of vehicular, bicycle, and pedestrian traffic, as well as space for three-wheelers and bicycle storage (see "Pedestrian and Bicycle Circulation" in chapter 9).

Amenities and Detailing

1. Specific recreational and sport facilities are best determined by residents, as interest in particular activities may vary. Recreation that involves socializing, however, is generally the most popular.

2. The setting is most important for generating use. Opportunities to watch and to be watched, amenities for comfort, shade, ample seating, and easy access are essential.

3. Special detailing for recreational facilities and equipment, such as finely graded playing surfaces or brightly colored equipment, may encourage participation even by those with some infirmity.

4. Recreational activities and equipment should not involve isometric exercises, as they raise blood pressure [7].

5. Resting and viewing areas in shade and sun are particularly important for vicarious participation and for those who tire more easily.

Enjoying the Outdoors from Inside

Viewing outdoor activity and nature from inside a building is an extremely popular activity, especially among the less active and those who are housebound during harsh winter months. Consequently, the overall site plan and layout of activity areas should enhance indoor spaces or provide exceptional views from them.

The physical and visual relationship between indoor and outdoor areas is not only stressed for enjoyable observation of the outdoors, but also for encouraging older people to use the outdoors. Unfortunately, this relationship has generally received the least attention of any design aspect in housing for the elderly. Views are one important connection to outdoor activity, serving as a window to the world for the more frail, as well as promoting a sense of safety and security outdoors.

Views for interest and enjoyment of the outdoors consist of two major components: (1) what is being viewed and (2) how it is being viewed. Views of activity and change are generally the most popular; observation from a seated position in a favorite chair is popular. Other aspects of indoor–outdoor relationships were examined in chapter 5, including access, the relationship between types of indoor and outdoor spaces, and transitions.

Location

1. The orientation of buildings and the location of outdoor activity areas should provide views of activity, action, and change, especially from indoor common spaces and residential units. These are generally the most popular. Some potential areas offering activity for watching include the surrounding neighborhood, building entries, major walkways, and frequently used recreational areas. Wildlife and natural scenic beauty have great appeal. Even delivery and service areas, normally considered visual blights, may be of interest.

2. The layout and general geometry of outdoor areas is an important element in views from upper-story windows and balconies of mid- to high-rise buildings. A strong geometry on the ground plane, with a central or focal element, may add interest when seen from upper-story windows [8]. The placement of outdoor activity areas and viewing angle

from upper-story windows should also be considered; areas adjacent to the building may not be visible from upper stories, and primarily westerly views may be obscured by glare (see fig. 8–6).

Spatial Characteristics

1. Architectural devices can enhance outdoor views without actual exit. A solarium, for example, can be modified for outdoor exposure during good weather (see fig. 8–7).

Amenities and Detailing

1. Plant materials may be placed to open or frame a view (see "Windows and Glazed Surfaces" in chapter 10). Dense trees in front of windows or the line of sight to activity areas may obscure a view.

2. Detailing to reduce window glare, such as extended overhangs and window glazing, are essential, as older people are generally more sensitive to glare.

3. The height and design of balcony railings and windowsills should allow one to see the outdoors

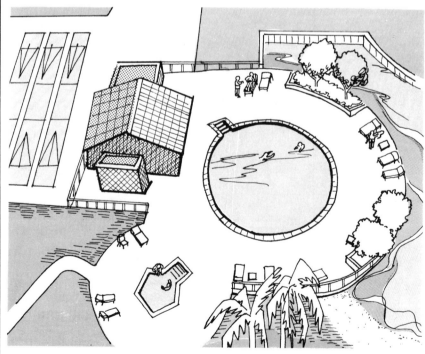

8-6.
A strong geometry on the ground plane (and activity) adds interest to views from upper-story apartments at the Waterford life-care community in Juno Beach, Florida.

from a seated position (see "Windows and Glazed Surfaces" in chapter 10 and "Unit Patios and Balconies" in chapter 9).

4. Balconies and patios provide unique viewing opportunities. They should be large enough to allow for comfortable seating, wheelchair access, and general movement, as well as for personalization of the

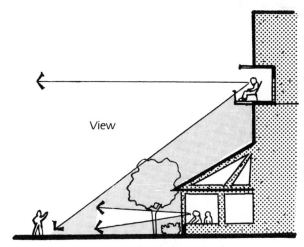

View

Area Not Visible From Upper Stories

8-7.
Architectural elements to moderate climate and control glare are essential for comfortable viewing. The placement of outdoor activity areas and plant materials should take into consideration viewing angle—areas close to the building are not visible from upper-story windows.

space (see "Unit Patios and Balconies" in chapter 9).

5. Night lighting can provide dramatic and scenic interest as well as safety and security.

References

1. Lawton, M. Powell. "Public Behavior of Older People in Congregate Housing." In *Proceedings of the 1st Annual Environmental Design Research Association Conference,* edited by H. Sanoff and S. Cohen. Chapel Hill, NC: The Conference, 1970.

2. ——. "Public Behavior of Older People."

3. Zeisel, J., G. Epp, and S. Demos. *Low Rise Housing for Older People.* U.S. Department of Housing and Urban Development, Office of Policy Development and Research. HUD-483(TQ)-76. Washington, DC: U.S. Government Printing Office, 1977.

4. Carstens, D., and E. Makowski. *Residents' Use of the Outdoors Adjacent to Elderly Public Housing: Small Town Example.* Urbana Department of Landscape Architecture, University of Illinois, 1980.

5. Carstens, D. "Behavioral Research Applied to the Redesign of Exterior Spaces: Housing for the Elderly." In *Proceedings of the 13th International Conference of the Environmental Design Research Association,* edited by P. Bart, A. Chen, and G. Francescato. College Park, MD: EDRA, 1982.

6. Carstens and Makowski. *Residents' Use of the Outdoors.*

7. Atchely, Robert C. *The Social Forces in Later Life: An Introduction to Social Gerontology.* Belmont, CA: Wadsworth Press, 1972.

CHAPTER

Site Design Elements for Recreation and Pleasure

A wide variety of recreational and social activities appeals to the senior citizen, from simply watching others to horseback riding. Many factors, however, will affect recreational preferences, including ability level, socioeconomic background, and previous recreational activities.

The site design elements addressed in this chapter reflect very basic site components around which more specific recreational facilities may be added, such as riding stables, lawn bowls, and golf courses. These specific facilities should be determined on a project-by-project basis.

Outdoor areas designed specifically for recreation, however, are not the sole site of activity. Borrowed activity from areas of frequent everyday use, such as dining rooms, cafes, laundry and mail areas, and major pedestrian routes increases the likelihood of outdoor space use. Main building entries in particular are often the hub of activity, offering a continual flow of passersby with whom one can meet and talk.

In this chapter, important recommendations are made for the location, design, and detailing of common site elements for recreation and pleasure:

- shared patios and terraces
- rooftop developments
- unit patios and balconies
- gardens and nature areas
- resident gardening areas
- pedestrian and bicycle circulation
- lawn areas for recreation
- play areas for children

Shared Patios and Terraces

Patios and terraces that are shared by residents of a unit cluster or the project as a whole can be centers for both informal small group socializing and large group activities. Casual use, dances, barbeques, and club luncheons are but a few of the potential activities for these areas. When appropriately located, designed, and detailed, these areas may be frequented by less able residents, who require easy access, comfort, and security.

The type of development (e.g., low- or high-rise) may have important implications for the location, design, and use of shared patios. When panoramic views are a possibility or when limited ground-level space is available, rooftop patios may be an option.

On larger low-rise and mixed developments, dispersal of activity throughout the site is a potential problem. A centrally located patio can serve as a focal point for development-wide recreation. It can provide a unifying element on-site, tying together the site and site-based activity. Smaller shared patios may be developed for use by residents of a particular cluster of low-rise units, enhancing their sense of community within the larger development.

In contrast, mid- to high-rise developments often include a strong indoor center of activity, especially on small sites with a single building. Shared patios developed as an extension of indoor activity have the potential to generate high levels of use. In this situation, an architectural type of solution such as a solarium or courtyard is appropriate to enhance the indoor–outdoor relationship as well as comfort—especially for the less able. A creative architectural solution may also be needed to provide adequate outdoor space where ground-level space is limited. Options for intimacy, however, should be maintained.

With all shared patios and terraces a special challenge is to create a sense of intimacy for small group and individual use while providing adequate space for large group activities. This may be particularly important for small sites, where only a single communal patio may be possible due to space limitations.

Some major design considerations for shared patios and terraces are outlined below.

Location—Indoor Relationships

1. Patios located near central points of indoor activity and facilities will generate higher levels of use. Patio spaces, particularly for less able older people, require minimizing the amount of physical and psychological commitment necessary to use the space. Some good connections include the following (see fig. 9–1):

- Connection to community recreation or social centers.
- Easy access from indoor common spaces, such as lounges, dining halls, and so on, as well as kitchens and restrooms, support casual as well as planned patio use by both small and large groups.
- A location that is highly visible from indoor areas frequented by staff and residents, such as the lounge and office, ensures visual surveillance and reduces residents' concern over not being seen if they fall or are bothered by strangers.
- Connection to laundry rooms, craft areas, and main corridors within the building promotes informal drop-in use of patios.

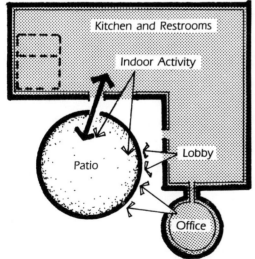

9-1.
A patio location for ease of access to and from indoor activity centers enhances use of both. Visual surveillance from areas frequented by staff (e.g., office) and residents maximizes safety and security.

2. Shared patios, for mid- to high-rise buildings in particular, may be developed as an extension of indoor activity spaces. A solarium or extended roof overhang, can provide a comfortable transition from the mass and architecture of the building to the outdoors.

3. A secure and protected location, such as the pocket created by an L-shaped building, or a cluster of units, is an ideal way of establishing connections. Courtyards, for example, with a dual orientation toward activity (e.g., the street) and protection—afforded by the surrounding building—can offer a sense of security important for socializing, especially among the less able, while providing interesting views of activity (see fig. 9–2).

Location—Outdoor Relationships

1. A central location near nodes of outdoor activity and recreation is ideal for shared patios; views of activity add interest and a "reason" for use. Proximity to recreational facilities, such as lawn bowls, a bocce court, and swimming pools, is a good option.

2. Shared patios, for larger low-rise and mixed developments, when centrally located, may serve as a focal point for activity, tying the development together and providing a sense of place.

3. A location near walkway intersections, particularly those leading to and from activity, supports drop-in use. A patio near walkways leading to parking lots, residential clusters, or community buildings, for example, offers greater activity and informal meeting opportunities (see figs. 9–3 and 9–5).

Spatial Characteristics

1. The appropriate size for a patio is determined by many factors. As a general guide, approximately 13 square feet of paved outdoor common space per unit is recommended [1]. Many variables, however, may influence frequency of use and whether patios are used by large or small groups. These variables have implications for both the size and number of patios needed. A large recreationally based retirement community with active programming, for example, is likely to place heavy demands on patio use for both small and very large groups. Some common variables that can potentially influence patio use are summa-

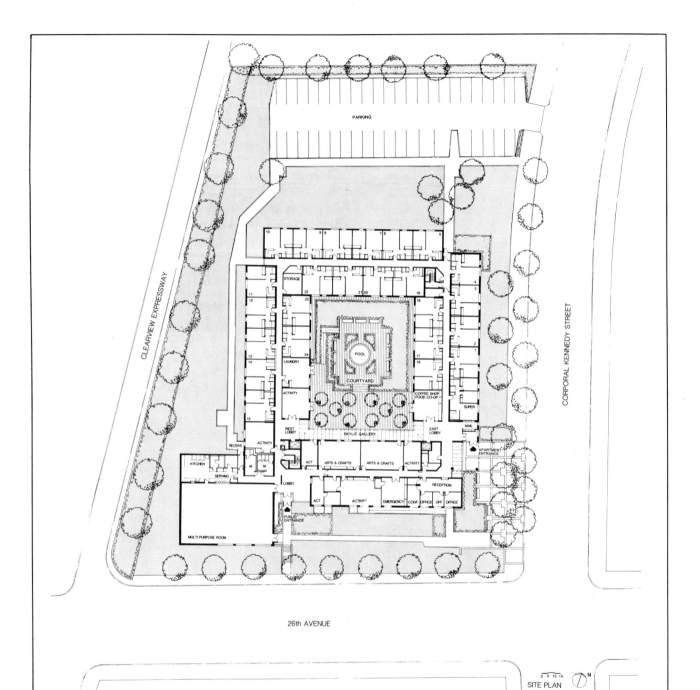

PARKING

CLEARVIEW EXPRESSWAY

CORPORAL KENNEDY STREET

STORAGE

LAUNDRY

ACTIVITY

POOL

COURTYARD

COFFEE SHOP
FOOD CO-OP

SUPER

MAIL

WEST
LOBBY

EAST
LOBBY

SKYLIT GALLERY

RECEIVE

ACTIVITY

KITCHEN

SERVING

M W

ACT

ARTS & CRAFTS

ARTS & CRAFTS

ACTIVITY

APARTMENT
ENTRANCE

LOBBY

ACT

ACTIVITY

EMERGENCY

CONF

OFFICE

OFF

OFFICE

RECEPTION

PUBLIC
ENTRANCE

MULTI PURPOSE ROOM

26th AVENUE

SITE PLAN   0 5 10 15   N

9-2.
Scheuer House, Queens, New York: Easy access to this inner courtyard from indoor activity generators, such as the coffee shop and laundry room, is ideal. A skylit gallery to the south extends seasonal enjoyment. A stronger connection between the courtyard and building entries/lobbies could prove beneficial for courtyard use. The Gruzen Partnership, Architects and Planners, New York.
Reprinted with permission.

92

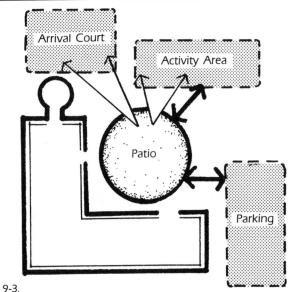

9-3.
Connections to indoor activity enhance patio use. A location near walkway intersections leading to residential units, parking lots, and activity centers is ideal. Views of activity add interest.

rized in table 9–1. It is important to keep in mind, however, that flexibility of space is a key factor.

2. A flexible patio design can provide a smaller scale of space and a sense of intimacy for individual socializing while retaining adequate space for large group activities such as barbeques, dances, or displays. One design solution is the use of smaller subspaces that adjoin, offering a sense of security and intimacy (important for small groups) within a larger space (see fig. 9–4).

3. In general, a smaller, intimate space with defined edges is most suitable for small group conversation and socializing. A maximum conversation distance comfortable for many older people is approximately 6 feet—less for those with visual or hearing impairments.

4. Shared patios should have a variety of spaces for privacy, intimacy, and for meeting others, from a private nook to side-line seating and seating in the middle of the action (see fig. 9–4). This is essential where private outdoor spaces are not available.

Table 9–1 FACTORS INFLUENCING TYPE OF PATIO USE AND SPACE REQUIREMENTS*

Factors Increasing Patio Use**	Effect Upon Use and Space Requirements
Sense of community	Space needed for moderate levels of individual and small and large group use
Strong activity programming	Space needed for frequent large and small group activities and community events
Connection to food service/cafe	Space needed for heavy use by individuals and small groups around mealtime, possibly also for large group dining and other food-related events
Connection to indoor common areas (e.g., lounge)	Space needed for moderate levels of individual and small group use; large group use for special events is likely, especially if activity programming exists
Connection to laundry facilities, craft rooms, and units	Space needed for moderate levels of informal individual and small group use
Connection to mail area	Space needed for moderate to heavy use by individuals and small groups at mail delivery time
Connection to major access route	Space needed for moderate to heavy "drop-in" use by individuals and small groups

*Approximately 13 square feet of paved outdoor common space per unit is generally recommended. Many factors, however, can impact the amount of space required, including the type of use expected (e.g., small or large group) and anticipated activities (e.g., reading or dining).

**These examples are for illustrative purposes. The actual demand for patio space is influenced by many interacting factors.

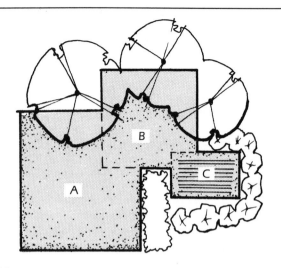

5. Walkways that pass through or by shared patio areas should be subtly separated from seating areas. This arrangement ensures some measure of privacy for those passing by and for those who are seated. Offensive surveillance can be a problem (see fig. 9–5).

Amenities and Detailing

1. An ample area for seating and activities both under cover and in sun and shade increases comfort.

2. A greater level of detail is more appropriate for patio areas. Sensory losses associated with aging and the greater amount of time that many older people spend in the same location increase the importance of visual variety and sensory stimulation that may be

9-4.
The spatial characteristics of patios should provide for intimacy as well as for large group use. In this arrangement, smaller, more intimate patio areas (A, B, C) connect to accommodate large groups when demand exists. A variety of landscape and overhead treatments (e.g., arbor) define subareas and add human scale.

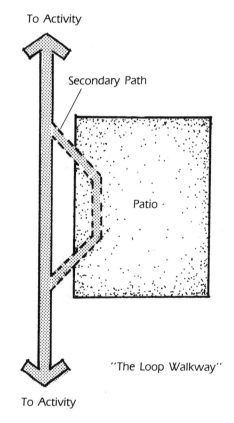

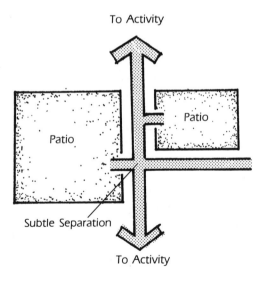

9-5a and b.
Walkway intersections are ideal locations for patios, enhancing drop-in use. Those passing by, however, should not be required to walk directly through the patio; a subtle separation or secondary walkway enables drop-in use without direct confrontation or isolation.

had through such detailing as fountains, use of color, textures, and so on. Detailing that relates to residents' past experiences and residential environment may be appropriate.

3. Exposure to sun, wind, and extremes in weather must be moderated. Approximately half of the patio area should be shaded, using architectural or landscape elements. Too much wind, sun, shade, heat, or cold, as well as bothersome insects may reduce outdoor use.

Some examples of landscape treatment and architectural devices to control and moderate exposure to weather include the following (see figs. 9–6, 9–7):

- Arbors with the slats oriented for maximum shade during midday to early afternoon.
- Umbrella tables.
- A screened porch to moderate climate and control insects.
- Landscape elements such as trees, shrubs, vines, earth berms, and water features, may be used to moderate temperature and to control glare and wind. Vines on a large building face, for example, may reduce glare and heat.

4. Comfortable seating and site furniture, such as tables, are critical for patio use:

- Fixed seating should offer opportunities for both right-angle conversation seating and activity-oriented seating.
- Movable seating and site furniture are preferable. These accommodate the closer conversation distance of older people who are hard of hearing or have poor vision, allowing for easier conversation and a sense of closeness. Movable furniture may also be arranged to accommodate any number of people and be oriented for changes in sun and shade patterns.
- The problem of theft, associated with movable seating, may be partially overcome in an inner courtyard or by hiring interested residents to take charge of storing furniture at night.
- A nearby storage area for furniture and recreational equipment owned by residents is ideal.

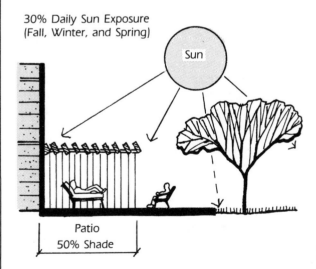

30% Daily Sun Exposure
(Fall, Winter, and Spring)

Patio
50% Shade

9-6.
Choices for seating in sun and shade are musts for comfort. Patio location, orientation (not primarily western or northern exposure), and detailing are key for moderating temperature and glare.

Reflective Heat and Glare Absorbed

9-7.
Landscape treatment should control wind, reflective glare, and heat.

- The design of seating for easy movement in and out of the seat, comfort, and safety is critical for encouraging patio use. Seating must have contoured backs and armrests (see "Seating" in chapter 10).

5. Other amenities and detailing of interest that support individual and group patio use include:

- recreational facilities, such as shuffleboard and game tables
- raised flower beds that allow close viewing without stooping (see "Planters and Planting Beds" in chapter 10)
- bird feeders, birdbaths, and so on
- barbeques that are easy to use (gas or electric are preferable)
- availability of electricity, water faucets, and drinking fountains
- night lighting (see chapter 10)
- plant materials for color, texture, form, seasonal interest, and attraction of wildlife

6. Paving must be nonslip and nonglare for safety and ease of use (see "Pedestrian and Bicycle Circulation," below).

Case Example: Shared Patios and Terraces

White Sands of La Jolla,
La Jolla, California
Owner and Developer: Southern California Presbyterian Homes, Inc.

Originally designed as one of the grand beach-front hotels, the site was converted several decades ago into a multilevel care facility (semi-independent to skilled nursing). The large patios and terraces surrounding the structure are seldom used by residents, perhaps due to failing health and poorer mobility as well as to the design itself. Yet these patios and terraces indirectly serve important needs, both in their "attracting power" for visiting grandchildren and in the image they create for the project as a whole.

Some problem areas and development potentials for three main patio areas are discussed below (see figs. 9–8, 9–9). Special areas of concern for this group of mixed-ability levels are connections to indoor spaces, spatial scale, and elements for comfort and access.

1. Spatial characteristics and location
In general, all three patio areas present the same large and open spatial scale. In addition, the large amount of continuous concrete patio area diffuses activity, especially as many of the approximately 250 residents are frail and do not venture far from the personal care and skilled nursing floors. The patio expanse also creates glare. A progression of spaces for large to intimate gatherings—a progression that relates to the type of adjacent indoor use—would provide greater options for residents. Some potential areas could include:

- a small seating area adjacent to the library, for reading, retreat, and indirect watching of the shuffleboard activity
- a slightly larger sitting area connecting the lounge and shuffleboard courts, addressing the needs of people watchers
- small seating areas near the entries to each building wing to make outdoor access easier for the less agile

2. The poolside patio
Although used by only a handful of residents, the pool area encourages visits from friends and relatives (especially grandchildren) while lending a "resort" atmosphere to the project—one that residents relish. Elements for comfort and protection from sun are needed.

3. The shuffleboard patio
The shuffleboard patio is the focus for after-meals gatherings since, of all the patios, it is the most central to indoor social spaces. Full-length glass windows (northern exposure) and seating in the adjacent lounge offer a stopping-off point en route from the dining room for watching the men play their 9:00 A.M. shuffleboard games. The interaction between display and watching enhances use of both indoor and outdoor spaces and boosts the pride of the players.

- A comfortable indoor–outdoor transition with seating for small groups, protection from weather, and

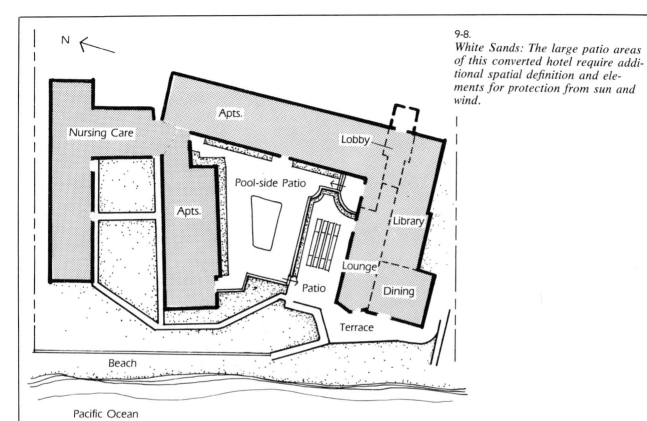

Nursing Care

Apts.

Apts.

Pool-side Patio

Lobby

Library

Lounge

Patio

Dining

Terrace

Beach

Pacific Ocean

9-8.
White Sands: The large patio areas of this converted hotel require additional spatial definition and elements for protection from sun and wind.

9-9.
White Sands: The large expanse of patio space offers spectacular views but is seldom used by residents. The pool does draw visits from grandchildren, a plus for residents, while the shuffleboard courts are part of an after-breakfast ritual of talent display.

views of the courts (while not obscuring views from inside) would be ideal.

- Shaded seating and drinking fountains are needed for the players.

4. The ocean-side terrace

This terrace is rarely used on an impromptu basis, as it is more removed from traffic flow and activity. Its westerly exposure also makes comfort a potential concern. Connection to the dining room, however, enables terrace use for lunches during good weather. The association of life with the ocean and knowing that the opportunity is there to watch and hear its breakers and smell the sea breezes are very important to many residents.

- Connection to the dining room and the exceptional ocean view offer two assets to build upon for informal small group use and for large food-related events, perhaps even a small sidewalk cafe.
- Spatial manipulation to create small alcoves along the water's edge would better accommodate intimate small group use, while not conflicting with larger group needs.
- Amenities for food-related events that would further enhance the dining room connection could include space heaters, special night lighting, barbeque pits, serving areas, and so on.
- Elements for comfort and protection from weather are essential.

Case Example: Shared Courtyard Patio

Kings Road, East
West Hollywood, California
Architects: Bobrow/Thomas and Associates
and Charles Moore/Urban Innovations Group
Landscape Architects: Pam Burton and Company

This central courtyard patio is a focal point for the site-entry scheme and for informal socializing among residents. It provides a comfortable, more architectural, transition to the outdoors. Connections to activity and a comfortable scale of space for socializing within a secure area are key elements in its success (see figs. 9–10, 9–11).

1. Location
A central location near nodes of activity and major

pedestrian flow enhances drop-in use as well as security.

- The primary access route to units, through a covered open-air vestibule space within the courtyard, maximizes drop-in use and views of activity. A wrought-iron entry gate provides connecting views to the street.
- The courtyard is surrounded by activity generators that also enhance the sense of safety and security: the mail alcove, ceramics and activity buildings, and offices. Spatial definition provides a needed sense of intimacy and privacy for socializing.
- Views from adjacent unit patios and open galleries on the second and third floors enable previewing of the space, while the large shade tree mediates the view and the feeling of being overexposed. The low-level walls separating unit patios from the courtyard, however, do not provide adequate privacy for units (the design intent was for unit patios to be an extension of public, not private space).
- The courtyard is not equally accessible from all units—residents of adjacent ground-floor units may feel a stronger sense of ownership over the space than those in the back of the project or those on the upper stories, where access to the courtyard is indirect.

2. Spatial characteristics and detailing for intimacy
The general layout, design, and detailing of the courtyard help to define subareas within the courtyard, providing a sense of intimacy and needed separation for the seating area.

- The overall size and scale of the courtyard (and subareas within it) comfortably accommodate this smaller project (approximately 50 units), without seeming too crowded or too large and void of activity.
- Landscape elements, such as the central grassed area and a large tree, subtly separate pedestrian routes from seating areas while providing an intimate vertical scale and needed shade.
- Umbrella tables and movable seating add color and contribute to comfort and flexibility of use.
- Architectural fenestration, alcoves, and texture add interest and warmth.

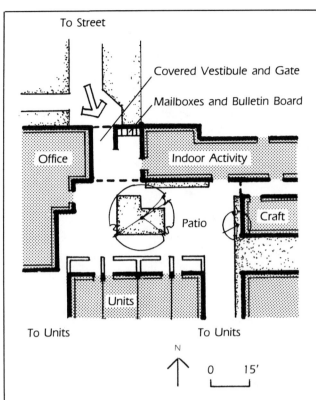

To Street

Covered Vestibule and Gate

Mailboxes and Bulletin Board

Office

Indoor Activity

Patio

Craft

Units

To Units

To Units

N

0   15'

9-10.
Kings Road, East: A shared courtyard patio provides an intimate place to sit and watch those coming and going, to wait for mail, and socialize.

Case Example: Inner Courtyard With a Dual Orientation

San Rafael Commons, San Rafael, California
Architects: Kaplan, McLaughlin Diaz; Ellis Kaplan, partner-in-charge
Original Evaluation: Kathryn H. Anthony, Ph.D., University of Illinois at Urbana-Champaign

Although the general layout of facilities at this project is noteworthy—particularly the relationship between the courtyard, community room, and street—greater spatial definition is needed to support courtyard use.

Residents like many of the architectural and landscape architectural features, such as views of the courtyard from unit windows and the open galleries. The courtyard, however, serves primarily as an access route; few stop to sit and enjoy the outdoor space. Lack of intimate seating areas and semiprivate spaces were seen as important drawbacks during the evaluation of this project. Major assets of and problem areas in this courtyard space are noted below (see fig. 9–12).

1. Location for protection and connection to activity.

The courtyard arrangement provides a protected outdoor space with connections to key on- and off-site activity generators.

9-11.
Kings Road, East: The courtyard and adjacent unit patios provide a convenient and intimate place for drop-in socializing. Greater privacy for unit patios is desirable. One resident, however, selected her unit for the view—she monitors everyone coming and going through the entry gate. Photo courtesy of Ed Lubieniecki.
Reprinted with permission.

99

- A location along pedestrian routes connecting key facilities (units, parking, the site entry, mail area, and community room) maximizes opportunities for drop-in use of the courtyard.
- The relationship between the courtyard and community room offers a dual orientation for views and access both to the active street and protected outdoor courtyard; choices are maximized.
- Entrance to the courtyard space from the street is controlled, but allows for views. Although it is a prime location for seating, with the adjacent mail area, street, and community room, no chairs or benches are available. The area also creates a wind-tunnel effect.

- Open galleries surrounding the courtyard on upper stories provide opportunities for viewing and drop-in use.

2. Spatial definition for a variety of spaces is needed.

While residents greatly enjoy the view of the courtyard from their units, few actually stop in the courtyard while passing through.

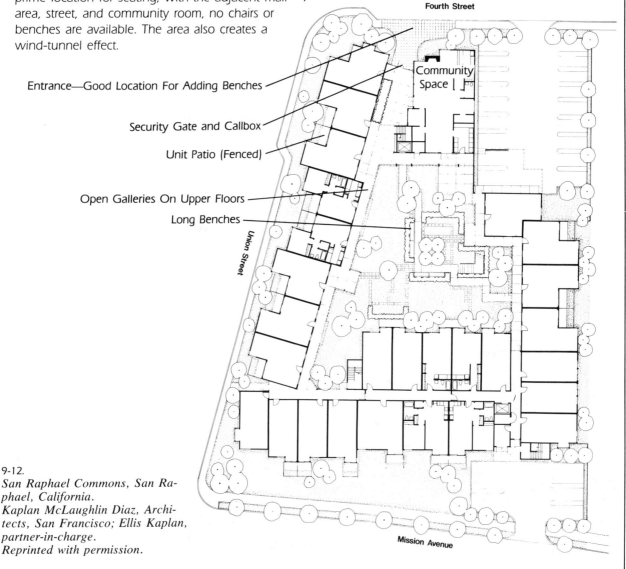

Entrance—Good Location For Adding Benches

Security Gate and Callbox

Unit Patio (Fenced)

Open Galleries On Upper Floors

Long Benches

Fourth Street

Community Space

Union Street

Mission Avenue

9-12.
San Raphael Commons, San Raphael, California.
Kaplan McLaughlin Diaz, Architects, San Francisco; Ellis Kaplan, partner-in-charge.
Reprinted with permission.

- The courtyard is too open and undefined for comfortable sitting and socializing. Although a pattern is created on the ground plane with planting and paving (which provides an interesting view from upper stories), these elements do little to define intimate areas within the space or to establish larger areas for group activities that could "spill over" from the community room.
- Few semiprivate or transitional spaces exist between the privacy of the units and the public courtyard and community room. Previewing and overhead protection are available (with the galleries), but no comfortable areas are available to sit or pause in a halfway zone. A hierarchy of spaces is essential.
- The two sets of benches, located directly in the center of the open space, are overexposed. In addition, their length (too long) and placement (not at right angles) make conversation more difficult and less intimate. Residents like to look at the benches, but few actually use them.

Rooftop Developments

Rooftop developments pose many potential design and use problems that are difficult to overcome. However, such developments may be appropriate in several situations to maximize exceptional views, both on the ground plane and distant views, and to provide outdoor space for developments that offer little or no ground-level outdoor space (most likely in a dense urban area). In neighborhoods with definite security problems and in those cases where secure space such as an inner courtyard is not available at ground level, rooftops offer a safe and secure outdoor environment. Activity on the roof, however, may reduce opportunities for community contact.

Several important factors for rooftop developments must be addressed. Rooftop developments often tend to be removed from the general activity within the building, becoming an unused appendage to the building rather than an extension of activity. Rooftop and indoor spaces must be planned together to develop a symbiotic relationship among access, views, and concentrations of activity. Where indoor spaces do not provide a natural flow of movement and activity from a focal point within the building to the roof, use of rooftop space is likely to suffer.

Another important point to consider for rooftops is physical comfort, especially protection from harsh winds, excessive sun, heat, and glare.

Where rooftops are appropriate, they may accommodate many types of activity, from resident gardening to pleasure gardens, patios, and recreation. It is wise to allow for a variety of subsidiary uses. Many sources are available for general design information on rooftop developments [2]. A few special issues for rooftops where older people are concerned are outlined below.

Location

1. A location near centers of indoor activity, with easy and direct visual and physical access, is essential. Indoor activity spaces adjoining the rooftop development are ideal (see figs. 9–13, 9–14).

2. Protection from harsh winds, too much sun, glare, or shade is a must; the location and orientation of surrounding buildings play an important part in this.

3. Maximize exceptional views, especially for those who may spend longer periods of time seated in the same location.

Spatial Characteristics

1. Rooftop developments must feel safe and secure. Vertical elements, edge definition, and a protected seating area may lend a sense of safety and security.

2. Like shared patios, rooftop developments often need to accommodate a wide range of activities, from large events, such as July 4th fireworks, to an intimate twosome enjoying the view, or a single person gardening. Flexibility of space to accommodate residents' interests encourages use by all. Thus a variety of spaces for these activities is ideal (see "Shared Patios and Terraces," above).

Amenities and Detailing

1. Amenities and detailing for comfort and ease of access and use, among others, are important. Some

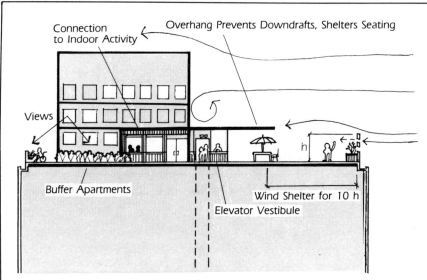

Connection to Indoor Activity

Overhang Prevents Downdrafts, Shelters Seating

Views

Buffer Apartments

Wind Shelter for 10 h

Elevator Vestibule

h

9-13.
Rooftops can accommodate a variety of activities, especially when limited outdoor space is available at grade. Connection to indoor activity, protected access and seating areas, and a variety of defined areas on the roof maximize use. Visual surveillance and edge and vertical definition enhance a sense of safety and security. Elements for comfort, protection from wind and sun are essential.

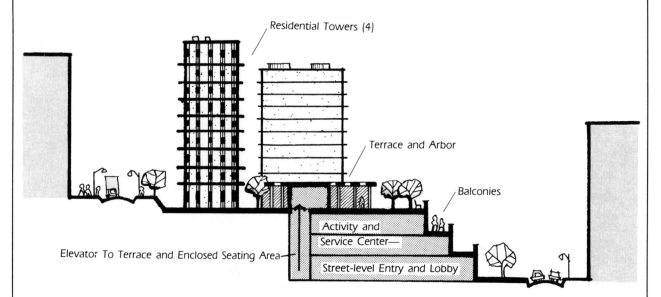

Residential Towers (4)

Terrace and Arbor

Balconies

Activity and Service Center—

Elevator To Terrace and Enclosed Seating Area

Street-level Entry and Lobby

9-14.
An urban site often requires an innovative architectural solution for outdoor spaces. The terrace at Angelus Plaza, in downtown Los Angeles, provides premium outdoor space on top of a five-story interconnecting activity/service center, lined by sixteen-to seventeen-story residential towers (1,000 units). Terrace use, however, is primarily limited to a few who enjoy the view and programmed events; it also serves as an access way between units and the street-level entry. Unfortunately,

key elements that would have connected activity and provided human scale were eliminated from the preliminary plans to meet budget constraints. These elements (not shown) were to include an on-terrace dining room, atrium/spa, and neighborhood spaces.
Architects: Daniel L. Dworski and Associates, Los Angeles.
Landscape Architects: Emmet Wemple and Associates, Los Angeles.

suggested facilities for most types of rooftop uses include:

- Easy access to restrooms and drinking fountains is necessary.
- Comfortable seating under cover, in shade and sun, is a must. Seating with arms and backrests is essential. Movable chairs and tables are preferable.
- Walking surfaces should be nonslip and nonglare.
- Night lighting for special events, such as a moon-gazing festival, adds flexibility of use.

2. Resident rooftop gardening requires many special considerations to ensure success, including the following (see also the case example below, Woolf House):

- Ample storage space, potting tables, resting places (seating in shade), and water sources are essential.
- Raised gardening beds minimize stooping and are accessible by the handicapped (see "Planters and Planting Beds" in chapter 10).
- Tiered shelves for potted plants and greenhouses for growing exotic plants and starting seedlings increase garden versatility.
- Educating residents about rooftop gardening and the properties of lightweight soil mixes is essential for successful gardening.
- Management of rooftop gardens, allocation of space, and the possibility for shared equipment are especially important due to limited space (see "Gardens and Nature Areas," below).

3. To maximize exceptional views, railings and ballustrades should allow for viewing from a seated position. Solid ballustrades (24-inch maximum height) with glassed or open railings extending above (to a minimum height of 42 inches) will allow for viewing.

Case Example: Rooftop Gardening

Woolf House, San Francisco, California
Architects: Robert Herman Associates
Original evaluation: Diana Colby

This nine-story redevelopment project houses 182 units, a lounge, glass-covered dining and sitting areas, on-grade outdoor recreation and gardening areas (recently added), as well as the roof garden.

Highly successful, this project illustrates the need for flexibility in design as well as management and education about rooftop gardening.

The success of a neighborhood community garden and a survey of seniors in the area prior to redevelopment spurred the development of this rooftop for gardening. A little more than a year after completion, a survey of the residents suggests that it is an asset to the development and a success. Some of the highlights of the rooftop garden and the evaluation are summarized below (see fig. 9–15).

1. The gardeners
The success of the rooftop gardening might be attributed to the cultural predeliction of residents toward gardening. Seventy-five percent are Chinese, whose traditions include small-area gardening, although the gardens are an important part of the project for residents of all ethnic groups [3]. The majority of gardeners had gardened before their move into the project, confirming other research that indicates a continuity of activity patterns into old age—if physical ability permits.

2. A sense of safety and security
Due to several design features, the Woolf House roof does not feel exposed or threatening.

- The undulating line of the 4-foot-high parapet walls alternating with open railings that allow for viewing contribute to a sense of security by breaking up the space. The ninth-floor wall also provides scale and enclosure.
- The location of the greenhouses defines an edge and adds enclosure.
- The garden is visible from apartment windows on the ninth floor, thus increasing surveillance.

3. Comfort and protection from wind
Wind was a special concern for this San Francisco rooftop. Consultation with a wind expert resulted in the following design responses:

- The leeward side of the roof, the windiest, was not used, while the garden beds were placed on the southwest side.
- Potting greenhouses minimize the reverse wind currents.

4. Access

Principal access to the roof from the ninth-floor corridor and elevator is convenient, but does not present a strong connection to indoor spaces.

- The addition of indoor community space on the ninth floor, connecting to the garden, would increase the flexibility and comfort of rooftop use.

5. Planters, greenhouses, and gardening amenities

Amenities for gardening on the roof include raised planters, greenhouses, watering hoses, garbage cans, and a light over each access door.

- Eight rows of raised staggered beds on a north–south axis maximize exposure to sunlight and access by the handicapped. Although shallow (from 18 inches to 8 inches deep) due to weight limitations, the beds are highly successful.
- The four greenhouses have been less successful

and are used primarily for storage of tools, soil conditioners, shoes, and so on. Management of and education about roof garden and greenhouse use, as well as additional storage space, may increase use.

- Additional gardening facilities for ease of use and safety could also include tiered shelves for potted plants (one corner of the roof has been claimed for such storage), a shaded potting bench, storage, night lighting, a water fountain, and shaded seating/resting area.

6. Management and programming

The need for garden management and resident education concerning rooftops was indicated by the survey.

- Education (through fliers, tours, guest speakers, and so on) about the many possibilities for greenhouse use is needed.

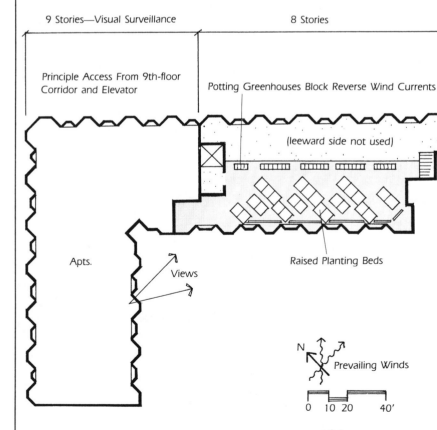

9 Stories—Visual Surveillance

8 Stories

Principle Access From 9th-floor Corridor and Elevator

Potting Greenhouses Block Reverse Wind Currents

(leeward side not used)

Apts.

Views

Raised Planting Beds

N

Prevailing Winds

0 10 20   40'

9-15.

Woolf House: The rooftop feels safe and secure with visual surveillance, protection from strong winds, and a defined edge. Highly successful for gardening, the rooftop is also used for viewing and simply as a feature to show off to visitors. Additional facilities for comfort and flexibility of use are needed.

- Assignment of greenhouse space in conjunction with the beds for starting early vegetables and for plants that require more heat was suggested.
- Education about the lightweight U.C. soil mix used for planters is needed to alleviate residents' doubt about the richness of the soil. At present, residents cart soil conditioners up eight stories, placing greater demands on storage and increasing the weight load.

Unit Patios and Balconies

Private balconies and patios for residential units present opportunities for the less able to enjoy the outdoors and watch activity from a comfortable and secure place readily accessible from the unit. Balconies and patios can also offer places for personalization and casual socializing, both of which may be quite limited in planned housing. If well designed, such private outdoor areas can physically and perceptually extend the living area, which is often quite small in retirement housing.

Location

1. Patios and balconies should be directly accessible from indoor living spaces; connection to the living room is ideal.

- Easy access to the kitchen increases the flexibility of use.
- Balconies off living rooms should not block views of activity areas below. They may be moved slightly to the side to enable viewing.

2. It is important to orient patios and balconies for protection from extremes in weather. An orientation for sun exposure of 30 percent each day during spring, summer, and fall months is often recommended [4]. Adequate shade, however, is also necessary; 50 percent of the patio area in shade is ideal and may be achieved through the use of arbors, for example. Protection from strong winds is also an important consideration for balconies.

3. Balconies above the twelfth floor often feel unsafe. They may be justified for exceptional views or when little outdoor space is available. Above the twentieth floor, the sense of vertigo, strong winds, and other undesirable elements makes balconies most impractical.

4. A location that offers views of activity and change is ideal. Views and access between a patio and a walkway, for example, can encourage drop-in socializing (see figs. 9–16, 9–17).

- A distance of 20 feet (minimum distance for privacy) to 100 feet (maximum) between unit patios/balconies and activity areas will enable most residents to recognize the presence of activity or identify individuals.

Spatial Characteristics

1. Privacy should be maintained for balconies and on-grade patios while providing views of activity. Visual privacy from neighboring patios and balconies may be provided through recessing, screening walls and planting, or a physical separation of approximately 20 feet (see fig. 9–16).

2. On-grade patios should be well defined from public walkways, other units, and activity spaces, but not isolated from views.

- Security and privacy may be particularly difficult with on-grade patios. Patios may be partially or totally enclosed if security is a special concern.

3. Access from on-grade patios to adjacent community outdoor space is desirable; steps should be avoided. A patio with views of and access to a communal walkway, for example, may increase opportunities for meeting and socializing with others who pass by (see "Low-rise Unit Clustering" in chapter 6).

4. Unit patios and balconies should be large enough for several people to sit and maneuver in comfortably. Space for such personal belongings as plants and outdoor furniture is desirable. Size also affects how safe a balcony feels. The Michigan State Housing Development Authority recommends the following minimum dimensions (see fig. 9–18) [5]:

- On-grade patios with one dimension of at least 12 feet and with the length extending the full width of the unit (100-square-foot minimum area).
- Balconies with a minimum clear dimension of 5

feet; a total of 50 square feet clear for one-bedroom units; 60 square feet clear for two-bedroom units.

5. Minimum clearances for the handicapped are noted below. Additional clearance is always desirable, particularly for older people, who may have difficulty

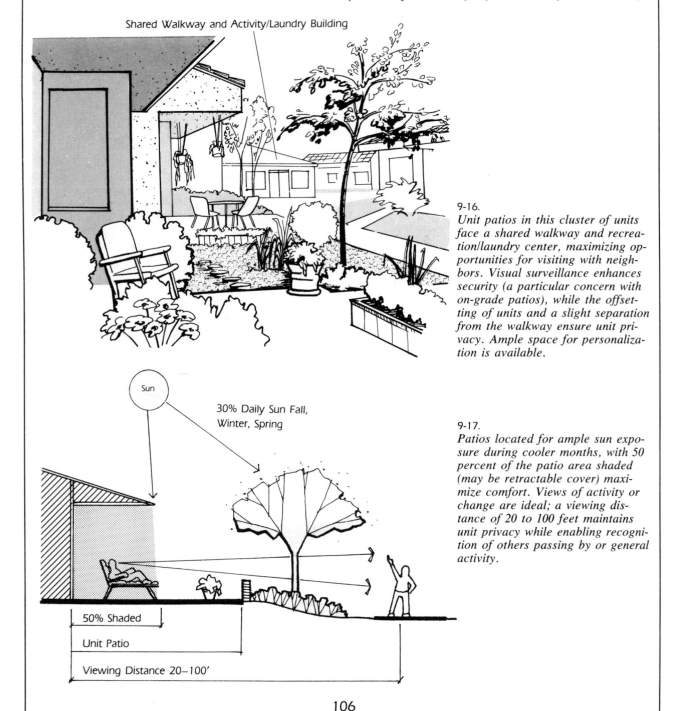

Shared Walkway and Activity/Laundry Building

9-16.
Unit patios in this cluster of units face a shared walkway and recreation/laundry center, maximizing opportunities for visiting with neighbors. Visual surveillance enhances security (a particular concern with on-grade patios), while the offsetting of units and a slight separation from the walkway ensure unit privacy. Ample space for personalization is available.

Sun

30% Daily Sun Fall, Winter, Spring

9-17.
Patios located for ample sun exposure during cooler months, with 50 percent of the patio area shaded (may be retractable cover) maximize comfort. Views of activity or change are ideal; a viewing distance of 20 to 100 feet maintains unit privacy while enabling recognition of others passing by or general activity.

50% Shaded

Unit Patio

Viewing Distance 20–100'

maneuvering a wheelchair or walker [6]:

- A minimum clear space of 60 by 60 inches is required for a smooth-pivot U-turn in a wheelchair; a clear space of 78 inches in the line of travel is best.
- A clear width of 32 inches (minimum) is required for wheelchair access through a passage such as a door; 36 inches for a longer run, such as a corridor.

6. A design that provides the option for enclosing or screening patios and balconies is desirable, particularly in regions with inclement weather or where insects may be bothersome (see fig. 9–19).

Amenities and Detailing

1. Nonslip, nonglare walking surfaces are very important (see "Pedestrian and Bicycle Circulation," below).

- Broomed or brushed concrete (stained) is a good surface, as well as brick (if concrete is laid to ensure a continuous surface).
- Exposed aggregate is satisfactory if small river-washed stones of 3/8-inch to 1/2-inch grade (maximum) are used and if stones are not overexposed.
- Tile becomes too slippery when wet.
- Wood decks should be treated; plank spacing at 1/2 inch or less is maneuverable for wheelchairs.

2. Overhead cover for shade and protection from weather is a must for comfort. It has to be wide enough for several people to be seated under cover and in shade. Arbors, partial enclosure, and awnings are a few options.

3. Balcony railings or solid balustrades must be sturdy and provide a comfortable grip rail. Where solid balustrades are used, a height of 24 inches, with an open handrail extending a minimum of 42 inches above the balcony surface, allows for viewing while providing protection. Fifty inches is more desirable (see fig. 9–20) [7].

4. Shelves for plants and other items may encourage personalization. Shelves must be sturdy, as residents may lean on them for support.

5. Lighting is desirable for patios and balconies.

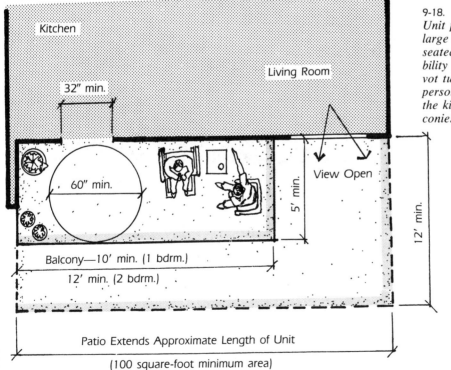

9-18.
Unit patios and balconies must be large enough for several people seated, for wheelchair maneuverability (60 inches min. clear for a pivot turn), and for the addition of personal items. Easy access from the kitchen and living room (balconies not to block view) is ideal.

Kitchen

Living Room

32" min.

60" min.

View Open

5' min.

12' min.

Balcony—10' min. (1 bdrm.)

12' min. (2 bdrm.)

Patio Extends Approximate Length of Unit

(100 square-foot minimum area)

9-19.
These balconies are easily enclosed with blinds or glass, extending the living space and providing greater climate control (note that the top balcony is enclosed with glass). Standard working drawings for enclosure are provided by the management, thereby ensuring architectural continuity.

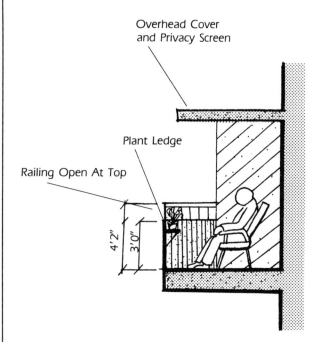

Overhead Cover and Privacy Screen

Plant Ledge

Railing Open At Top

4'2"

3'0"

9-20.
To enable viewing from a seated position, while ensuring safety, balcony railings should be 4 feet, 2 inches in height but open above 3 feet for viewing. A ledge for plants is ideal. After: Isaac Green et al. Housing for the Elderly: The Development and Design Process. *New York: Van Nostrand Reinhold, 1975, 87.*

Light switches should be located directly inside the unit by the door (see "Outdoor Lighting" in chapter 10).

6. Weatherproof electrical outlets increase convenience.

7. Doorways should have a minimum clear width of 32 inches, with thresholds level or beveled (8 percent maximum slope) (see "Doors and Door Handles" in chapter 10).

Gardens and Nature Areas

Ideally, a variety of garden and nature areas should be available for strolling and visual enjoyment. A garden is something that people of all ability levels can enjoy; it provides an important connection to nature and a reason for outdoor use. Gardens for enjoyment may be especially important for less able seniors and those living in developments where personal outdoor space is not available. Nature areas may also provide a place for needed solitude, especially in high-density developments. Some important considerations are outlined below.

Location

Garden areas for pleasure, within view from indoor common spaces and/or units, offer increased opportunities for enjoyment. Other garden areas, such as nature areas, may be more distant from the buildings for a quiet walk or exploration—perhaps on a part of the site set aside for its unique natural features (see fig. 9–21).

Spatial Characteristics

1. Different types of garden areas, such as formal gardens and nature walks, provide greater variety for outdoor spaces (see fig. 9–21).

2. Spatial and edge definition of gardens, with a sense of scale and enclosure achieved through plant-

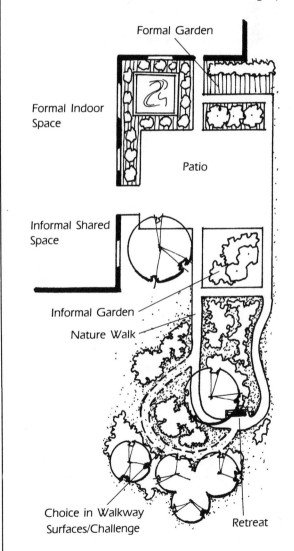

Formal Garden

Formal Indoor Space

Patio

Informal Shared Space

Informal Garden

Nature Walk

Choice in Walkway Surfaces/Challenge

Retreat

ing, and so on, is generally appropriate. Some researchers suggest that, more than younger adults do, older people prefer a formal garden, secure, defined, and detailed space. Variety, however, may accommodate all preferences.

3. Street noises and other obtrusive sounds should be minimized through site planning, planting, berming, and so on.

Amenities and Detailing

1. Garden areas for pleasure should present a rich visual and sensory experience. Vegetation with seasonal color and interesting form, as well as auditory, olfactory, and tactual elements, adds interest and stimulation.

2. Both sunny and shady seating areas in a garden assure comfortable viewing and resting.

3. Paved walkways through garden areas encourage use and exploration, especially by less agile and by nonambulatory residents (see fig. 9–21). Options for walking surfaces that offer greater challenge, such as gravel, may be included, but should not be the only access route (see "Pedestrian and Bicycle Circulation," below).

4. Detailing for interest and sensory stimulation, such as fountains and pools, is desirable. Sculpture is a good option if high-maintenance pools and fountains are not feasible. Wind sculpture, for example, may provide visual, auditory, and tactual interest.

5. Raised planters allow for easy viewing without stooping. Low-level planters and edging should be avoided; they may cause a fall because they are not easily seen (see "Planters and Planting Beds" in chapter 10).

9-21.
Easy access to a variety of garden areas offering seasonal and sensory interest are ideal for those who depend more upon their immediate surroundings for daily activity. Garden views may also reinforce use of indoor spaces.

Case Example: A Therapeutic Park for the Mentally Frail

Sunset Haven Home for the Aged
Welland, Ontario, Canada
Developer: Senior Citizens' Department,
Regional Municipality of Niagara, and
the Provincial Ministry of Community and Social
Services

Therapeutic "parks," designed to meet the needs of the mentally and physically frail, are becoming a reality in homes for the aged. No longer just a medical problem, the mental frailness associated with aging is being recognized as an issue for environmental design.

One example is a recently completed park for residents of a special-care unit at a home for the aged in Ontario, Canada. This example brings to our attention how simple design elements can help mentally frail older people recognize their own actions in the environment and heighten their awareness of the surroundings.

The therapeutic park lies within a 30,000-square-foot area between two wings of the home. It is one of three developed by the Senior Citizens' Department of the Regional Municipality of Niagara in conjunction with the Activation Consultants of the Provincial Ministry of Community and Social Services.

The design focuses upon the social, medical, psychological, and environmental needs of the mentally and physically frail. Some issues addressed in this small space include:

- Offering a variety of environments
- Maximizing physical and mental stimulation
- Providing for freedom of physical movement while giving protection without undue restraint

Although relatively new, the park seems to be a success. Subjective observations by the Senior Citizens Department and project staff indicate positive changes in resident morale, activation, staff involvement, and/or acceptance and family participation [8]. They note that these changes indicate greater appreciation of the outdoors, greater mobility among residents, increased social interaction, and enriched daily life experiences, in addition to providing staff with a wider variety of settings for reality orientation classes. A few of the facilities, their design, and role in the park are discussed below (see figs. 9–22, 9–23).

1. Gazebo
A focal point in the park, the gazebo provides a shaded area for privacy, as well as a stimulating area for staff-led reality orientation classes. For the class, the gazebo is equipped with benches, portable barbeque, blackboard, and bulletin board.

To increase the feeling of open expanses and reduce the sense of confinement the gazebo uses latticework and an octagonal dimension that allows for a division outward and inward. Located beyond the ends of the two main nursing wings, the gazebo provides residents with a clear view of the surrounding neighborhood and street activity.

2. Fencing and edge condition
While containing the area was considered important for residents' safety, an effort was also made to reduce the sense of being fenced in. The park is enclosed on two sides by the building wings. Lattice-type fences enclose the other sides while adding decoration and visual stimulation.

3. Walkways
A variety of walkway surfaces adds visual, tactual, and acoustical stimulation while reinforcing the activity of walking. Well-textured surfaces allow residents to feel the concrete under foot while reducing the possibility of slipping. A wooden bridge heightens the acoustical stimulation of walking, reinforcing the link between activity and the environment.

4. Japanese theme garden
A different kind of environment is experienced in the Japanese theme garden, with the touch and sound of running water, large stones, and sculpture.

5. Artifacts "garden"
In one corner of the park, a special display of artifacts provides residents with the opportunity to relate to their past external surroundings. Such artifacts include a one-hundred-year-old plow and cultivator and an old-fashioned water pump. Other elements around the site, such as a sundial and wall mural, act as focal points.

6. Therapeutic garden

The therapeutic garden is designed to enhance the feeling of touch. Raised gardening planters, narrow at the bottom and sloping wider at the top, allow for use and close examination by those in wheelchairs.

- Furnishings include brightly colored rocking chairs and swing sets, offering a safe source of motion.
- Blondie, the pet dog, shares the park with residents, while birds at the feeder are visible all year from indoors. The use of pets in similar settings has stimulated resident responsiveness to therapy and has given pleasure to residents.

Resident Gardening Areas

Gardening provides exercise, contact with nature, and the personal reward and satisfaction of its produce. Interest in gardening varies from one building to an-

9-22.
Sunset Haven Home for the Aged: The therapeutic garden provides a variety of elements for sensory stimulation to help the mentally frail recognize their own actions in the environment. The wooden bridge, for example, enables residents to hear their own footsteps, reinforcing the action of walking. Photo courtesy of Senior Citizens Department, Regional Municipality of Niagara, Ontario, Canada. Reprinted with permission.

9-23.
Sunset Haven Home for the Aged: Reality orientation classes are held in the Pavilion. Although an enclosed and protected space was needed for safety, the use of latticework reduces the feeling of being fenced in. Photo courtesy of Senior Citizens Department, Regional Municipality of Niagara, Ontario, Canada. Reprinted with permission.

other and may change over time. Thus before setting aside large areas for garden plots, it is best to survey residents' interest. Providing a small gardening area and allowing for additional space when needed is a good option. Residents' health and ability levels may also influence demand, although facilities for comfort and protection from the sun may encourage use by all. Some design and management considerations for gardening areas are outlined below.

Location

1. Small resident gardening areas located near residential units are most accessible and easiest to monitor. If poorly maintained, however, this location can present special problems for aesthetics. Management of gardens, particularly when they are near residential and activity areas, is essential (see "Management," below).

2. Where interest is very strong and residents are very able, larger gardening centers may be located farther away from units. A location removed from activity, where gardeners need not worry about the visual impact of the garden, is ideal for the avid gardener.

3. Gardening areas should not dominate views or formal entries and activity spaces, as general interest and upkeep levels may change over time.

4. Garden plots must be located for ample sun!

Spatial Characteristics

1. Small garden plots that obviously "belong" to a building, a cluster of units, or a single unit are ideal, increasing a sense of ownership and control. Visual screening from public areas, however, may be necessary.

2. It is impossible to prescribe an ideal size for garden plots, although much can be grown on a small plot. Plot sizes of 5 by 10 feet have been found to be too large for some older people, while avid gardeners may find a 20-by-40-foot area ideal. The ability level and interest of residents are determining factors, as are garden location and purpose. Flexibility is the key.

3. The layout of larger gardening centers should allow for easy vehicular access for dropping off mate-rials nearby individual plots. Access to individual plots should not require walking over a neighboring plot.

Amenities and Detailing

1. Facilities and detailing to increase ease of use and comfort for gardening areas and plots include the following:

- raised planting beds accessible by the handicapped (see "Planters and Planting Beds" in chapter 10)
- shaded seating
- easy access to water sources
- drinking fountains (see "Drinking Fountains" in chapter 10)
- locking storage sheds for community or individual use
- working areas with raised tables (in shade)
- lighting for evening harvest (desirable)

Management

1. Some options for management of gardens are outlined below, although each project presents its own set of management problems.

- Where general interest and upkeep is very low, small garden areas near activity centers can be managed by a few residents who love gardening, assisted by others whose interest varies. By delegating responsibility, this method increases the likelihood that a small plot will be visually appealing.
- Minimal rental fees for garden plots are an option. The fees may be used to purchase community tools and to maintain facilities.
- Storage of individual tools, soil builders, and so on, is often a problem. Community-owned tools, locked in a shed, may alleviate much of the storage problem. Individual supplies, such as fertilizers and stakes, may be stored in small chests adjacent to or located directly on each garden plot.

Case Example: A Gardening Center for the Avid Gardener

Leisure World–Laguna Hills
Laguna Hills, California
Landscape Architect: P.O.D., Santa Ana, California

The two garden centers at this "active" retirement community are exceedingly popular. The more recent one, approximately five acres, provides 500 garden plots in addition to potting sheds, greenhouses, and restrooms. It is designed and detailed for ease of use and comfort, while maintaining a "working" atmosphere that many residents enjoy. Due to its location, size, and limited provisions for the handicapped, however, this garden is for active and avid gardeners (see figs. 9–24, 9–25, 9–26). Each residential unit also has some form of private outdoor space.

1. A location for working

- Removed from residential and social areas (not within walking distance), and with a "country" atmosphere, the area is ideal for real gardening, without attention to looks. Many gardeners delight in the opportunity to get away and work.

2. Access and circulation

- A loop access road and parking throughout the garden center ensure easy drop-off of materials near the plots.
- An office and greenhouse by the entry provide a centralized social and welcome area as well as an access control point.

- Major concrete access walks and minor gravel walks create a regular grid pattern, defining plot boundaries while providing direct and easy access.

3. Facilities for gardening

- Four pavilions and a large greenhouse are easily reached from the road and main walks. These provide shaded seating and tables, tool storage, and water fountains.
- Under the pavilion roofs, shaded seating areas (picnic benches) and cooled drinking fountains provide a comfortable resting spot, although benches with backs might be much appreciated.
- Soil-building material, donated by the adjacent stables, is stored in bins around the site.
- The separation of garden plots on level terrain from tree-growing areas on the terraced slope assures ample sun for vegetables and flowers.

4. Management and allocation of gardening space

- The plots, 10 by 20 feet, are rented for a small yearly fee (approximately $10). Many gardeners rent several plots for themselves, while others may form a group of two to four people, working them together. Though some plots have turned to weeds,

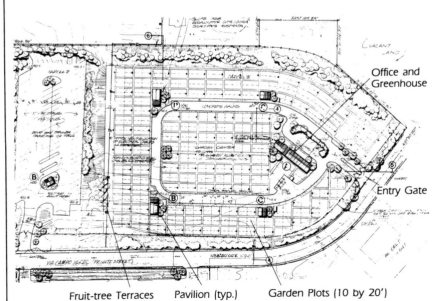

Office and Greenhouse

Entry Gate

Fruit-tree Terraces   Pavilion (typ.)   Garden Plots (10 by 20')

9-24.
Leisure World: The five-acre Garden Center provides a working retreat for the avid gardener where "formal display" is not a concern. Every plot is rented.
P.O.D., Inc., Landscape Architects, Santa Ana, California.
Reprinted with permission.

9-25.
Leisure World: Garden plots located around a loop road and a paved walkway system make transportation of materials easy. The four pavilions provide comfortable and shady places to relax, with tables (although of fixed tablebench type), restrooms, and cooled drinking fountains. Shared tools, purchased with rental fees, are stored inside.

9-26.
Leisure World: Garden plots are the sole responsibility of the renter. Many residents add irrigation systems, fencing, mini storage sheds, and so on. Some plots have been raised.

the nature of this "working" garden reduces concern over aesthetics.

• Residents are responsible for every aspect of their own garden plot: building fences and trellises, soil building, watering, and so on. Some have even put in irrigation/sprinkler systems and raised their plots.

• Storage of personal items (stakes, fertilizers, and so on) in resident-built storage chests on individual plots seems to work well when combined with communal tools stored in centralized sheds.

Pedestrian and Bicycle Circulation

The location and design of walkways and bicycle paths for older people should receive special attention for four reasons: (1) walking is a popular activity among many older adults; (2) mobility problems are frequent among the elderly; (3) walking and bicycling offer opportunities for access to and participation in many activities; and (4) walking and bicycling are generally healthy—regular walking, for example, may improve muscular control and mobility.

Although many older people enjoy walking for exercise and pleasure, concern over the negotiability and safety of walking routes may limit use. Bicycling (including three-wheelers), popular in many regions of the United States, involves a number of the same concerns as walking. Mobility problems, poor sense of balance, declining vision (in particular, depth perception, peripheral vision for the perception of movement, and discrimination of fine detail), combined with slower reaction times and decreased confidence, all affect the ease and safety of walking and bicycling. In addition, the design and layout of circulation routes can affect the older person's ability to find his or her way to on- and off-site facilities; this is a special concern for larger sites and for those developments housing the more frail older person.

Some special concepts for the layout and design of circulation systems include: (1) walkways and bicycle paths as a collector system for meeting others; (2) circulation loops that include options for length and difficulty of route; (3) a pattern of circulation that is easy to identify; (4) a system of hierarchies, from major access routes to cluster, unit, and pleasure routes; and (5) a location for views of activity, as well as safety and security. Topography, in addition to such detailing and amenities as walking surfaces and resting spots, is equally important for a well-designed circulation system.

Location

1. The layout of walkway and bicycle systems should provide a pattern that is easy to recognize and identify, especially on larger sites (see "Circulation" in chapter 6).

2. Direct and easy access to facilities on- and off-site is especially important. Grading criteria for walkways are noted below [9]; provisions for ramps and stairs must be made where slopes exceed those recommended (see fig. 9–27).

- Major on-site walkways at building entries should not exceed a 2.5 percent slope (no ramps, steps, or curbs should be located in arrival court areas).
- Other major access routes between on-site facilities should not exceed a 5 percent slope (steps and ramps may be used, but they are not desirable along major connecting routes).
- Major access routes to off-site facilities should not exceed a 5 percent cumulative slope (10 percent maximum slope for a maximum run of 75 feet).
- Indirect access routes that are level (or less than a 5 percent slope) may be preferred by those with ambulatory difficulties over shorter routes with maximum grades; such alternatives should be available.

3. Major access routes within sight of the building(s) or other areas frequented by residents and staff promote safety and security. They should not be isolated or removed from view, as use may decline due to residents' concern over not being seen if they fall or are bothered by strangers (see fig. 9–28).

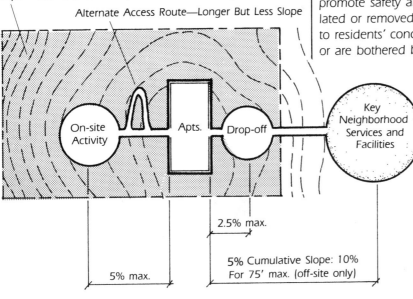

Slope > 5%—For Secondary/Pleasure Routes Only

Alternate Access Route—Longer But Less Slope

On-site Activity

Apts.

Drop-off

Key Neighborhood Services and Facilities

2.5% max.

5% max.

5% Cumulative Slope: 10% For 75′ max. (off-site only)

9-27.
Maximum walkway gradients to on- and off-site facilities may be difficult for some to negotiate; alternate routes that are longer but less than the maximum grade may be preferred. Steps and ramps may be used along most routes, but they must not be used at the building entry and drop-off area.

115

4. Walking routes for pleasure that begin at frequently used building entries are ideal. Residents often wait at the building entry for someone to offer assistance for a short walk (see fig. 9–28).

5. Walkway and bicycle routes should not pass through or by areas on- and off-site that pose a threat to safety and security.

6. Major circulation routes that pass by areas of on-site and neighborhood activity, "collecting" people en route, are often favored by older people. They offer increased opportunities for meeting others and watching activity (see fig. 9–28).

7. Some pleasure routes may offer opportunities for quiet retreat, such as one that passes through a garden or nature area. Opportunities for privacy and solitude may be limited in planned housing (see fig. 9–28).

8. Separate pedestrian and bicycle systems reduce the potential for accidents. Crossing of pedestrian, bicycle, and automobile routes should be kept to a minimum (see "Pedestrian Street Crossings" in chapter 10).

Spatial Characteristics

1. Circulation routes developed as a system of hierarchies, from major public routes for access to communal facilities to cluster and unit access routes, assist in wayfinding. This arrangement may also increase control over access to semiprivate spaces. Spatial characteristics, such as walkway width and landscape treatment, should support the overall pattern hierarchy.

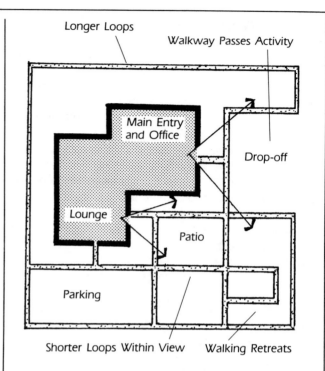

9-28.
A series of connecting walkway loops, offering choice in length and difficulty of route as well as visual surveillance from inside, encourages use by the less able. Options for passing activity and for retreat are ideal.

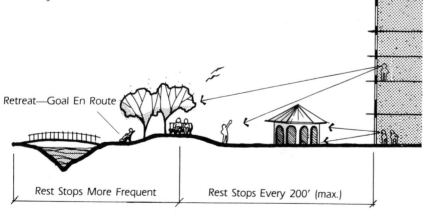

9-29.
Shorter walking routes closer to the building may be frequented by less able residents, although more distant goals and retreats encourage exploration. Rest stops approximately every 200 feet are desirable; changes in grade and walkways more removed from view require more frequent resting spots.

2. Circulation routes for pleasure and exercise may be developed as a series of walkways that connect to form "walking loops." This arrangement provides options for variety and for length and difficulty of route for all ability levels (see fig. 9–28).

Amenities and Detailing

1. Goals along routes are important for encouraging walking and bicycling for pleasure. Public mailboxes, seating areas, or a unique feature may serve as a "goal," encouraging exploration.

2. Rest stops with shade and seating should be located along walkways. A distance of approximately 200 feet between resting spots is recommended [10]. Many factors, however, may affect how frequently rest spots are needed, such as the general ability level of residents, climate, topography, visibility, and goals en route.

Walkway intersections and areas overlooking activity are likely locations for seating/resting areas—choices, however, are desirable (see fig. 9–29).

3. In harsh climates, major access routes between on-site facilities may be covered or enclosed for protection from weather. Extended roof overhangs and breezeways and glassed-in walkways connecting facilities are some examples of protection.

4. Surface quality and ground-plane elements are very important for negotiability and safety. Older people are very aware of ground-plane elements and textures. Some may make adjustments in their use of the outdoors to compensate for a ground plane that is difficult to negotiate. Some older people look directly down in front of their feet to *see* the ground plane, drawing their attention away from the surrounding environment. This decreases opportunities for visual appreciation of the outdoors and reduces safety. Surface quality is a prime concern for main access routes and building entries.

Some important considerations for surface quality and ground-plane elements include the following:

- Changes in elevation should be avoided for major access routes, particularly for building entries.
- Walking surfaces should be made of predictable, nonslip, and nonglare substances such as stained broom-finished concrete. Brick is preferable to tile, which may become slippery when wet. Brick laid on concrete is better than brick on sand, as it is more stable. Exposed aggregate, if used, should not be overexposed; small river-washed stones are easier to negotiate than large or rough stones.
- Irregular textures, jointing, and other protrusions on the ground surface should be avoided or be very obvious (see fig. 9–30).
- Grates and drainage structures along walkways pose safety problems for those who use canes and walkers; they should be avoided in pedestrian areas.
- Good surface drainage is basic, particularly at building entries. Downspouts and sheet drainage should not discharge onto walks.
- In colder climates, sun exposure to aid in melting snow and space for snow removal and piling are musts.
- Wet leaves on a ground surface pose a safety hazard. This problem is double sided: the use of trees is a frequent response to older people's need for shade, yet fallen leaves pose hazards for negotiability and are a concern of many older people. The use of small-leafed or evergreen trees, as well as nonslip paving along major walking routes, may resolve this problem in part. The unique qualities of certain trees and their leaves are also a consideration; for example, linden seeds are extremely slippery, as are maple leaves, which lie flat, while the curl of oak leaves makes them easier to kick away or sweep (see fig. 9–30).

5. All steps, ramps, and areas of transition to traffic must be clearly marked. Changes in pavement color and/or texture may be used to signal a change in elevation or upcoming traffic. For maximum effectiveness, however, management should inform residents about these more subtle signals. Some pavement textures and ground-plane treatments are more easily "read" by those with visual impairments (see "Pedestrian Crossing Areas" and "Ramps and Stairs" in chapter 10).

6. Special consideration for the design of pedestrian crossings and the timing of pedestrian crossing signals is important for those who walk with canes

9-30.
The "flagging" of a sprinkler head at one project reflects the extreme hazard that low-level objects pose for the older walker. Wet leaves (particularly larger leaves) and irregular surfaces are also hazardous.

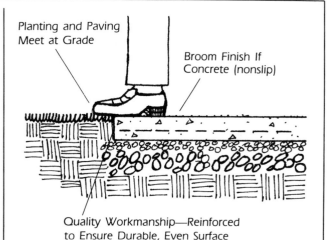

Planting and Paving Meet at Grade

Broom Finish If Concrete (nonslip)

Quality Workmanship—Reinforced to Ensure Durable, Even Surface

9-31.
A nonslip, nonglare, even walking surface is essential for safety. No edging should be used where planting meets a walking surface.

and walkers, those who are visually and physically handicapped, as well as those who walk more slowly (see "Pedestrian Crossing Areas" in chapter 10).

7. Planters and planting beds along walkways should be raised for easy visibility or should be at grade to avoid the possibility of tripping (see "Planters and Planting Beds" in chapter 10). Raised edging should not be used (see fig. 9–31).

8. Walkways must be wide enough to accommodate two people side by side. A minimum width of 6 feet is recommended for major routes and 5 feet, minimum, for minor routes [11]. Width may also be used to delineate public, cluster, and private walkways.

9. Provisions for bicycles should include bicycle routes with ample separation from pedestrian traffic and ample width for the sway of bicycles along the route. Minimum widths are outlined below, but additional width is recommended [12].

- One-way bicycle routes, 5-feet wide with a 29-inch buffer between routes, will allow two standard bicycles minimal space to pass and 18 inches' leeway for a single bicycle. Additional space for three-

wheelers is desirable.
- Two-way routes, 8 feet wide, provide a comfortable minimum width for double-lane traffic.
- Bicycle racks at all buildings, and for large sites, at recreational areas are desirable if bicycle riding is anticipated. Visitors may also require racks. Bicycle racks under cover or security lockers are ideal for storage (three-wheelers require more space).

10. Night lighting is a priority for a well-designed circulation system, especially for the visually and physically handicapped (see "Outdoor Lighting" in chapter 10).

Case Example: Walkway Loops for Enjoyment and Exercise

Ottawa Congregate Housing
Ottawa, Illinois
Landscape Architects: Diane Carstens and Charles Burger, University of Illinois

The many options for short walking routes available on this site and the special considerations for safety and security directly address the ability level of residents in this congregate housing project. Key elements are noted below (see fig. 9–32).

1. Layout of walkway loops

- A series of walkway loops connect to offer the greatest number of choices for length and difficulty of route (in this case through changes in grade and direction of travel).
- Walkway loops begin at frequently used indoor spaces and pass by areas of activity (e.g., delivery areas, entry, and the neighborhood), promoting safety and security while adding interest to the route.

2. Amenities and detailing

- Small seating areas offset from the public sidewalk and landscaped with flowering trees provide goals for walking and a safe place to sit and watch the activity. Most of the seats are visible from the office or lounge. The arrangement works well in this small midwestern town; however, in many neighborhoods, additional measures would be necessary to ensure safety, security, and control over use.
- Small-leafed (or evergreen) trees along the walkways and patio, broom-finished concrete, and bedding areas at grade reduce the possibility of a fall.

Lawn Areas for Recreation

Lawns not only provide a pleasing setting for activity, but also allow the flexibility of additional space for future recreational demands and large group and impromptu activities.

In addition to the functional aspects of lawns, expanses of green grass impart many images of "the good life," such as social and economic status, the suburban home, and family life. Lawns, however, are not a necessary site component, particularly when

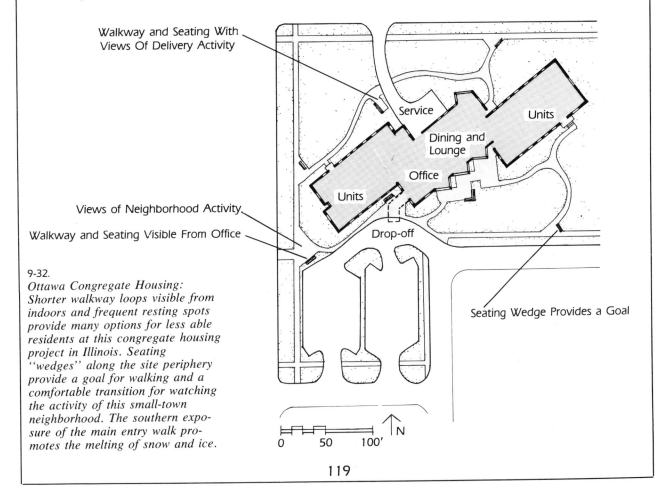

Walkway and Seating With Views Of Delivery Activity

Service

Units

Dining and Lounge

Office

Units

Views of Neighborhood Activity

Walkway and Seating Visible From Office

Drop-off

Seating Wedge Provides a Goal

9-32.
Ottawa Congregate Housing: Shorter walkway loops visible from indoors and frequent resting spots provide many options for less able residents at this congregate housing project in Illinois. Seating "wedges" along the site periphery provide a goal for walking and a comfortable transition for watching the activity of this small-town neighborhood. The southern exposure of the main entry walk promotes the melting of snow and ice.

0   50   100'   ↑N

they are replaced by local images, such as a desert landscape or an urban landscape. Some design considerations in planning lawn areas for recreation are outlined below.

Location

1. Lawn areas for recreation may be located at some distance from the building(s), but near major paved activity areas. The less agile generally prefer not to walk on an irregular ground surface, favoring paved surfaces close to the building. However, a lawn located near a major activity area, like a patio, may serve as additional space for group activities too large for the patio (see fig. 9–33).

2. Lawn areas for recreation that are visible from other activity and seating areas provide opportunities for vicarious participation.

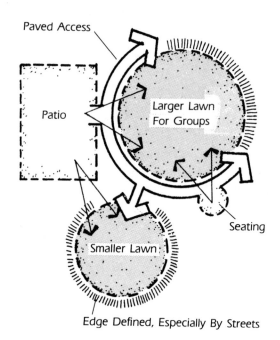

9-33.
Larger lawn areas adjacent to activity centers provide flexibility for spillover activity and large group events. Smaller lawns for retreat and small group use are ideal.

Spatial Characteristics

1. Ideally, both small and large lawn areas should be available for recreation. Larger lawn areas may accommodate large group activities and community events, such as arts and crafts shows, as well as provide additional space for future recreational demands. A smaller lawn area may serve as a retreat and for small group use and recreation, such as for a croquet game or picnic (see fig. 9–33).

2. Clearly defined edges and boundaries of lawn areas (particularly where they meet the street) increase safety and security as well as the sense of control over the space.

Amenities and Detailing

1. Paved seating areas, in sun and shade, and walkways nearby can provide a variety of viewing opportunities for less able residents who cannot negotiate a soft ground surface. They also serve as resting places from which to view the activity of others—an important type of participation for many older people.

2. Where paving meets the lawn surface, edges that meet at grade reduce the possibility of tripping. That is, lawns should not be edged.

3. A finely graded and well-groomed lawn surface is essential for easy and safe walking.

Play Areas for Children

Outdoor play areas for children may be welcomed by many residents with visiting grandchildren and others desiring increased contact with the young. Privacy, control over actual contact with the children, and noise, however, are very real concerns of many older people. If outdoor play areas are provided on-site, some special considerations are musts.

Location

1. The location and layout should ensure separate adult and child territories (see fig. 9–34) [13]. Where day-care centers are provided, child and adult areas should function independently.

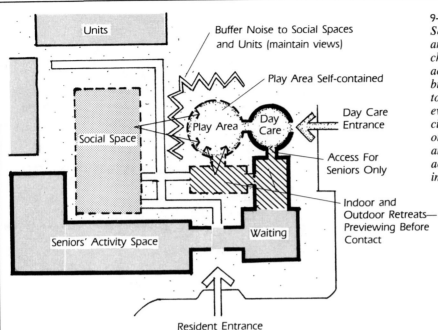

Units

Buffer Noise to Social Spaces
and Units (maintain views)

Play Area Self-contained

Play Area

Day Care

Social Space

Day Care Entrance

Access For
Seniors Only

Indoor and
Outdoor Retreats—
Previewing Before
Contact

Seniors' Activity Space

Waiting

Resident Entrance

9-34.
Separate entrances and activity areas for residents and day-care children maximize choices for inter-action and reduce congestion at building entries. Visual connections to child areas add interest; how-ever, noise reaching units and so-cial spaces must be controlled with-out isolation. Self-contained child areas, nearby seating, and retreats accessible only to seniors are important.

2. A location to reduce or buffer noise, especially near residential units and social spaces (e.g., patios), is important.

Spatial Characteristics

1. Common ground for compatible activities is de-sirable; however, the older person should not be re-quired to pass through children's areas to get to any on-site facilities (see fig. 9–34).

2. Refuge for the elderly is imperative, and access to "their" territory must be under residents' control [14]. A viewing area removed from the play area is one way to establish such refuge. Where day-care centers exist, an adult area removed from the children's area allows opportunity for rest and relaxation.

3. Providing opportunities for visual contact with children before physical contact allows for evaluation and preparation before interaction.

Amenities and Detailing

1. Amenities and detailing for comfort, ease of use, and access, as well as safety, are musts. Comfortable

seating areas, nonslip and nonglare walking surfaces, and other measures are basic.

2. Some researchers suggest that the physical ca-pabilities and requirements of young children are sim-ilar to those of a handicapped older person. Such fac-tors as eye height (of a wheelchair-bound adult) and hand coordination and strength (assuming the older person has arthritic hands) are analogous [15]. Al-though further research is needed, this may have val-uable implications for the design of combined child–senior centers.

References

1. Green, Isaac, et al. *Housing for the Elderly: The Devel-opment and Design Process.* New York: Van Nostrand Reinhold, 1975.

2. Central Mortgage and Housing Corporation. *Roof Decks Design Guidelines.* NH18-2/1. Ottawa, Ontario: CMHC National Office, 1979.

3. Colby, Diane. *Post-occupancy Evaluation of the Woolf House Roofgarden.* Berkeley: University of California, 1983.

4. Green et al., *Housing for the Elderly.*

5. ———. *Housing for the Elderly.*

6. American National Standards Institute. *Specifications for Making Buildings and Facilities Accessible to and Usable by Physically Handicapped People.* A117.1-1980. New York: ANSI, 1980.

7. Green et al. *Housing for the Elderly.*

8. Rapelje, D., P. Papp, and L. Crawford. *A Therapeutic Park for the Mentally Frail Resident of an Ontario Home for Senior Citizens.* Welland, Ontario: Senior Citizens Department, Regional Municipality of Niagara, n.d.

9. Green et al. *Housing for the Elderly.*

10. Zeisel, J., G. Epp, and S. Demos. *Low Rise Housing for Older People.* U.S. Department of Housing and Urban Development, Office of Policy Development and Research. HUD-483(TQ)-76. Washington, DC: U.S. Government Printing Office, 1977.

11. Green et al. *Housing for the Elderly.*

12. Untermann, Richard K. "Pedestrian Circulation." In *Handbook of Landscape Architectural Construction,* edited by J. Carpenter. Washington, DC: Landscape Architecture Foundation, 1976, 235–397.

13. Steinfeld, Edward H. "Physical Planning for Increased Cross-Generational Contact." In *Proceedings of the 4th Annual Environmental Design Research Conference,* edited by W.F.E. Preiser. Stroudsburg, PA: Dowden, Hutchinson & Ross, 1973.

14. ———. "Physical Planning for Increased Cross-Generational Contact."

15. Belles, Bill. *An Architectural Analysis of Intergenerational Facilities Combining Child Care Centers with Elderly Care Facilities.* Urbana Department of Architecture, University of Illinois, 1980.

CHAPTER
10
Amenities and Design Detailing

Design detailing is of prime importance for those people who experience sensory, cognitive, and other physiological changes with age.

Recommendations for the detailing of amenities and the design of special-use areas are covered in this chapter. The focus is on concerns frequently encountered by the designer that require in-depth discussion and specifications:

- seating
- tables
- outdoor lighting
- planters and planting beds
- raised planters for gardening
- ramps and stairs
- handrails
- doors and door handles
- windows and glazed surfaces
- outdoor signs
- pedestrian street crossings
- drinking fountains
- special considerations for canes, walkers, and wheelchairs

Seating

Chair and bench design is very important for older people who may spend great amounts of time seated. Muscle fatigue, general decline of muscle strength, compression of tissues, lessened flexibility, and other physiological changes associated with aging all create problems for older people in getting in and out of chairs and in sitting for periods of time. Thus, it is better to supply a few comfortable seats than to provide many uncomfortable slab-type benches that would rarely be used. Outdoor use, however, may be related to the number of seats provided [1] (see figs. 10–1, 10–2). Design and detailing considerations for seating are outlined below.

General

1. Movable seating (single chairs) is generally better than fixed seating. It enables a range of groupings according to changing patterns of sun, shade, activity, and number in the group.

2. Selecting a variety of comfortable chair designs or chair models accommodates those with differing needs, body builds, and disabilities (such as arthritis of the spine).

Placement

1. Two popular seating arrangements are those oriented toward activity, and right-angle seating that enables a closeness important for conversation. Older people tend to sit close together when conversing, perhaps compensating for poorer vision and hearing.

2. A defined space, with a sense of intimacy and security, is generally the most appropriate location for seating, especially for conversation. Seating in very open areas generally feels overexposed and uncomfortable. (For specific seating locations, refer to the appropriate use area in the site-design chapters.)

3. Choices for seating in shade and in sun, as well as protection from harsh winds, are essential for comfort.

4. For those in wheelchairs, an adequate paved surface (32-inch minimum width) next to benches is necessary for participation in a conversation (see fig. 10–3). A minimum area of 60 inches in diameter allows for a pivot turn (60 × 78 inches is a better minimum).

Backrests and Armrests

1. The most important criterion for bench and chair design is the inclusion of armrests and backrests. Seating that includes these features is often expensive but is critical for outdoor use and comfort (see figs. 10–4, 10–5).

- Backrests should be continuous, giving support to the lower part of the back as well as the shoulder region. A well-designed backrest is essential, due to decreased flexibility of the spine and fatigue experienced when leaning forward for any length of time [2].

10-1.
Comfortable seating has arms and full back support. Movable or fixed right-angle seating makes conversation easier.

10-2.
Concrete slab benches are extremely uncomfortable, cold, and difficult to get up from, especially if there is no kickspace underneath.

10-3.
Clearance for wheelchairs next to benches makes conversation easier.
After: American National Standards Institute. Specifications for Making Buildings and Facilities Accessible to and Usable by Physically Handicapped People. *New York: ANSI, 1980, 51.*

- The leading edge of the armrest should extend to the leading edge of the seat and provide a firm, rounded gripping surface. Decreased muscle strength in the legs and difficulty in angling the legs under the seat make it difficult for older people to lift themselves out of the seat [3]. Thus many older people use armrests to pull themselves out of the seat.

Seat

1. For easy movement in and out of the chair, the seat should not tilt too far backward off the horizontal nor be too high or too low [4] (see figs. 10–4, 10–5).

2. A seat with a high or abrupt leading edge may cut off circulation. Ninety percent of today's population from 75 to 91 years of age is between 4 feet 7 inches and 5 feet 4 1/2 inches in height. For these individuals (mostly women), the leading edge of the seat should not be more than 17 inches above the ground plane [5] (see figs. 10–4, 10–5).

3. The seat should be made of soft material or wood. Hard materials and those that conduct heat and cold, such as concrete, should be avoided. Padding or cushions are desirable. When seated, 60 percent of the weight load rests at the base of the hip-

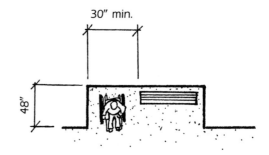

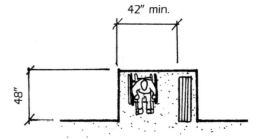

bone [6]; therefore, a soft seating surface is preferable for older people, who generally have less fatty muscle tissue in this area to disperse the weight load (see figs. 10–4, 10–5).

Legs

Chairs should be stable, with nonprotruding legs to reduce the possibility of tripping.

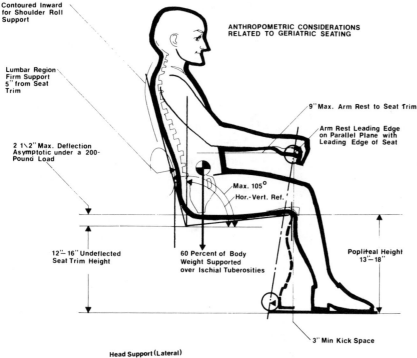

ANTHROPOMETRIC CONSIDERATIONS RELATED TO GERIATRIC SEATING

Contoured Inward for Shoulder Roll Support

Lumbar Region Firm Support 5" from Seat Trim

2 1\2" Max. Deflection Asymptotic under a 200-Pound Load

12"–16" Undeflected Seat Trim Height

60 Percent of Body Weight Supported over Ischial Tuberosities

Max. 105° Hor.-Vert. Ref.

9" Max. Arm Rest to Seat Trim

Arm Rest Leading Edge on Parallel Plane with Leading Edge of Seat

Popliteal Height 13"–18"

3" Min Kick Space

10-4.
Anthropometric criteria for seating; these address age-related changes in physiology and the fact that today's older people are generally shorter than the younger generation.
Source: Joseph A. Koncelik. Designing the Open Nursing Home. Stroudsburg, PA.: Dowden Hutchinson & Ross, 1976, 123. Reprinted with permission.

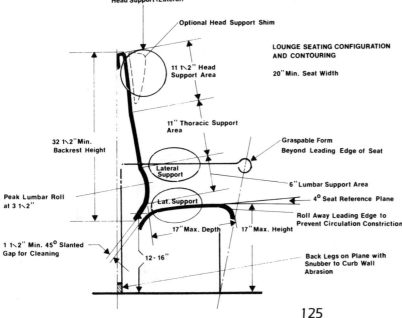

LOUNGE SEATING CONFIGURATION AND CONTOURING

20" Min. Seat Width

Head Support (Lateral)

Optional Head Support Shim

11 1\2" Head Support Area

11" Thoracic Support Area

32 1\2" Min. Backrest Height

Lateral Support

Peak Lumbar Roll at 3 1\2"

Lat. Support

1 1\2" Min. 45° Slanted Gap for Cleaning

17" Max. Depth

12 - 16"

17" Max. Height

Graspable Form Beyond Leading Edge of Seat

6" Lumbar Support Area

4° Seat Reference Plane

Roll Away Leading Edge to Prevent Circulation Constriction

Back Legs on Plane with Snubber to Curb Wall Abrasion

10-5.
Seating design criteria for indoor lounge chairs are applicable to outdoor seating, although such a chair (or bench) is impossible to find in today's market. Base-level features, which are available, must include full back support (including the lower spine), armrests, a seating height of 17 inches, and a rolled leading edge to the seat.
Source: Joseph A. Koncelik. Designing the Open Nursing Home. Stroudsburg, PA.: Dowden Hutchinson & Ross, 1976, 122.

Tables

Outdoor tables increase the range of possibilities for such outdoor activities as picnics, card games, and socializing. They can help to define space and create a sense of intimacy. Some special considerations for table type and detailing are outlined below.

Size and Configuration

1. There is much debate over the appropriate size and configuration of tables. Round tables are flexible in the number of people that can be seated, while square tables, for example, provide an easily definable seating "place" and may be combined to accommodate large groups. A variety of sizes and shapes may be the best option.

2. A table should be a separate unit from the chairs to ensure easy access and flexibility in seating arrangements. Fixed table–bench combinations are very difficult for many older people to get in and out of.

3. A table height of approximately 29 to 30 inches allows for easy penetration of most chairs and wheelchairs (27-inch minimum for penetration of knees) (see fig. 10–6).

4. A clear floor space of 30 inches wide and 48 inches deep is required for wheelchair clearance at a table; 19 inches (maximum) of the depth may fall underneath the table (see fig. 10–7).

5. The table must be stable, as older persons tend to use it for balance and assistance in seating. Lightweight tables are desirable for easy movement. Table legs should not protrude beyond the table-top edge, or they should be well marked (see fig. 10–6).

Table Top

1. The edge of the table should be smoothed or slightly rolled (not cut square) for safety and to provide an ample gripping surface.

2. The surface should not be white or too reflective, as glare from natural lighting is a problem for aging eyes and for the visually handicapped.

Outdoor Lighting

Lighting may be used to accentuate an area or focal point, to define an area or edge of an area, and to provide security. In general, higher levels of illumination are required for aging eyes. Poor lighting design may compound many of the visual problems associated with aging, such as faulty depth perception and the misperception of a change in elevation. Some special considerations for outdoor lighting are outlined below.

Nonglare Surface

27" min. (29–30" best)

10-6.
Tables, as separate units from chairs, with nonprotruding legs (but extremely stable) and clearance underneath are best for the less agile. Nonglare surfaces and a rolled edge maximize comfort and safety.

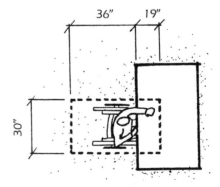

36"   19"

30"

10-7.
Clearance for wheelchairs at a table requires an area 30 inches wide and 55 inches deep (including a 19-inch-deep clear space for knees).

126

Lighting for Different Areas On-site

1. Different areas on-site have differing light requirements for security. Some feature areas may be suitable for accent lighting.

- Higher-intensity lighting for security is recommended for drop-off areas, building entries, and parking lots.
- Steps, ramps, curb cuts, and hazardous areas also require special lighting.
- There should be adequate light for special events and gatherings around patio areas and other outdoor activity spaces. Decorative lighting to accentuate night views from indoors may also be incorporated into the lighting scheme (see fig. 10–8).

Light Fixture Type and Placement

1. Lighting, particularly in high-movement areas, should illuminate the periphery of the area to help define the pavement edge and prevent harsh shadows (see fig. 10–9).

2. Light standards placed to provide an overlap will reduce glare and hot spots (see fig. 10–9).

3. Light fixtures should minimize the light source to pedestrians and vehicles (see fig. 10–9).

- Globe fixtures should have deflection devices that direct light down rather than up and out.
- Lighting placed at a lower level is best for those who use walkers and wheelchairs; light from high-level fixtures may be blocked by their bodies, casting a shadow directly in front of them.

Planters and Planting Beds

Planters and planting beds add interest and detailing to the landscape and may offer opportunities for close-up viewing of plants.

Special considerations for viewing and safety are outlined below.

General

1. Decorative planters and planting beds should be either a minimum of 30 inches in height or unprotected at grade to reduce the possibility of tripping. It is better to have the landscaping trampled than to have a resident trip and fall (see fig. 10–10). Other considerations for planter height include the following [7, 8]:

- Planters 32 to 48 inches in height can serve as a handrest for most semiambulant people.
- Five-foot walls (minimum height) aid the visually impaired in detecting deflected sounds, but obscure views for the sighted.
- A maximum planter height of approximately 40 inches enhances visibility for the handicapped (eye height is generally between 43 to 51 inches; average height 48 inches).
- A plant material height of approximately 25 to 35 inches enables those in wheelchairs to touch and smell the flowers. The ideal planter height will depend upon the height of plant materials used (working planter height is discussed below).

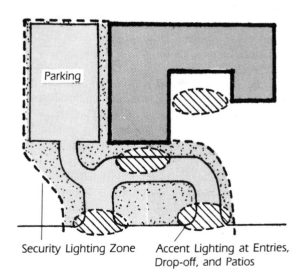

Security Lighting Zone   Accent Lighting at Entries, Drop-off, and Patios

10-8.
Lighting enhances real and perceived security. Accent lighting at key decision-making points facilitates wayfinding as well as safety.
After: Isaac Green et al. Housing for the Elderly: The Development and Design Process. *New York: Van Nostrand Reinhold, 1975, 125.*

Raised Planters for Gardening

Raised working planters, for use by both ambulatory and nonambulatory persons, may take many forms. If seats are provided, raised planters designed for wheelchair access can also meet the needs of those who use walkers or who cannot stand or stoop for periods of time.

The ideal type and height of planters for use by those in wheelchairs depend upon individual preferences and abilities as well as the chair dimensions. Thus, a variety of designs and heights is the best op-

tion. Some planter designs and important dimension criteria are discussed below.

Planter Design

1. Alcove-type planters provide a greater working area that is easily accessible from a stationary position, while keeping wheelchairs out of the flow of

10-9.
Lighting that reduces glare to pedestrians and defines the pavement edge enhances safety and negotiability. Low-level lighting is important for those who use walkers or wheelchairs, as their bodies block high-level lighting, casting a shadow directly in front.

Low-level Lighting With Deflection Device

Overlap Reduces Glare and Hot Spots

Periphery Lighting Defines Pavement Edge, Avoids Deep Shadows

10-10.
Raised planters or planting at grade is best; low-level planters and edging are not easily seen and can cause a fall; planters above 40 inches may obscure views.

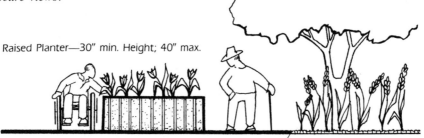

Raised Planter—30" min. Height; 40" max.

Planting Meets Paving at Grade—No Edging

traffic. Alcoves, however, may limit conversation and restrict movement. Adequate space for maneuverability and for setting down working materials is desirable (see fig. 10–11).

2. Parallel-approach planters allow for easy movement and increased conversation opportunities, although wheelchairs may obstruct the flow of traffic (see fig. 10–12). When knee space is provided underneath, the range of possible working positions from a wheelchair is increased.

3. Raised potting tables allow knee clearance and can offer a variety of lower working heights often desired for heavier work, as no planting bed depth is required.

4. The required clear floor space for wheelchair access depends upon the planter design (see figs. 10–11, 10–12) [9].

- Shallow alcoves (24 inches or less for a forward approach; 15 inches or less for a parallel approach) and nonalcove-type working areas require a minimum paved clear space 48 inches deep and 30 inches wide.
- Deeper alcoves require additional clear paved surface for maneuverability in addition to space for resting supplies and equipment.
- Planters with clear space for knees also require a 48-by-30-inch clear space; however, up to 19 inches of the depth may extend underneath the planter.

Clearances and Working Surfaces

1. Knee clearance underneath a planter increases the range of working-surface reach and enables a frontal working position that makes material manipulation easier. The height required for knee clearance and the depth of planting beds, however, dictate the minimum working surface height, which is often higher than many desire.

Some people prefer a lower working surface, which is impossible to achieve when providing clearance for wheelchair armrests or even for knees. These people often prefer to pull their chair back from the planter, enabling use of a lower surface. Thus a variety of options may be best:

- A clearance of 31 to 31 1/2 inches for standard, fixed-armrest wheelchairs allows 1 to 1 1/2 inches free space.
- Knee clearance of 27 inches is minimum, and 29 inches better.
- Minimum clearance for part of the extending foreleg allows a lower working surface height.
- Planters that bevel outward at the top are desirable (see clearance requirements, below).

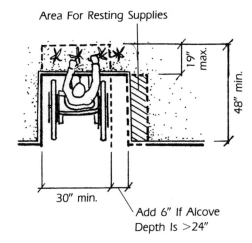

Area For Resting Supplies

19" max.

48" min.

30" min.

Add 6" If Alcove Depth Is >24"

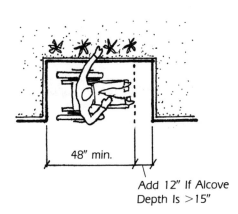

48" min.

Add 12" If Alcove Depth Is >15"

10-11.
Alcove-type planters provide a greater working area within easy reach for gardening. Adequate clearance and additional space for resting working materials (even shelving) are ideal (maximum side reach over a planter is 24 inches).

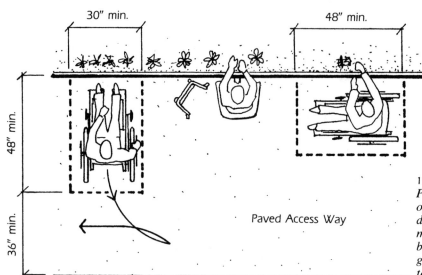

30" min.   48" min.

48" min.

36" min.

Paved Access Way

10-12.
Parallel-approach planters maximize opportunities for socializing while gardening; however, adequate clearance must be available for those passing by. Raised planters may also make gardening easier for the semiambulatory, especially if chairs are available.

2. The height, placement, and size of working surfaces and storage areas are critical factors for easy use from a wheelchair (see figs. 10–13, 10–14). Important dimension criteria for working-surface reach from a wheelchair are outlined below; length of reach may decrease with age or infirmity [10, 11].

- For manual work over an obstacle (or planter), short people generally prefer a working surface height of 26 inches; tall people prefer 30 inches. This height increases by approximately 3 inches for light, detailed work.
- Maximum horizontal side reach is approximately 24 inches (range: 22 to 27 inches).
- Maximum horizontal forward reach over a table or planter is approximately 25 to 31 inches.
- Vertical side reach for a shelf or planter is approximately 54 inches, maximum height, and 9 to 10 inches for lowest side reach.
- Average height for a front reach upward is approximately 48 inches.

Ramps and Stairs

Access to and around outdoor areas is critical for outdoor use. Whenever possible, changes in grade that require ramps and stairs (more than a 5 percent slope) should be avoided, especially at building entry and drop-off areas. Where changes in grade are necessary, both ramps and stairs must be provided; ramps are difficult for ambulatory people to negotiate, as the rise of a ramp changes the walking gait. Those who use walkers and canes also have special needs for stair design.

General

1. Where changes in grade are absolutely necessary, both ramps and stairs should be provided.

2. Nonslip and nonglare surfaces are imperative for ramps and stairs.

3. Steps and ramps should be well marked and lighted:

- Lighting should illuminate the top and bottom of steps and ramps, as well as ramp edges.
- Low-level lighting directed toward the stair riser and illuminating the tread increases safety, especially for those using walking aids, whose bodies will block light from higher-level fixtures.
- A textured paving surface, between 24 to 48 inches in front of stairs and ramps, allows the visually im-

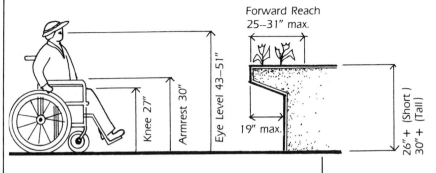

Forward Reach 25–31" max.

Knee 27"
Armrest 30"
Eye Level 43–51"
19" max.

26" + (Short)
30" + (Tall)

10-13.
Clearance underneath raised planters will affect working-surface height; preferred heights vary according to the individual's size and the type of work (higher for light work). Choices should be available.

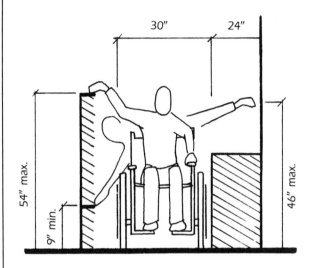

30"   24"

54" max.
9" min.
46" max.

10-14.
High and low limits for side reach may actually be less than shown for infirm elderly and those who are smaller than average.
After: American National Standards Institute. Specifications for Making Buildings and Facilities Accessible to and Usable by Physically Handicapped People. New York: ANSI, 1980, 18.

paired enough time to recognize the signal, complete their step, and stop before arriving at the hazard [12].

4. Handrails are a basic requirement for all steps and ramps (see figs. 10–15, 10–16 and "Handrails," below).

● Handrails should extend 1 foot beyond the length of the ramp or stair. One handrail on each side is desirable.

● Railing supports should be located outside of ramp guards and running surface.
● Handrails along both sides of the change in grade are desirable. A double rail (along both sides), one at approximately 32 inches above grade (36-inch maximum) and another at approximately 26 inches (30-inch maximum), is best [13].

Ramps

1. A gradient greater than 5 percent should be considered a ramp. These are some basic requirements for ramps (see fig. 10–15):

● Ramp gradients should not exceed 8.33 percent (1:12).
● A level approach of 6 feet should be available at the top and bottom of each ramp.

2. A minimum ramp width of 5 feet is adequate for general purposes, as it allows space for assistance, irregular travel path, or two chairs or those using walkers to pass cautiously (6-foot width is best for passing). A ramp width for a single chair is between 4 feet and 4 feet 6 inches (3-foot 6-inch minimum).

3. A maximum ramp length of 30 feet is often recommended, although this length may prove impassable for the more frail person, especially on steep gradients. If a longer ramp is absolutely necessary, a level resting platform of approximately 5 feet clear length at 15-foot intervals is suggested.

4. Curbs or ramp guards (2 to 2 1/2 inches, minimum height) that extend along the sides of a ramp prevent overrun and assist in emergency stopping (see fig. 10–15).

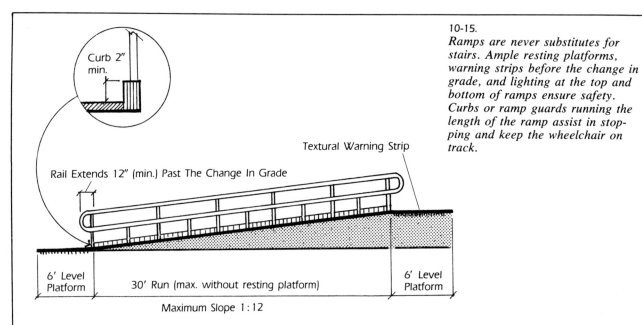

Curb 2" min.

10-15.
Ramps are never substitutes for stairs. Ample resting platforms, warning strips before the change in grade, and lighting at the top and bottom of ramps ensure safety. Curbs or ramp guards running the length of the ramp assist in stopping and keep the wheelchair on track.

Textural Warning Strip

Rail Extends 12" (min.) Past The Change In Grade

6' Level Platform   30' Run (max. without resting platform)   6' Level Platform

Maximum Slope 1:12

Stairs

1. Stair runs should be as short as possible, but not fewer than 3 steps (see fig. 10–16).

- Single and double stairs are hazardous and should be avoided, as they are not easily detected, especially by the visually impaired.
- As a general guide, 10 risers between landings are an absolute maximum. A run of 5 is better.

2. Treads and risers should be uniform throughout the sequence; standard formulas should be used for calculation. Some special needs of less agile older people include the following (see figs. 10–16, 10–17):

- Standard 5- to 6-inch risers (6 1/2-inch maximum) ensure familiarity for the visually impaired and are passable for most people using walkers who must lift the walker over the rise (a 4-inch rise is easiest for this group).
- Stair treads should be no less than 11 inches deep (12-inch treads are best for fuller placement of the foot).
- Where frequent use of walkers is anticipated, a deeper tread is desirable. Although a 12-inch tread is often recommended, most standard walkers are approximately 19 to 20 inches deep at the base.

Thus, for stairs frequented by those with walkers, a tread depth of at least 20 inches will allow the base of the walker to rest upon a single stair. A standard step can generally be negotiated with assistance and the use of a handrail (leaving the walker behind), although freedom of travel is obviously limited.

3. Vertically splayed risers with nonprojecting beveled nosings are best for those who have ambulatory difficulties (see fig. 10–18).

- Open steps and those with abrupt, projecting nosings are a hazard for the less agile who may drag and catch one foot. A projecting nosing of 1/2 inch or less is passable.
- Contrasting colors on stair treads and risers may also aid in identification, although too many warning signals may promote an institutional image.

Handrails

Handrails are generally used by those who walk with some difficulty and by those who use wheelchairs. They offer both real and perceived safety and are often used to assist in wheelchair locomotion.

Handrails are necessary at changes in grade. They

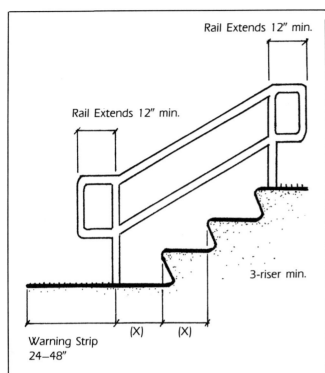

Rail Extends 12" min.

Rail Extends 12" min.

3-riser min.

(X) (X)

Warning Strip
24–48"

10-16.
Stair runs should be a minimum of three risers to en-sure recognition. Textural warning strips and railing ex-tensions allow ample time for the less agile and visually impaired to identify the change in grade and make nec-essary adjustments. (Note: X = width of tread).

are desirable where changes in the environment may cause confusion or require adjustment time, such as exiting from a dark room to the bright outdoor light. A landscape element (e.g., light standard) may serve as a grab post where handrails are not feasible (see also "Ramps and Stairs," above).

Placement

1. The standard height of handrails varies from 26 to 39 inches. For use by ambulatory and nonambula-tory residents, two handrails are optimal: one at 32 inches and the other at approximately 26 inches [14] (see fig. 10–19).

2. The length of the handrail should extend 1 foot past the change in grade. Where handrails are free-standing, the projecting end of the rail should not

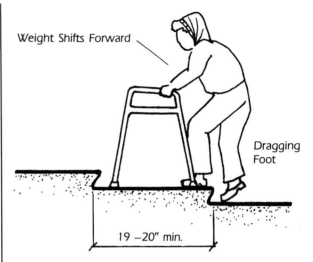

Weight Shifts Forward

Dragging Foot

19 –20" min.

10-17.
Standard treads assure familiarity for those with visual impairments, but present a barrier to independent movement with a walker. A wider stair run, accommo-dating the full base of the walker (generally 19–20 inches min.) is ideal for this group.

protrude abruptly. A curved or bowed rail ending is one option.

Detailing

1. A handrail easiest to grip (even for those with prosthetic devices) has a diameter of approximately 2 3/4 inches and is mounted approximately 2 inches from the wall [15] (see fig. 10–19).

2. Indirect lighting should be used for greatest visibility.

3. Handrail material impervious to weather is pref-erable. Metal becomes cold and slippery when wet; thus, plastic or a vinyl coating should be considered.

4. A coded system of textural markings along hand-rails may help the visually impaired identify the be-ginning and end of a set of stairs, a change in direc-tion, or the location of facilities.

Doors and Door Handles

The design of doors and door handles may facilitate safe and easy access to outdoor areas. Arthritis, failing eyesight, and other age-related infirmities may affect the older person's ability to open and close a door. Some important considerations for doors are outlined below.

Door Type

1. The ease of opening a manual door is inversely related to its width (and weight); however, a door must be wide enough for a single wheelchair to pass. Lightweight doors are easiest to open.

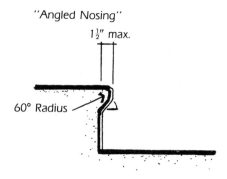

"Angled Nosing"

$1\frac{1}{2}$" max.

60° Radius

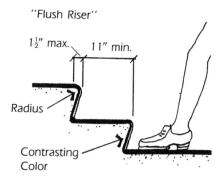

"Flush Riser"

$1\frac{1}{2}$" max.   11" min.

Radius

Contrasting Color

10-18.
Vertically splayed risers with nonprojecting beveled nosings ($1\frac{1}{2}$ inches max.), flush, or rounded nosings are best, as the less agile may drag one foot. Contrasting color of riser and tread helps identify stairs; nonslip surfaces are basic.
After: American National Standards Institute. Specifications for Making Buildings and Facilities Accessible to and Usable by Physically Handicapped People. *New York: ANSI, 1980, 28.*

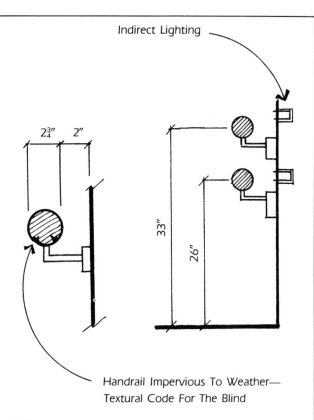

Indirect Lighting

$2\frac{3}{4}$"   2"

33"

26"

Handrail Impervious To Weather— Textural Code For The Blind

10-19.
Round handrails at approximately 33 inches for the ambulatory and 26 inches for the handicapped are easiest to grasp. Textural codes may signal an upcoming hazard or help identify a location for the visually impaired.

2. Power-assisted doors should require a constant but not excessive pressure for opening. A door that suddenly lurches open under pressure is dangerous.

3. Powered swinging doors, although easy to open, may create a dangerous situation for the unsuspecting person on the other side. Slowly opening low-powered automatic doors and clear marking of the door path are essential.

4. Powered sliding doors alleviate the problem of a swinging door, but they often require more maintenance.

5. Glass doors allow viewing; however, they present special problems for safety and for control of glare (see figs. 10–20, 10–21). Some special considerations include the following:

- Full-length glass doors can create excessive glare and are hazardous for those who use wheelchairs, as foot rests protrude out from the chair and may shatter glass. Some disabled people may push the door open with their chair or walker, so kickplates (especially for swinging doors) and marking to identify the glass area are essential. Window treatment to reduce glare is also necessary.
- A door with a glazed upper half (36 inches above the floor, maximum) is a good option, allowing previewing without the problems of full-length glass.
- Glass doors should be located to minimize direct exposure to glare from major access routes and activity areas (a diagonal exposure to the light source is best). A gradual transition in exposure to the light source provides time for adjustment of the eye.

Detailing

1. A minimum door width of 32 inches is required for access by a single wheelchair; 60 inches for two.

2. A level threshold reduces the possibility of tripping and ensures wheelchair access. When a raised threshold is necessary, it should be beveled (8 percent maximum slope) and at a height no greater than 3/4 inch for sliding doors; 1/2 inch for other types [16].

3. Kickplates are particularly important for hinged doors, especially for persons who use walkers or wheelchairs. Kickplates should cover the approximate door width up to a height of 16 inches from the bottom.

4. Door handles must provide sufficient gripping surface and be easy to open with the hand or forearm. A lever handle is a good option (see fig. 10–21).

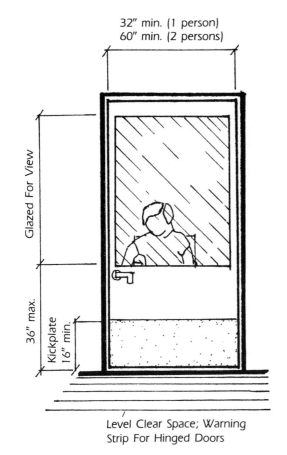

32" min. (1 person)
60" min. (2 persons)

Glazed For View

36" max.

Kickplate 16" min.

Level Clear Space; Warning
Strip For Hinged Doors

10-20.
Glazed doors enable previewing; however, a solid lower portion is necessary for hinged doors used by those with walking aids or wheelchairs. A level clear space 60 inches deep, with an additional 24-inch clear width opposite the hinged side, is necessary for safety (for most door types). Clear marking of the door path is essential for power-assisted hinged doors.

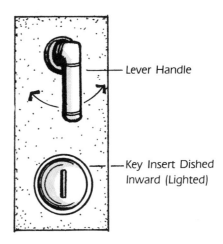

Lever Handle

Key Insert Dished
Inward (Lighted)

10-21.
Lever-type door handles are easiest for those with arthritis. Dished key inserts guide the key.

5. Key inserts should be designed for easy identification and key insertion. A lighted key insert, which is dished inward to guide the key, is ideal (see fig. 10–21).

Windows and Glazed Surfaces

Older people value windows because they allow enjoyment of the outdoors and views of activity from the comfort of being indoors. Special care must be taken to reduce glare, which can make identification of objects and people very difficult for aging eyes. Window placement, surface treatment, and other detailing can improve viewing as well as reduce glare.

Window Placement

1. Window placement should minimize direct exposure of major room entries to intense glare (fig. 10–22).

- A diagonal exposure to the light source reduces initial exposure to glare, allowing time for adjustment to changes in illumination.

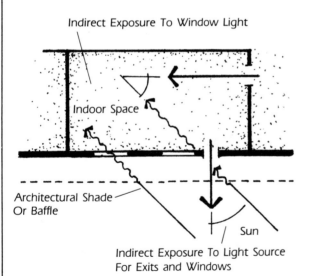

Indirect Exposure To Window Light

Indoor Space

Architectural Shade Or Baffle

Sun

Indirect Exposure To Light Source For Exits and Windows

10-22.
Indirect exposure to light sources for primary window views and entrances/exits reduces glare and allows time for adjustment to changes in illumination.

- A gradual transition in exposure to intense light allows time for adjustment to illumination.
- The interior decor, such as nonreflective floor surfaces, also plays an important role in glare reduction.

2. Placement of dwelling-unit windows should ensure privacy, while enhancing views of activity, pathways, and scenic beauty. Some ideal window placements include the following (see fig. 10–23):

- At least one living-room window should be low enough to allow the outside ground level to be seen from a seated position.
- Kitchen windows should be placed to illuminate the working area and sink. Views from the kitchen table are desirable.
- Dining-room windows offering views from the dining table are ideal.
- Bedroom windows should be high enough to accommodate furniture. One window should be low enough so that the bedridden can easily see outdoors. Privacy from those passing by is also a special concern.
- Unit privacy is important, especially for the bedroom. An adequate setback from outdoor pathways, a change in grade, or plant materials can ensure privacy from those outdoors while maintaining views from inside.

3. The appropriate placement of common-space windows can serve as a drawing card for activity, enlivening both indoor and outdoor spaces. Such windows can also provide comfortable spots for relaxing alone. Some good locations for shared windows include the following:

- Windows that connect indoor and outdoor activity spaces set the stage for social routines and encourage participation. A window seating area along the dining-area access route, for example, can provide the perfect setting to sit and watch men display their shuffleboard skills after breakfast.
- Windows overlooking the main entry/drop-off area should be large and low enough for a number of residents to watch for rides and visitors from a seated position.

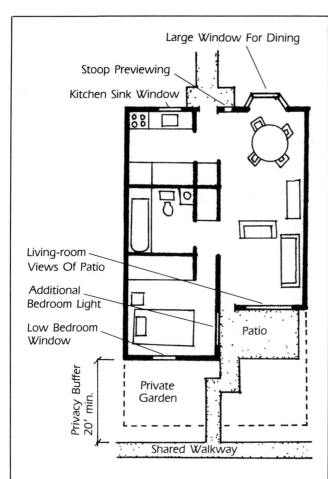

Large Window For Dining

Stoop Previewing

Kitchen Sink Window

Living-room Views Of Patio

Additional Bedroom Light

Low Bedroom Window

Privacy Buffer 20' min.

Patio

Private Garden

Shared Walkway

10-23.
Unit window placement is important for the views as well as light. Window placement and landscape treatment should ensure bedroom privacy; one low-level window for viewing from bed is desirable.

- An intimate window alcove, slightly offset from an activity area, nursing station, or corridor, is a perfect place to relax alone or with a few friends and enjoy the outdoor view.

Window Detailing

1. A maximum window sill height of 3 1/2 feet allows for viewing from a seated position; many older people enjoy watching outdoor activity from a favorite chair (see fig. 10–24) [17].

2. Plant materials can frame or open the view. Low-level planting should not obstruct vision (see fig. 10–24).

3. Windows and screens should be easy to open and clean without requiring fine muscle control and dexterity or gross muscular strength. This is a frequently desired improvement among older people.

4. Inside window ledges of approximately 1 foot in depth may serve as a place for planters as well as a support for balance while observing the outdoors (see fig. 10–24).

Detailing to Reduce Glare

1. Window tinting and glazing, screens, and blinds may be used to control the quality and quantity of light and reduce glare.

2. Such architectural detailing as overhangs and arbors as well as the use of trees can reduce glare while maintaining visibility.

Outdoor Signs

Signs should support the site-development scheme and aid residents and visitors in locating the site and facilities. Signs may identify the site entry, offer direction and information at building entries, direct traffic, and provide information about facilities. The need for too many signs, however, indicates a poor site-development scheme and may lend an undesirable institutional character to the site. Important considerations for the size and design of signs, based upon the perceptual requirements of older people, are outlined below.

General

1. Signs should be developed as a consistent system, with a consistent pattern and hierarchy as well as legibility [18]. This makes sign identification easier and reduces clutter.

2. Signs, particularly those at the site and building entries, are important for creating an image for the project as a whole (see fig. 10–25).

3. Placement of pedestrian signs should ensure easy identification without obstructing walkways (see fig. 10–26).

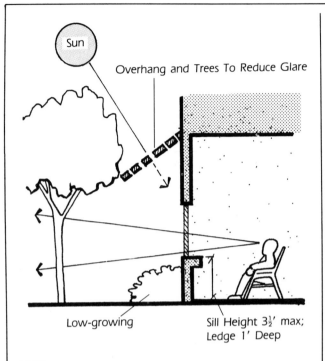

10-24.
Many older people spend considerable time viewing the outdoors from a seated position. Windowsill height, plant materials for opening or framing a view, and elements to reduce glare enhance viewing.

Sun

Overhang and Trees To Reduce Glare

Low-growing

Sill Height 3½' max; Ledge 1' Deep

- For those with visual impairments, signs with raised lettering, at a height of approximately 5 feet above grade, can be "read" by touch [19].
- Signs that hang should allow a clear space of between 6 1/2 to 7 feet above grade to ensure safety [20].

Size of Signs, Letters, and Symbols

1. The appropriate size of the sign and lettering is dependent upon the speed and distance of viewing. In general, oversized is better than undersized. Signs for pedestrians may be sized similarly to signs viewed from a car traveling 15 miles per hour. Some recommendations for entrance signs are outlined in fig. 10–27.

2. Size may also be used to indicate the relative importance of the message: larger signs for a primary message and smaller signs for less important messages.

Letter Style and Symbols

1. Lettering styles should be bold without serifs; Helvetica or Futura typefaces are ideal. Lettering on signs should not be extended or condensed, as these are difficult to read (see fig. 10–28).

10-25.
The image that an entry sign creates for the project is important. Residents at this project have donated funds to replace the existing bright blue-and-white translucent plastic sign shown here with one "like those fancy apartments have," made of wrought iron and wood.

2. Letters should be spaced similarly to the spacing on typewritten material—closely or loosely spaced letters are more difficult to read (see fig. 10–28).

3. White lettering or images on a black or dark-

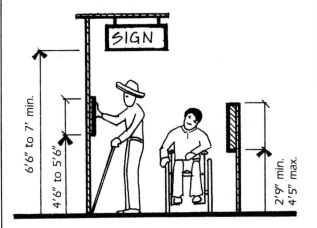

10-26.
Signs should be located where they can be read easily, but should be outside of the pedestrian path to ensure safety. Ideal sign heights that are easily "read" by the blind (left) and handicapped (right) are noted above.

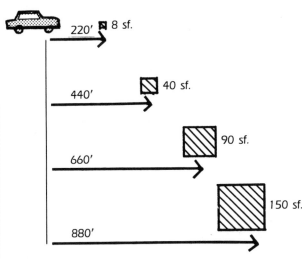

10-27.
The appropriate size of entrance signs for easy recognition and legibility is influenced by the distance of viewing. After: Isaac Green et al. Housing for the Elderly: The Development and Design Process. *New York: Van Nostrand Reinhold, 1975, 136.*

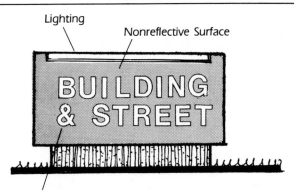

Bold Letters (No Serifs), White On Dark Background

10-28.
Age-related changes in vision require that signs be clear, legible, and well illuminated.

blue background are best for legibility. If dark letters are used, they should be on a neutral gray background to reduce glare. If color is used, warmer colors are preferable; blue and green color combinations should be avoided, as they are not easily distinguished [21].

4. Symbols as well as textures, raised letters and images that support the message, may aid those with visual impairments.

- Raised letters are preferable to braille, which only 7 percent of the blind population can read [22].
- In general, smaller raised letters are easier for the blind to feel than larger letters.
- Incised characters present maintenance problems, as they can fill with dirt and other material.

Surface Material and Other Detailing

1. The surface material should be durable and nonreflective.

2. There should be lighting on signs for easy identification at night.

Pedestrian Street Crossings

Crossing the street can pose many hazards for the older pedestrian as well as for the physically and visually handicapped, yet street crossing is essential for reaching neighborhood services and facilities.

139

The pedestrian casualty rate is highest in the age groups of 5 to 14 years and 65 years or older; 7 out of 10 pedestrian accidents involving the elderly occur at intersection crosswalks [23]. Less accurate depth perception, decreased peripheral vision, slower reaction time, and poorer hearing may all contribute to these accidents. In addition to traffic accidents, older people are more likely to be caught halfway across the street when the signal changes. Ambulatory, handicapped, and visually impaired older pedestrians may also find signals difficult to read, curbs and ramps difficult to pass (or see), and heavy pedestrian and vehicular traffic confusing. If safety and neighborhood access are to be ensured, the design and detailing of pedestrian crossings along neighboring roads must address the needs of those who walk more slowly or have ambulatory and visual impairments.

Five basic ways to make street crossing easier are (1) to reduce the distance (and exposure time) for pedestrians across traffic lanes; (2) increase the time provided at crossing signals; (3) reduce or mark potential barriers (e.g., curbs); (4) increase visibility; and (5) limit traffic or modify traffic flow along major pedestrian access routes. Some special considerations are outlined below.

Distance Across Traffic Lanes

1. Extended pedestrian crossing areas are a safe and effective way to reduce the distance across traffic lanes. They reduce exposure time to traffic and ensure a safe place for waiting (see figs. 10–29, 10–30).

- When combined with one-way turn or three-way intersections, where pedestrians do not have to cross in the same direction as left-turning vehicles, extended crossing areas substantially increase pedestrian safety. Vehicles turning left across the intersection are particularly hazardous for pedestrians traveling in the same direction.
- Extended crossing areas with reduced radius at nonturning intersections can help direct traffic.
- Extended crossing areas require special attention to drainage patterns; water and drain inlets should be located outside of the pedestrian area.

2. For very wide and heavy traffic streets, walk-through islands also reduce the effective distance across traffic lanes, although they are generally less satisfactory than extended crossings. Safe waiting at the island must be assured. Crossing areas through the island should be at grade and provide ample space for safe waiting (see fig. 10–29).

Lighting

1. Light standards placed to backlight the pedestrian to traffic approaching from the intersection or to vehicles turning toward the crossing increase visibility and safety (see fig. 10–31). Approximately 70 percent of intersection accidents involving pedestrians occur at night due to poor lighting [24]. Older people often have poorer night vision and reaction time. Their eyes adjust more slowly to changes in illumination.

Pedestrian Crossing Signals

1. An auditory signal (such as a buzz or clicking when crossing is safe) aids the visually impaired; lower-pitched signals are often more easily heard than high-pitched sounds.

2. The standard timing of pedestrian crossing signals may not provide enough time for the slower walker and handicapped person to cross the street before the signal changes. Average walking speeds decline with old age, although both slow and fast walkers can be found in all age groups.

The timing of pedestrian crossing signals should take into account the following walking speeds [25]:

- A minimum walking speed for most fairly able ambulatory older people is between 210 and 240 feet per minute (average of 215 feet per minute for a 75-year-old), versus 254 to 270 feet per minute for the average pedestrian.
- A minimum walking speed for most handicapped and less agile seniors is approximately 150 feet per minute. This speed is similar to that of a crowd exiting a stadium. Speeds below 145 feet per minute represent restricted shuffling; however, some disabled people may walk a short distance at a rate of 90 feet per minute (on level terrain) and at a rate of 100 feet every two minutes for distances

greater than 100 feet (assuming a two-minute resting period every 100 feet) [26].

- Changes in grade, irregular terrain, inclement weather, and the carrying of packages further reduce walking speeds. Those who are unsure of their balance may also stop while other pedestrians pass.

Curb Ramps

The most appropriate type of curb ramp and its location are influenced by many surrounding conditions, including the width of adjacent sidewalks and streets, drainage patterns, and the location of drainage inlets and grates. Thus, no single ramp design is appropriate for each situation. Some special considerations for older people are outlined below (see figs. 10–32, 10–33, 10–34).

1. Gradients and dimensions are important elements of ramp design for ambulatory, nonambulatory, and visually impaired older pedestrians. A Federal Highway Administration (FHwA) study completed in 1980 indicated several hazards with many common gradient and dimension standards for ramps [27, 28]. The results of this study suggest the following:

- American National Standards Institute (ANSI) standards require a maximum curb ramp slope of 1:12. Steeper slopes of 1:8 for 3-inch curbs and 1:10 at 6-inch curbs are permitted under certain circumstances. These steeper slopes, however, may prove impassable for some wheelchair users.
- Vertical curb returns and steep side flares can present a hazard for both ambulatory pedestrians and wheelchair users. Some recommended slopes include ramp flares used by wheelchairs to enter or exit a ramp no steeper than 1:12 and ramp flares within the path of pedestrians that do not exceed a slope of 1:10 (1:8 outside of the pedestrian path).

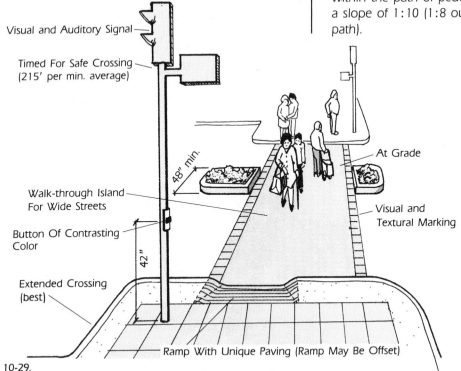

Visual and Auditory Signal

Timed For Safe Crossing (215' per min. average)

48" min.

At Grade

Walk-through Island For Wide Streets

Button Of Contrasting Color

42"

Visual and Textural Marking

Extended Crossing (best)

Ramp With Unique Paving (Ramp May Be Offset)

10-29.
Extend pedestrian crossings, defined routes, and signals timed for the slower walker increase the safety of street crossing. Offsetting curb ramps from the intersection provides greater curb definition for the blind and ample space for the ambulatory. See text for appropriate paving materials.

- Sufficient traffic-free overrun, or stopping platform distance, for most wheelchair users is 53 inches at the base of the ramp, 54.4 inches at the top.

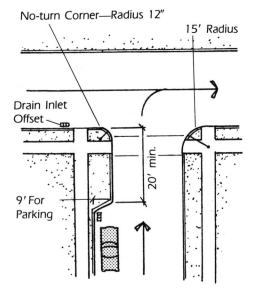

10-30.
Extended pedestrian crossings, three-way intersections (versus four-way), and pedestrian crossings that do not require passing in front of left-turning vehicles all increase pedestrian safety.

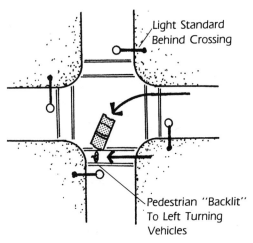

10-31.
Lighting located beyond the crosswalk to backlight or shadow the crossing pedestrian increases safety, especially with left-turning vehicles.

- The angle between the curb and street (or gutter), if too acute, can catch the footplates of wheelchairs. A maximum slope of 1:20 for the intersecting gutter and 1:8 for the ramp reduces this problem.

2. A curb ramp width of 36 inches is often recommended, although some states require a 40-inch width. Wider curb ramps are desirable for heavy traffic areas; however, the option for stepping off of the curb must be available.

Curb Ramps and the Visually Impaired

1. Ramps pose special problems for the visually impaired, as the clarity and alignment of the curb edge is often used for orientation (see figs. 10–32, 10–33, 10–34).

- A lip at the bottom of the ramp does not substantially aid the visually impaired pedestrian and may pose a problem for wheelchair users [29].
- Paired ramps (with flared sides), swept-corner ramps, and wraparound ramps present problems for the visually impaired due to the lack of curb definition for orientation. A slight off-setting of the curb ramp away from the intersection is best.
- Changes in pavement treatment may help to identify the curb edge (see number 2 below).

2. Changes in paving material, texture, and color for the entire ramp (including flares) provide sensory clues to aid the visually impaired. The results of the FHwA study revealed that certain paving treatments are more easily discriminated by the visually impaired [30]:

- Changes from brushed concrete to thermoplastic strips, nicked concrete, exposed pea gravel aggregate, and pliant polymer were distinguished by more than 85 percent of the totally blind people surveyed.
- Changes to mortared brick paving, solid thermoplastic, Kushioncote, and scored concrete were distinguished by 70–80 percent.
- Changes to asphalt or burlap-textured concrete were detected by fewer than 70 percent.

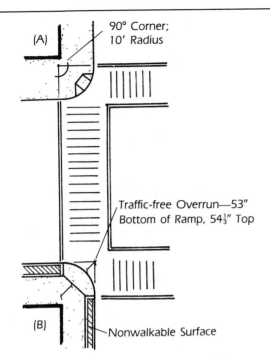

90° Corner; 10' Radius

(A)

Traffic-free Overrun—53"
Bottom of Ramp, 54⅓" Top

(B)

Nonwalkable Surface

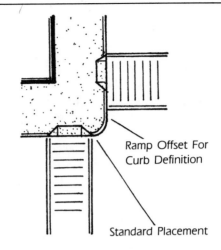

Ramp Offset For Curb Definition

Standard Placement

10-33.
Paired flared curb ramps present the fewest problems for the disabled, especially if the ramps are totally recessed and utilities are outside of the pedestrian flow. Sufficient walkway to keep the two ramps separate is needed. Greater curb definition through offsetting assists the visually impaired.

10-32.
(A) Single diagonal flared curb ramps are least costly and most efficient on narrow sidewalks. (B) Wraparound ramps do not require wheelchair users to change direction to enter the ramp, but may confuse the blind. Clear changes in pavement and control of perpendicular pedestrian movement are essential. Both ramp types require ample overrun area and appropriate drainage patterns.

10-34.
(A) Vertical curb returns are extremely hazardous unless planting or walls discourage perpendicular pedestrian approach. (B) Ramp flares should not exceed 1:12 if used by wheelchairs for entrance and exit; 1:10 if within the pedestrian path.

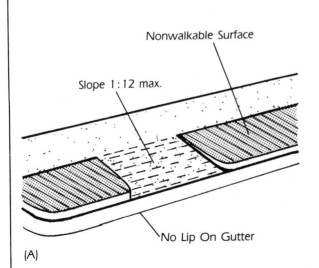

Nonwalkable Surface

Slope 1:12 max.

No Lip On Gutter

(A)

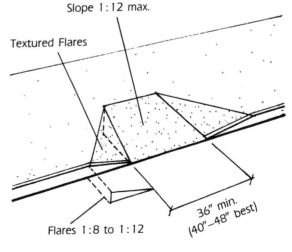

Slope 1:12 max.

Textured Flares

Flares 1:8 to 1:12

36" min. (40"–48" best)

(B)

Drinking Fountains

Easy access to drinking fountains outdoors means much to older people, who may find it more difficult to get to an indoor fountain. Some medications require an increased intake of water. Thus, drinking fountains should be easy for everyone (including the handicapped) to use and should be accessible from all major outdoor activity areas. Some special considerations for drinking fountains are outlined below.

1. A hand lever operable with the forearm or a push-type control is best for those with arthritis or some other handicap.

2. The height and design of fountains should be easy for both ambulatory and nonambulatory residents to use (see fig. 10–35).

- For those who use wheelchairs, a minimum vertical clear space of 27 inches is needed for knee clearance; a horizontal clear space of 17 to 19 inches is required for penetration under the fountain [31].
- Dual spouts at 36 and 30 inches above grade are best, although a single spout at 36 inches is manageable [32].
- Spouts located at the front of the unit, with a water trajectory basically parallel to the front of the unit, make access easier.

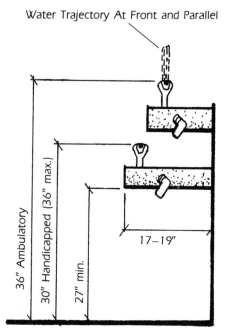

Water Trajectory At Front and Parallel

36" Ambulatory

30" Handicapped (36" max.)

27" min.

17–19"

10-35.
Easy access to drinking fountains is essential for older people, who are more sensitive to heat, take medications requiring increased water intake, and for those who cannot easily get to indoor fountains.

Special Considerations for Canes, Walkers, and Wheelchairs

Many design and detailing considerations for those who use canes, walkers, and wheelchairs have been covered throughout this chapter. The use of walking aids increases substantially after the age of 75; these people are often weak and tire easily; therefore, in addition to eliminating environmental barriers, elements that contribute comfort and conservation of energy are needed. Some common environmental constraints are noted below (see fig. 10–36).

1. Walkway

- A width of less than 5 feet is inadequate to allow nonhandicapped walkers to pass slower, handicapped persons.
- Slopes greater than 3 percent without frequent level rest areas and slopes greater than 5 percent, with or without rest areas, are difficult to negotiate.

2. Paving and walking surfaces

- Rough or uneven surfaces can trip the less agile, catch a cane tip or walker, and bump a wheelchair.
- Smooth nonporous surfaces provide inadequate traction underfoot or for wheelchairs, canes, and walkers.
- Soft or loose surface material (gravel, grass, and so on) provides inadequate support for canes, walkers, and wheelchair traction.
- Wood decking with plank spacing greater than 1/2 inch (3/8 inch is desirable) can catch the tip of canes and walkers as well as wheelchair wheels.
- Adverse weather (rain, snow) creates additional problems for walking; semiporous walking surfaces reduce the possibility of slipping.

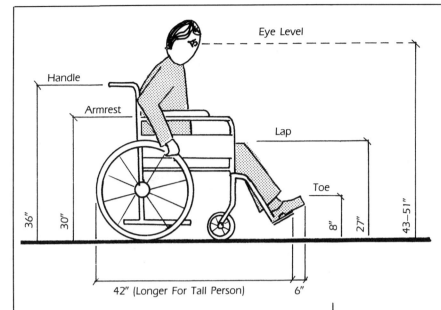

Handle

Armrest

Eye Level

Lap

Toe

36"

30"

8"

27"

43–51"

42" (Longer For Tall Person)

6"

10-36.
Dimensions of wheelchairs vary according to type and manufacturer. A standard adult-sized wheelchair is pictured.
After: American National Standards Institute. Specifications for Making Buildings and Facilities Accessible to and Usable by Physically Handicapped People. *New York: ANSI, 1980, 61.*

- Inadequate edge definition is hazardous for the visually impaired.
- Edging or paving that does not meet planting at grade can cause falls.

3. Drainage structure grates may catch the tips of canes and walkers, shoe heels, and the wheels of wheelchairs.

4. Stairs

- Inadequate stair width prevents nonhandicapped persons from passing by those using walkers and canes.
- Treads less than 12 inches are too shallow for placing the foot fully on the tread and too shallow for walkers.
- Treads should not, however, be too deep for those using a cane to step up comfortably.
- Riser height must not be insurmountable; a 5- to 6-inch riser is desirable, as it assures familiarity for the visually impaired; however, those with canes and especially walkers would probably find a 4-inch riser easier.
- Length of run must not be too long to mount comfortably; nor should it be too short to identify easily (10 risers maximum, 3 risers minimum).

- Lack of color contrast makes identification of tread and riser difficult.
- Projected nosings or open steps can catch a dragging foot.
- Inadequate lighting of treads and the top and bottom of a run is hazardous.
- Insufficient warning signals are dangerous for the visually impaired.

5. Low-level and high-level obstacles within the pedestrian path are hazardous.

6. Benches

- Benches placed too infrequently along walkways are inconvenient.
- Benches too high, too low, without armrests or backs are uncomfortable and possibly dangerous.
- Inadequate space next to benches and tables impedes comfortable conversation from a wheelchair and prevents resting a walker while seated.

7. Lighting

- Insufficient illumination levels present hazards.
- Overhead lighting may be blocked by the body or wheelchair, casting a shadow underfoot.

8. Inadequate space for maneuverability around obstacles and for loading and unloading from a car is a danger and inconvenience.

9. Doors should not be difficult to open for those using walkers or wheelchairs, or even canes.

10. Drinking fountains that are inaccessible (too high, too low, providing inadequate clearance underneath and adjacent) and infrequent make for uncomfortable, even hazardous conditions.

References

1. Lawton, M. Powell. "Public Behavior of Older People in Congregate Housing." In *Proceedings of the 1st Annual Environmental Design Research Association Conference,* edited by H. Sanoff and S. Cohen. Chapel Hill, NC: The Conference, 1970.

2. Koncelik, Joseph A. *Designing the Open Nursing Home.* Community Development Series no. 27. Stroudsburg, PA: Dowden, Hutchinson & Ross, 1976.

3. ———. *Designing the Open Nursing Home.*

4. ———. *Designing the Open Nursing Home.*

5. ———. *Designing the Open Nursing Home.*

6. ———. *Designing the Open Nursing Home.*

7. Office of Policy Development and Research, Department of Housing and Urban Development. *Access to the Environment,* vol. 1. Prepared by the American Society of Landscape Architects Foundation under contract H-2002-R with the Office of Policy Development and Research, Department of Housing and Urban·Development; and the Architectural and Transportation Barriers Compliance Board. New York: American National Standards Institute, 1977.

8. American National Standards Institute. *Specifications for Making Buildings and Facilities Accessible to and Usable by Physically Handicapped People.* A117.1-1980. New York: ANSI, 1980.

9. ———. *Specifications for Making Buildings and Facilities Accessible.*

10. ———. *Specifications for Making Buildings and Facilities Accessible.*

11. Koncelik, Joseph A. *Aging and the Product Environment.* Environmental Design Series, vol. 1. Stroudsburg, PA: Dowden, Hutchinson & Ross, 1983.

12. American National Standards. *Specifications for Making Buildings and Facilities Accessible.*

13. Koncelik. *Designing the Open Nursing Home.*

14. ———. *Designing the Open Nursing Home.*

15. ———. *Designing the Open Nursing Home.*

16. American National Standards. *Specifications for Making Buildings and Facilities Accessible.*

17. Green et al. *Housing for the Elderly: The Development and Design Process.* New York: Van Nostrand Reinhold, 1975.

18. ———. *Housing for the Elderly.*

19. American National Standards. *Specifications for Making Buildings and Facilities Accessible.*

20. ———. *Specifications for Making Buildings and Facilities Accessible.*

21. Green et al. *Housing for the Elderly.*

22. Office of Policy Development and Research. *Access to the Environment.*

23. Untermann, Richard K. "Pedestrian Circulation." In *Handbook of Landscape Architectual Construction,* edited by J. Carpenter. Washington, DC: Landscape Architecture Foundation, 1976, 235–397.

24. ———. "Pedestrian Circulation."

25. Fruin, John J. (telephone interview, January 1983).

26. ———. *Pedestrian Planning and Design.* New York: Metropolitan Association of Urban Designers and Environmental Planners, 1971.

27. Templer, John. *Provisions for Elderly and Handicapped Pedestrians.* Federal Highway Administration report no. FHwA-RD-79, 1, 2, 3, 1980. Cited in L. Jewell. "Curb Ramps at Intersections." *Landscape Architecture.* 72, no. 6 (1982): 87–89.

28. American Natonal Standards. *Specifications for Making Buildings and Facilities Accessible.*

29. Templer. *Provisions for Elderly and Handicapped Pedestrians.*

30. ———. *Provisions for Elderly and Handicapped Pedestrians.*

31. American National Standards. *Specifications for Making Buildings and Facilities Accessible.*

32. Office of Policy Development and Research. *Access to the Environment.*

Summary and Conclusions

Many service and housing alternatives for seniors are evolving today, enabling a closer match between individual needs and preferences on the one hand and housing provisions on the other. As a person ages, certain design elements may become increasingly important, such as those that contribute to comfort, safety and security, ease of access, and socializing. Appropriate design can facilitate rich social and recreational experiences, personal growth, and challenge among older people of all ages and ability levels.

The influence of management and activity programming on residents' satisfaction with and use of the built environment is also of prime concern to designers. Ongoing reviews of project management, programming, and the design itself must become integral parts of housing provision, both before and after construction. Diversity among the older population and the fact that the circumstances of residents (both individually and as a group) often change over time underscore the need for periodic review.

In this section, key design components for the development of successful outdoor spaces are summarized, and future trends that affect design are discussed. Although general principles of design for the aging apply to most housing developments, no specific design solution is appropriate for every situation—flexibility and sensitivity to the special needs of each prospective resident group are essential. A discussion of new trends among the aging population, housing provision, services, and programs highlights the important interplay between the individual and the physical and social environment.

Summary by Design Stage

Many topics have been covered throughout this book, including aspects of the aging process that affect design, general issues and concerns, spatial organization schemes, recreational outdoor use, site-planning patterns, site-activity components, and design detailing. In this summary chapter, major issues and design considerations are drawn together and reviewed by design stage:

1. Site development patterns: Development type, on-site and neighborhood conditions
2. Site-planning elements: Location and general issues, spatial quality, amenities, and detailing
3. Special amenities and detailing

For easy reference, information is presented in tabular form.

Site-Development Patterns

The overall site-planning scheme, or pattern, is an important part of designing for older people. Behavioral issues must be addressed during the site-planning phase as well as in detailing. Several factors that may affect the site development pattern were examined: (1) the type and size of development (e.g., high rise or low rise, small or large site); (2) neighborhood conditions; and (3) on-site conditions.

Some concerns for several development types are summarized in table 11–1.

On-site conditions and the surrounding neighborhood may also affect the site-planning scheme and the way in which needs of older people are addressed. This is particularly true for those sites and neighborhoods that have a strong physical and/or social character, such as extremes in topography or problems with security. Site-planning goals and patterns that respond to the needs of older people are summarized in table 11–2.

Site-planning Elements

The location of specific site-planning elements, their spatial quality, amenities, and detailing can affect safety and security, ease of access, comfort, and many other factors important for older people's use of the outdoors.

Special concerns for the location of site-planning elements are summarized in table 11–3. In table 11–4, important spatial qualities, amenities, and detailing are summarized for each site element.

Amenities and Detailing

Amenities and detailing deserve special consideration for older people who may experience sensory, cognitive, and other physiological changes with age. Appropriate amenities and detailing may increase the confidence and ease of outdoor use for seniors by responding to their special needs. Detailing, for example, may facilitate wayfinding by offering visual, auditory and tactual clues that can be "read" regardless of the specific sensory losses experienced by the individual. Comfort, safety, conversation, and general enjoyment of the outdoors, among other things, may be facilitated by appropriate design detailing. Some important considerations are outlined in table 11–5.

Table 11-1 SITE DEVELOPMENT PATTERNS AND DEVELOPMENT TYPE

Development Type	Special Concerns	Recommendations
Mid- to high-rise buildings	Strong indoor center of activity reduces opportunity for outdoor use	• Connect outdoor activity spaces to indoor activity • Provide easy access to outdoors • Maximize views to outdoors
	Mass of the building, especially on a small site, overpowers outdoor spaces	• Architectural type of solution for activity areas near the building to establish a human scale and create transition
Small site	Strong physical/social neighborhood characteristics may have a strong impact on the site and residents due to proximity	• Attention to neighborhood scale and image, security, etc.
Low-rise and mixed developments (large site)	Lower density of development disperses activity	• Centralize activity • Provide focal point/unifying elements
	Larger scale of development and variety of spaces is confusing	• Facilitate wayfinding • Define activity spaces (especially on large open sites) • Create a sense of place
	Outdoor spaces serve as the connecting fabric on-site, generating use	• Capitalize upon natural pedestrian flows for social/activity spaces
Several levels of care on-site	Shared facilities among all levels of care risk the association of proximity to the more frail with personal closeness to death and dying	Options in response include: • Separate zones/facilities for one or all levels of care • Proximity but design differentiation creating separate identities for each level • Some shared facilities
	Separate facilities risk isolation of friends; eventual move to greater care may be more traumatic; segregation unnatural	Options in response include: • Shared housing/facilities • Some shared facilities • Proximity but design differentiation between levels of care
	Special concerns for the less able—safety, security, access, and comfort	Options in response include: • Locate care facilities away from potential safety problems or confusing areas • Develop close to services • Define outdoor spaces • Locate the frail close to the more able for perceived safety and security

Table 11–2 SITE DEVELOPMENT PATTERNS: ON-SITE AND NEIGHBORHOOD CONDITIONS

Neighborhood Issues	Recommendations
Access	• Maximize access to neighborhood services and facilities (grocery and drugstores, public transportation, activity centers, and places of worship, etc.) • Access routes to neighborhood services not greater than 5 percent cumulative slope [1]
Views	• Maximize exceptional off-site views (views of activity are often popular)
Safety and security	• Avoid orientation toward areas with safety and security problems (or establish buffer area)
On-Site Issues	**Recommendations**
Wayfinding	• Site-plan pattern should be easy to recognize and identify, particularly for larger sites (e.g., radial or linear arrangement)
Public to private spaces	• Create spatial hierarchy, from public to private, for a sense of ownership and control, wayfinding, and security
Safety and security	• Lay out major activity areas/access routes for visual surveillance • Define activity areas for sense of control and security
Centralized pattern	• Minimize distance required to access main facilities on-site, including parking to units • Provide visual connections between activity centers/use areas for security and to generate use • Reserve areas on-site for recreation/pleasure use • Maintain/enhance natural features • Create focal point for activity and a sense of place (especially for larger developments)
Circulation patterns	• Create an easily identifiable pattern (e.g., radial, axial) • Establish a hierarchy from public to private for security, sense of control, and ownership • Access to residential units must not require passing directly through activity spaces; access to activity must not require passing through semiprivate residential areas • Lay out for direct and easy access between major on- and off-site facilities/services • Lay out to maximize opportunities for meeting others, but maintain semiprivate areas • Minimize crossing of pedestrian, bicycle, and vehicle circulation systems • Locate major pedestrian routes for maximum visibility from indoor and outdoor activity spaces for security • Locate major pedestrian routes for maximum protection from extremes in climate • Major pedestrian routes on-site not to involve a slope greater than 5 percent [2] • Lay out pleasure routes with "goals" en route to encourage walking and add interest • Design walkway "loops" for exercise and pleasure with a variety of challenges (length, slope, surface) and choices for activity or retreat
Social spaces	• Connect indoor and outdoor activity to maximize use of both • Ensure visibility for security • Provide options for privacy, intimacy, and meeting others • Offer a smaller scale and sense of protection (e.g., from building edge) • Locate for protection from extremes in weather (30% daily sun exposure during fall, winter, and spring desirable) [3]
Low-rise unit clustering	• See recommendations above for wayfinding, security, and circulation • Maximize opportunities for meeting others from the cluster (e.g., U-shape layout with walkways converging on a central common space) • Ensure easy access between units, parking, and facilities • Cluster units for own identity and sense of place (up to approximately 20 units per cluster)

Table 11–3 LOCATION AND GENERAL ISSUES FOR SITE PLANNING ELEMENTS

1. *Site entry:* **Major Concerns—safety, ease of access, and identification**

   - Adequate (200 feet) sight distance in both directions along the street [4]
   - Site entry may be replaced by individual unit or cluster entries for those projects developed as a continuation of the neighborhood fabric
   - Choice between easy entry identification off a main street and the safety of a minor street [5]
   - Multiple entries may be required to provide easy and direct access to larger sites
   - Easy and direct access to neighborhood facilities

2. *Entry drive:* **Major Concerns—easy/direct access and safety**

   - Layout easy to recognize and identify
   - Not to mix one-way and two-way drives
   - Easy access to on- and off-site facilities
   - Close and convenient building access/drop-off

3. *Main entry/arrival court:* **Major Concerns—easy access, safety, comfort, views, and a "welcome" experience**

   Drop-off/Entryway:
   - Pivotal position in site entry scheme for monitoring site access and for service as welcome area
   - Close and convenient building access/drop-off
   - Orientation for maximum protection from harsh weather
   - In harsh climates, exposure to sun for accelerated melting of snow
   - Building access no greater than 2.5 percent slope (no steps) [6]
   - Easy access to other on- and off-site facilities
   - Right-side drop-off

   Seating/Waiting area:
   - Orientation for protection from weather (see "Drop-off/Entryway," above)
   - Easy access to building entry and drop-off area
   - View of incoming traffic

4. *Low-rise unit entries:* **Major Concerns—easy access and recognition, safety, security, and sense of entrance**

   - Location for maximum protection from extreme weather and in cold climates, sun exposure to accelerate melting of snow
   - Direct and easy access to connector walkways, unit parking (or drop-off area), and on-site facilities
   - Entrywalk may be developed off cluster walkways as extension of private space (20- to 100-foot viewing distance)
   - Front and back of unit differentiated

5. *Resident parking:* **Major Concerns—ease of access, security**

   - Close and easy building access
   - Visible, not isolated, for safety and security
   - Not to dominate views or main entries
   - Small cluster lots preferable to large
   - Parking for handicapped close to building
   - One-way and two-way aisles not to be mixed
   - Easily identified with building
   - Progression from building identification to drop-off area and parking

6. *Secondary building exits/entries:* **Major Concerns—ease of access, safety, and comfort**

   - Orientation for protection from weather
   - Easy access to parking/activity areas
   - Visible from indoor and outdoor activity centers (e.g., office)

Table 11–3 *Continued*

7. *Shared patios/social spaces:* **Major Concerns—safety, comfort, easy access, central to activity**
   - Centrally located near indoor and outdoor activity—focal point
   - Protected area (e.g., flanked by two sides of L-shaped building or cluster of units)
   - Easy access to outdoor and indoor activity areas and facilities
   - Walkways intersect at/near patio area
   - Orientation for protection from weather, excessive sun, or shade
   - Approximately 30 percent daily sun exposure fall, winter, spring [7]

8. *Unit patios and balconies:* **Major Concerns—easy access, comfort, privacy, and security**
   - Direct and easy access from indoor living spaces (e.g., living room)
   - Easy access to kitchen desirable
   - Orientation for protection from weather, excessive sun, or shade (approximately 30 percent daily sun exposure fall, winter, spring) [8]
   - Balcony location not to obscure views of outdoor activity
   - On-grade patios with setback from major activity spaces/walkways desirable (20–100 feet)
   - Balconies above twelfth floor may feel unsafe

9. *Lawn areas for recreation*
   - Some near major activity areas, such as patios for spillover activities
   - Others more distant for retreat and semiprivate activities

10. *Garden and nature areas*
    - Some close to buildings/units for easy access and views
    - Others farther away from activity centers for exploration and retreat

11. *Resident gardening areas:* **Major Concerns—access, easy of use, flexibility for changing demands**
    - Near residential units/buildings (large "working" gardens may be located farther away from units/buildings, in a separate zone)
    - Not to dominate views or activity areas
    - Ample sun

12. *Pedestrian and bicycle circulation:* **Major Concerns—negotiability, safety, easy and direct access**
    - Layout easy to identify/recognize
    - Easy and direct access to on- and off-site facilities
    - Slope not greater than 6 percent (overall) to neighborhood or 10 percent for a maximum of 75 feet; major on-site routes not greater than 5 percent (building entries 2.5 percent; no steps) [9]
    - Pass by areas of activity—"collecting" people en route, maximizing opportunities for meeting others, but not requiring access directly through semiprivate or activity spaces
    - Hierarchy of routes, from community wide to cluster and unit walkways

13. *Rooftop developments:* **Major Concerns—access, comfort, and safety**
    - Location near nodes of indoor activity, with easy visual and physical access
    - Protection from harsh winds, excessive sun, glare, etc.
    - Maximize exceptional views

14. *Service and delivery areas:* **Major Concerns—ease of use, safety**
    - Not to interfere with resident access to facilities
    - Consider image presented to community
    - Not to dominate views
    - Those for resident use easily reached from units

Table 11–3 *Continued*

15. *Play areas for children:* **Major Concerns—privacy, control over contact, control over noise**

- Separate adult and child territories [10]
- Location for noise control—buffer residential units and social spaces (e.g., patios)
- Access to residential areas not to require passing through play areas, but views desirable (with noise buffered)

Table 11–4 MAIN SPATIAL QUALITIES, AMENITIES, AND DETAILING

Site-planning Element	Qualities	Amenities and Detailing
Site entry	• Easy to recognize and identify (multiple entries differentiated from one another) • Spatial character compatible with site-development and neighborhood scale • Drop-off area(s) near building entries if no formal site entry (see drop-off area, below) • May be synoymous with main entry/arrival court (see below)	• Low-level planting or high-branching trees • Security and accent lighting • Signs to identify the entry, offer direction within large developments, visible from a distance • Seating/waiting area with cover, newspaper stands, etc. • Transit stop
Entry drive	• Buffered if near apartments • Direction easy to follow—guides driver (one-way roads may be confusing) • Adequate width for cars, buses, and ambulances • Easy turnaround	• Wide turning radii/drives—boulevard 20-foot (min.) width each way (15-foot-wide median); single two-way drive 24-foot (min.) width each way [11] • Lighting desirable • One-way stops clearly marked
Main entry/ arrival court- drop-off area	• Direct access to building • Visible from inside building • Adequate space for building access and seating (see seating area, below) • View between building entry and drop-off area • Pedestrian area defined • May be synonymous with site entry area (see above)	• Slope 2.5 percent maximum with no steps—bollards to control autos [12] • Tactile warning strip (3 feet wide) along passenger loading area • Special paving to define building entry walk • Access aisle at loading area approximately 4 feet wide • .Walkways (6-foot min. width) • No low-level protrusions (planters minimum of 30 inches in height or planting at grade—no edging) [13, 14] • Nonslip, nonglare paving—must be predictable • Security and accent lighting • Overhead cover to extend over drop-off area • Grip-raii and grab posts • Safe and easy-to-use door
Main entry/ arrival court- seating area	• Defined space • Subtle separation from entry walk • Views to building entry and drop-off area • Visible from indoor common spaces (e.g., lobby and office)	• Seating (right-angle and activity-oriented) • Seating choices undercover, in shade, and sun • Security and accent lighting

Table 11–4 *Continued*

Site-planning Element	Qualities	Amenities and Detailing
Low-rise unit entries	• Simple to identify and describe to others • Defined from cluster walkway • Visible from walkway/street (not isolated) • Adequate vestibule space for display, welcoming, and seating	• Detailing to suggest extent of area for personalization • Overhead cover/protection • Package ledge desirable • Railing desirable • Security and accent lighting • Nonslip, nonglare paving • No low-level protrusions or edging (see Main entry/arrival court-drop-off area, above) • Bicycle rack nearby desirable • Entry walk minimum width 5 feet • Access at grade (no steps) • Door and hardware safe and easy to use
Resident parking	• Close to building/units • Access may be more important than adequate setback and screening for aesthetics • Small cluster lots (versus large lots) or individual unit parking desirable • Layout easy to understand and follow—guides driver • One-way and two-way aisles not to be mixed • Drop-off area necessary where parking is not near building or unit entries (see drop-off area, above, and Secondary building exits/entries, below) • Lots oriented for direct pedestrian access routes in front of (not behind) cars	• Wide stalls, driving alleys, and turning radii desirable • Wheel stops clearly marked; placed for 32-inch access aisle to walkway • Low-growing and high-branching (6-foot minimum) plant materials [15] • Handicapped parking—direct access to walkway (not behind cars) at grade or ramped, stalls 8 feet wide with 5-foot aisle (shared) [16]
Secondary building exits/ entries	• Comfortable transition to outdoors • Protection from weather and glare • Easy visual and physical access (not isolated)	• Cover desirable • Package ledge • Grip rail • At grade or both steps and ramp • Easy-to-use door with window • Seating desirable • Security lighting
Pedestrian and bicycle circulation	• Pleasure "loops" to offer choice in length and difficulty of route, retreat, and activity • Major access routes visible from activity areas/ buildings • Physical separation between bicycle and pedestrian routes	• Nonslip, nonglare paving • Rest stops with shade and seating (every 200 feet average) • Goals en route (e.g., public mail boxes, seating area) • Security lighting for major access routes • Major walks—6-foot (min.) width; minor walks—5-foot (min.) [17]

Table 11–4 *Continued*

Site-planning Element	Qualities	Amenities and Detailing
Pedestrian and bicycle circulation		• Planting at grade or in raised planters (30-inch min. height)—no edging [18] • Plan for snow removal and exposure to melt snow and ice • Wet leaves are a potential hazard—small-leafed or evergreen trees along walks are best
Shaded patios	• Approximately 13 square feet of paved area (min.) per unit • Privacy/social interaction choices • Greater level of detail—tactual, visual, and auditory stimulation • Smaller intimate scale • Clusters of small areas may connect for larger group use • Views of activity • Noise control • Defined area/edges • Approximately 50 percent of area shaded	• Cover desirable (e.g., porch, arbor) • Right-angle and activity-oriented seating (movable preferable to fixed) • Easy access to restrooms • Access to kitchen desirable • Barbeque, water and electrical sources desirable • Drinking fountains • Nearby storage desirable • Accent lighting desirable • Nonslip, nonglare paving
Unit patios and balconies	• Spatial privacy • Security for on-grade patios (define from public areas or enclose, but retain views) • Large enough for several seated people, plants, etc. • On-grade patios minimum width 12 feet (100-square-foot min. area) [19] • Balconies 5 feet clear (min.); 50-square-foot min. (1 bedroom) or 60-square-foot (2 bedroom) [20] • On-grade access from patios to community space desirable • Balconies, in particular, must feel safe and secure • Approximately 50 percent of area shaded	• Option for screening or enclosing desirable • Nonslip, nonglare surface • Lighting (controls at inside of door) • Adequate cover overhead • Balcony railing height 42–50 inches to allow for viewing while seated; solid balustrades 24 inches high with open railing above [21] • Ledge for plants desirable
Lawn areas for recreation	• Both small and large lawns desirable • Defined space/edges • Views to and from activity areas (e.g., patio)	• Nearby seating with shade • Paved access route • Surface finely graded/groomed • Lawn to meet pavement at grade
Gardens and nature areas	• Rich sensory experience—visual, tactual and auditory interest • Variety of garden and nature areas desirable • Noise control	• Paved access a must, with options for more challenging surfaces/routes • Seating (sun and shade) • Plants for seasonal interest

Table 11–4 *Continued*

Site-planning Element	Qualities	Amenities and Detailing
Gardens and nature areas	• Some visible from indoors	• Some raised planters • Amenities and landscaping to attract wildlife (desirable)
Resident gardening areas	• Small gardens that obviously "belong" to a unit or cluster (desirable) • Larger gardening "centers" may be more removed from units • Plots of various sizes are desirable (5-foot by 10-foot plots that can be combined for a larger area are an option) • Layout for easy pedestrian access (vehicular for larger gardening centers)	• Paved access • Seating in shade and sun • Raised working area in shade (desirable) • Access to drinking fountain • Storage area nearby (locking desirable) • Raised planting beds accessible by the handicapped (desirable)
Rooftop development	• Must feel safe and secure • Accommodate a range of unanticipated activities • Protected from wind/sun	• Vertical elements and detailing to define edges • Covered seating in shade • Night lighting desirable • Nonslip, nonglare surfaces • Railings and balustrades to allow for viewing from a seated position (solid balustrades max. height 24 inches; glassed or open railings above to 42-inch, min.) [22].
Service and delivery areas	• Not visually dominating or totally isolated • Access at grade to service areas for resident use	• Security lighting • Nearby seating for viewing of frequently used delivery areas (desirable) • Traffic areas defined by special paving
Play areas for children	• Common ground for compatible activities [23] • Refuge for elderly • Viewing area for visual contact before physical contact • Noise control	• Amenities and detailing for comfort and safety: seating, shade, etc.

157

Table 11–5 AMENITIES AND DETAILING—SPECIAL CONSIDERATIONS

Areas of Concern	Recommendations
Spatial scale	• Smaller spaces with defined edges are more easily understood and claimed by the elderly; they may also reduce confusion and make conversation easier [24]
Level of detailing	• Older people may prefer a greater level of design detail than younger people due to sensory losses associated with the aging process (see Perception, below) [25]

Perception	• Some sensory clues may be more easily perceived by older people with declining vision
	• Tactual environments may be easier to "read"
	• Brighter colors in the red and orange range are easier to differentiate than darker colors in the blue-green range
	• Paving materials that are more easily differentiated by the visually impaired include changes from brushed concrete to [26]:
	    thermoplastic strips
	    knicked concrete
	    exposed pea gravel aggregate
	    pliant polymer

Lighting and glare	• Higher-density lighting is necessary for safety and security at drop-off areas, building entries, parking lots, and changes in grade • Decorative lighting for special events is ideal • Lighting in movement areas should illuminate the periphery of the paved area and avoid dark shadows • Glare and deep shadows present safety hazards because the aging eye does not readily adapt to changes in light and dark • Light standards should have deflection devices to reduce the light source and glare to pedestrians • Lighting overlap reduces glare and hot spots • Reflective surfaces should be avoided • Lighting fixtures placed at low level are best for illuminating the walking surface directly in front of those with walkers and wheelchairs (lighting from high fixtures is blocked by the body)
Climate control	• Architectural detailing and landscape treatment to moderate shade, sun, and wind are essential because older people are more sensitive to changes in temperature and glare
Paving	• Paved surfaces should be nonslip and nonglare, such as stained broom-finished concrete (see Perception, above) • Irregular surfaces and low-level protrusions on the ground plane should be avoided
Noise	• Noise control is essential, particularly in areas for socializing—background noises may distract and confuse the older person, making conversation difficult [27]
Seating	• The design of chairs and benches deserves special attention—a variety of seating types/models ensures comfort for all • Seating material should be wood or a material that does not conduct heat or cold; soft seating surfaces are best • Movable seating is desirable, as it accommodates any number of people and can be moved for sun or shade • Fixed seating should be at right angles or oriented toward activity • Chairs must be stable, with nonprotruding legs • A paved clear space next to benches is necessary for those in wheelchairs

Table 11–5 *Continued*

Areas of Concern	Recommendations
Planters	• Planters 30 inches high reduce the possibility of tripping; 32–48 inches for a handrest; 40 inches (max.) for views over top from a wheelchair [28]
Raised planters for use by the handicapped	• Parallel-approach and non-alcove-type planters allow for easy conversation and access, but limit working positions unless knee clearance is provided • Alcove-type planters limit conversation; with knee clearance, they enable a variety of working positions • A minimum clear floor space of 48 inches deep and 30 inches wide is required (more for deep alcoves); 19 inches of the depth may be under the planter.[29] • Desirable working surface height is between 26–30 inches [30] • Minimum clearance for knees is 27 inches (29 inches–2-inch clearance is best) [31] • A range in planter design, height, and knee clearance may be best, from full knee clearance to partial clearance, allowing for a choice of working surface heights • A maximum horizontal forward reach is 25–31 inches; horizontal side reach 24 inches (approx.); vertical side reach 54 inches (max. height), 9 inches max. lower reach [32] • Adjacent space for resting equipment is desirable
Stairs	• Stair sets of no fewer than three are essential for safety; 10 maximum for negotiability • Treads and risers must be uniform throughout the sequence • Stair risers of 6 inches with treads 12 inches deep are easier for the visually impaired; those with canes and walkers may find a 4-inch rise easiest; additional tread depth will assist those with walkers (many walkers are 19–20 inches deep at the base)—use standard formulas • Textured markers, 24–48 inches in front of stairs, warn pedestrians [33] • Vertically splayed, nonprojecting beveled nosings are best; open steps are hazardous • Nonslip, nonglare surfaces are essential • Handrails are essential, one on either side is often desirable • Lighting should illuminate the top and bottom of the run and the treads
Ramps	• Ramps are never a substitute for stairs; both should be provided • Ramps (greater than 5 percent slope) should not exceed 8.33 percent slope [34]; alternative routes that are longer but more level should be available • A level approach of 6 feet is necessary at the ramp top and bottom • A minimum ramp width of 5 feet allows two wheelchairs to pass cautiously • A maximum ramp length is 30 feet; where longer ramps are necessary, a level resting platform (60 inches clear length) at 15-foot intervals is suggested • Curbs or ramp guards (2 inches min. height) should extend the length of the ramp • Handrails are essential (see Handrails, below) • Nonslip, nonglare surfaces are important • A textured strip (24–48 inches in front of ramps) acts as a warning for the visually impaired • Lighting should illuminate the top, bottom, and edges of ramps (see Lighting, above)
Handrails	• Two handrails, one at 32 inches (for the ambulatory) and one at 26 inches (for wheelchair users) are best [35] • Surfaces should be impermeable to weather but not conduct heat or cold • Handrails should extend 1 foot beyond the change in grade; freestanding rails should not protrude abruptly • A rounded railing (approx. 2¾ inches in diameter) mounted approximately 2 inches from the wall is ideal [36]

Table 11–5 *Continued*

Areas of Concern	Recommendations
	• Indirect lighting is desirable • A textured code along handrails aids the visually impaired
Doors and handles	• Door type must be easy to open and safe: power-assisted doors must require constant pressure; powered swinging doors and full-length glass doors require a warning system • Powered and power-assisted doors (especially hinge type) require special attention for safety and predictability • A glazed upper half (36-inch max. above the floor) allows for previewing • Minimize direct exposure to glare from glassed doors (see Windows, below) • Minimum door width for a single wheelchair is 32 inches; 60 inches for two • A level threshold is best; a bevel (8 percent max.), at a maximum height of ¾ inch is passable • Kickplates, lever-type door handles, and easy key inserts are desirable
Windows	• Window placement should minimize direct exposure of indoor entryways to glare (a gradual transition in exposure and a diagonal exposure to the source are good options) • Detailing to reduce glare and baffle light is essential • Unit windows for viewing while seated at the dining and/or kitchen table, for viewing from the living room, and from a prone position in the bedroom are desirable • Window placement, detailing, and landscape treatment for privacy, especially in the bedroom, are important • Views from indoor common spaces to outdoor activity enhance use of both spaces • A window height of 3½ feet (max.) allows for viewing from a seated position • Window ledges 1 foot deep are ideal for plants and for leaning • A design for easy window opening and closing is necessary
Signs	• Outdoor signs at 5 feet (approx.) above grade are easiest for the visually impaired to read; for safety, hanging signs require a minimum clear space of 7 feet underneath [37] • Raised letters are better than braille; incised characters collect dirt • Bold letter styles, without serifs and not condensed or extended, are best • White images and letters on black or dark-blue background are easiest to read • Nonreflective surfaces and indirect lighting reduce glare
Pedestrian street crossings	• Reduced distance across major traffic lanes (e.g., curb widenings at crossing areas) increases safety • Time crossing signals for slower walking speeds (210–240 feet/minute for ambulatory; 90–150 feet/minute for the handicapped) [38] • Auditory crossing signals (e.g., clicker) aid the visually impaired • Curb ramp slopes greater than 1:12 may prove impassable for wheelchairs [39] • Curb-returns should not be steeper than 1:12 (for wheelchair access); 1:10 in the pedestrian path [40] • Sufficient traffic-free overrun is required at top and bottom of ramps • Change in paving material/texture for ramps and flares increases safety (see Perception, above)
Drinking fountains	• Hand levers operable with forearm, or push-type control are best • Dual spouts at 36 inches above grade are easiest for the ambulatory, and 30 inches for the nonambulatory; spouts at the front of the unit with water trajectory parallel to the unit front are best • Vertical clear space underneath (27 inches min.) and horizontal clear space (17–19 inches) are required for wheelchair penetration [41] • All major outdoor spaces require fountains

References

1. Green et al. *Housing for the Elderly: The Development and Design Process.* New York: Van Nostrand Reinhold, 1975.
2. ———. *Housing for the Elderly.*
3. ———. *Housing for the Elderly.*
4. ———. *Housing for the Elderly.*
5. ———. *Housing for the Elderly.*
6. ———. *Housing for the Elderly.*
7. ———. *Housing for the Elderly.*
8. ———. *Housing for the Elderly.*
9. ———. *Housing for the Elderly.*
10. Steinfeld, Edward H. "Physical Planning for Increased Cross-Generational Contact." In *Proceedings of the 4th Annual Environmental Design Research Conference,* edited by W.F.E. Preiser. Stroudsburg, PA: Dowden, Hutchinson & Ross, 1973.
11. Green et al. *Housing for the Elderly.*
12. ———. *Housing for the Elderly.*
13. Office of Policy Development and Research, Department of Housing and Urban Development. *Access to the Environment,* vol.1. Prepared by the American Society of Landscape Architects Foundation under contract H-2002-R with the Office of Policy Development Research, Department of Housing and Urban Development; and the Architectural and Transportation Barriers Compliance Board. New York: American National Standards Institute, 1977.
14. Green et al. *Housing for the Elderly.*
15. ———. *Housing for the Elderly.*
16. American National Standards Institute. *Specifications for Making Buildings and Facilities Accessible to and Usable by Physically Handicapped People.* A117.1-1980. New York: ANSI, 1980.
17. Green et al. *Housing for the Elderly.*
18. ———. *Housing for the Elderly.*
19. ———. *Housing for the Elderly.*
20. ———. *Housing for the Elderly.*
21. ———. *Housing for the Elderly.*
22. ———. *Housing for the Elderly.*
23. Steinfeld. "Physical Planning."
24. Pastalan, L. A. "How the Elderly Negotiate their Environment." Paper presented at Environment for the Aged: A Working Conference on Behavioral Research, Utilization and Environmental Policy, at San Juan, Puerto Rico, December 1971.
25. DeLong, A. J. "The Micro-Spatial Structure of the Older Person: Some Implications of Planning the Social and Physical Environment." In *Spatial Behavior of Older People,* edited by L. Pastalan and D. Carson. Ann Arbor: University of Michigan, 1970.
26. Templer, John. *Provisions for Elderly and Handicapped Pedestrians.* Federal Highway Administration report no. FHwA-RD-79, 1, 2, 3, 1980. Cited in L. Jewell. "Curb Ramps at Intersections." *Landscape Architecture.* 72, no. 6 (1982): 87–89.
27. Rabbit, Patrick. Cited in "The Twilight of Memory." *Time,* July 1981, 81.
28. Office of Policy Development and Research. *Access to the Environment.*
29. American National Standards. *Specifications for Making Buildings and Facilities Accessible.*
30. ———. *Specifications for Making Buildings and Facilities Accessible.*
31. ———. *Specifications for Making Buildings and Facilities Accessible.*
32. ———. *Specifications for Making Buildings and Facilities Accessible*
33. ———. *Specifications for Making Buildings and Facilities Accessible.*
34. ———. *Specifications for Making Buildings and Facilities Accessible.*
35. Koncelik, Joseph A. *Designing the Open Nursing Home.* Community Development Series no. 27. Stroudsburg, PA: Dowden, Hutchinson & Ross, 1976.
36. ———. *Designing the Open Nursing Home.*
37. Office of Policy Development and Research. *Access to the Environment.*
38. Fruin, John J. (telephone interview, January 1983).
39. Templer. *Provisions for Elderly and Handicapped Pedestrians.*
40. ———. *Provisions for Elderly and Handicapped Pedestrians.*
41. American National Standards. *Specifications for Making Buildings and Facilities Accessible.*

Conclusion

These are the headlines of just a few articles recently featured in major newspapers across the country; they point to the diversity of needs and circumstances among today's senior citizens:

Town Says Elderly are the "Industry"
Increasing Numbers of Aged Return North From
  Florida
Medical Students Learn to Understand the Aging
Elderly, Too, Find Pleasure at Campsites
Breaking Down Barriers for the Isolated Elderly

Advances in modern medicine and present life-style trends are directly affecting the older population and, in turn, the housing market for older persons. These trends and changes bring with them new roles and challenges for designers.

More healthful life-styles and improved medical care are contributing to create a new generation of active and more able elderly and to a rise in the percentage of people over 75 years of age, who are generally more frail. Also changing is the misconstrued notion that all seniors are alike, with similar needs. This new awareness is evidenced on a variety of levels, including the health care industries, service and recreation programs, and the housing market. Even the terms "young old" and "old old," increasingly common in discussions about older people, indicate a change from stereotypical conceptions of design for the elderly to ideas based on more individualized needs. Variety and flexibility are key concepts today.

The "new" generation of elderly is also better educated, possesses greater financial resources, and is demanding better housing, services, and products than previous generations have. In short, the "new old" will be tougher consumers—a situation that will have a positive impact on the market.

One response to these trends has been an explo-

sion in new housing and services alternatives. Options range from service-intensive housing (with greater flexibility in the service structure and design itself) to recreationally based programs and housing for active seniors of all ages. The rapidly evolving age-specific housing market now includes housing for those over 45 and for those over 65, in addition to a broader choice in housing types, including echo, shared, and congregate housing, among others. Of these housing types, those that enable continued independence and those that offer living arrangements integrated with existing neighborhoods (both in terms of design and life-style) are promising options yet little explored in the United States. Echo housing (or granny flats) is one alternative to promote independence and neighborhood integration. Zoning ordinances and concern over the aesthetic fit of temporary housing transplanted into residential backyards in established neighborhoods are a few of the concerns hindering their wide acceptance.

Also increasingly common are such programs as visiting nurse services, meals on wheels, senior day-care centers, summer camps, and summer schools for seniors at major universities. Even specially designed products for the less able are more routinely advertised in mail-order catalogs. Many senior employment and volunteer programs are also reacquainting the population as a whole with the vast resource of talent and experience that older people have to offer. Clearly, the realm of designing for the needs of older people extends to every aspect of the physical environment and benefits all.

Expertise on aging is indeed needed. Designing for senior citizens calls for an expertise beyond traditional design fields. It requires a holistic approach grounded in concepts from such areas as medicine, social gerontology, and psychology. The need for independence and self-esteem and the necessity of coping with mental confusion are but a few issues designers must address. The growing emphasis on services and activities also requires the designer to be aware of suitable programs and to be willing to cooperate with service programmers and providers. Even the basis for aesthetics is changing. The preferences of seniors themselves and an understanding of age-related changes in the sensory system are setting new criteria for design decisions.

Physical design reaches across a broad range of daily experiences, from selecting the products to be used to providing a setting for services and programs. If the goal is really to promote the optimal functioning of seniors, our vision must look beyond the confines of the built environment to the relationship between the individual and the physical as well as social environment.

Selected Bibliography

Many sources of information on environment and aging are available (see the appendix for agency and organization sources). This bibliography is a listing of general references that have been instrumental in the formulation of this particular work. Some have not been cited in the chapter references.

American National Standards Institute. *Specifications for Making Buildings and Facilities Accessible to and Usable by Physically Handicapped People.* A117.1-1980. New York: ANSI, 1980.

Atchely, Robert C. *The Social Forces in Later Life: An Introduction to Social Gerontology.* Belmont, CA: Wadsworth Press, 1972.

Bronson, E. P. "An Experiment in Intermediate Housing Facilities for the Elderly." *Gerontologist.* 12, no. 1, pt. 1 (spring 1972): 22–26.

Byerts, T. O. "Planning Environments for the Aged." In *Proceedings of the 4th Annual Environmental Design Research Conference,* edited by W.F.E. Preiser. Stroudsburg, PA: Dowden, Hutchinson & Ross, 1973.

Byerts, T. O., and Don Conway, eds. "Behavioral Requirements for Housing for the Elderly." Report from a Working Conference, sponsored by the American Institute of Architects, Association for the Study of Man–Environment Relations, Gerontological Society, and National Tenants Association, Washington, DC, June, 1972.

Carstens, Diane. "Behavioral Research Applied to the Redesign of Exterior Spaces: Housing for the Elderly." In *Proceedings of the 13th International Conference of the Environmental Design Research Association,* edited by P. Bart, A. Chen, and G. Francescato. College Park, MD: EDRA, 1982.

Central Mortgage and Housing Corporation, Minister of State of Affairs. *Housing the Elderly.* Canada: CMHC, 1975.

DeLong, A. J. "The Micro-Spatial Structure of the Older Person: Some Implications of Planning the Social and Physical Environment." In *Spatial Behavior of Older People,* edited by L. Pastalan and D. Carson. Ann Arbor: University of Michigan, 1970.

Gerontological Planning Associates. "An Architectural Program: A Model of Congregate Housing." Unpublished paper prepared for the First National Conference on Congregate Housing for Older People, International Center for Social Gerontology. Washington, DC, November 11 and 12, 1975.

Green, Isaac, et al. *Housing for the Elderly: The Development and Design Process.* New York: Van Nostrand Reinhold, 1975.

Howell, Sandra. *Designing for Aging: Patterns of Use.* Cambridge, MA: MIT Press, 1980.

Koncelik, Joseph A. *Aging and the Product Environment.* Environmental Design Series, vol. 1. Stroudsburg, PA: Dowden, Hutchinson & Ross, 1983.

————. *Designing the Open Nursing Home.* Community Development Series no. 27. Stroudsburg, PA: Dowden, Hutchinson & Ross, 1976.

Lawton, M. Powell. "Planner's Notebook: Planning Environments for Older People." *American Institute of Planners Journal.* 36 (1970): 127–29.

————. "Public Behavior of Older People in Congregate Housing." In *Proceedings of the 1st Annual Environmental Design Research Association Conference,* edited by H. Sanoff and S. Cohen. Chapel Hill, NC: The Conference, 1970.

————. *Planning and Managing Housing for the Elderly.* New York: John Wiley and Sons, 1975.

————. "Leisure Activities for the Aged." In *American Academy of Political and Social Sciences Annals.* 438 (July 1978): 71–80.

————. *Environment and Aging.* Monterey, CA: Brooks/Cole, 1980.

Lawton, M. Powell, Robert J. Newcomer, and Thomas O. Byerts, eds. *Community Planning for an Aging Society.* Stroudsburg, PA: Dowden, Hutchinson & Ross, 1976.

Nahemow, Lucille, and M. Powell Lawton. "Toward an Ecological Theory of Adaptation and Aging." In *Proceedings of the 4th Annual Environmental Design Research Conference,* edited by W.F.E. Preiser. Stroudsburg, PA: Dowden, Hutchinson & Ross, 1973.

Pastalan, Leon A. "Privacy Preferences Among Relocated Institutionalized Elderly." In *Proceedings of the 5th Annual Environmental Design Research Association Conference*, edited by D. Carson. Milwaukee, WI: The Conference, 1974.

Pastalan, Leon A. "How the Elderly Negotiate their Environment." Paper presented at Environment for the Aged: A Working Conference on Behavioral Research, Utilization, and Environmental Policy. San Juan, Puerto Rico, December 1971.

Pastalan, Leon A., and Daniel H. Carson, eds. *Spatial Behavior of Older People*. Ann Arbor: University of Michigan Press, 1970.

Sherman, S. R. "Provision of On-Site Services in Retirement Housing." *International Journal of Aging and Human Development*. 6, no. 3 (1975): 229–47.

———. "Leisure Activities in Retirement Housing." *Journal of Gerontology*. 29, no. 3 (1974): 325–35.

Urban Land Institute. *Housing for a Maturing Population*. Washington, DC: ULI, 1983.

Windley, Paul G. "Evaluative Research Begins with Use in Mind." In *Evaluative Research on Social Programs for the Elderly*. A report of the Seminar on Evaluative Research Sponsored by the Committee on Research and Development, Gerontological Society, Portland, Oregon, June 1973. DHEW Publication, No. (OHD) 77-20120. Washington, DC Department of Health, Education, and Welfare, 1977.

Zeisel, J., G. Epp, and S. Demos. *Low Rise Housing for Older People*. Department of Housing and Urban Development, Office of Policy Development and Research. HUD-483(TQ)-76. Washington, DC: United States Government Printing Office, 1977.

Appendix

For further information on environments and aging, the following agencies and organizations may be contacted:

Administration on Aging
Office of Human Development Services
200 Independence Avenue S.W.
Washington, DC 20201
(202) 245-7246

American Association of Homes for the Aging
Suite 7070
1050 Seventeenth Street N.W.
Washington, DC 20036
(202) 296-5960

American Association of Retired Persons (AARP)
1909 K Street N.W.
Washington, DC 20049
(202) 872-4700

American Institute of Architects (AIA)
AIA Database on Designing for Aging
1735 New York Avenue N.W.
Washington, DC 20006
(202) 626-7300

The Gerontological Society of America
Suite 300
1411 K Street N.W.
Washington, DC 20006
(202) 466-6750

Department of Housing and Urban Development
Information Center
451 Seventh Street S.W.
Washington, DC 20410
(202) 755-6420

National Center for a Barrier Free Environment
Suite 700
1015 15th Street N.W.
Washington, DC 20005
(202) 466-6896

The National Council on Aging
West Wing 100 Suite 208
600 Maryland Avenue S.W.
Washington, DC 20024
(202) 479-1200

Index

169